TEACHER THINKING:

A STUDY OF PRACTICAL KNOWLEDGE

Croom Helm Ltd, Provident House, Burrell Row,
Beckenham, Kent BR3 1AT

British Library Cataloguing in Publication Data

Elbaz, Freema
    Teacher thinking: a study of practical knowledge
    (Croom Helm curriculum policy and research series)
    1. Teaching
    I. Title
    371.3   LB1025.2
    ISBN 0-7099-0910-1

First published in the United States of America 1983
by Nichols Publishing Company, Post Office Box 96,
New York, NY 10024

Library of Congress Cataloging in Publication Data

Elbaz, Freema.
    Teacher thinking: a study of practical knowledge

    1. Teaching. 2. Curriculum planning.
I. Title.
LB1033.E37   1983   371.1'02   82-14418
ISBN 0-89397-144-8

Printed and bound in Great Britain by
Biddles Ltd, Guildford and King's Lynn

Teacher Thinking
A Study of Practical Knowledge

FREEMA ELBAZ

CROOM HELM
London & Canberra

NICHOLS PUBLISHING COMPANY
New York

CONTENTS

FOREWORD

Curriculum planning and development are activities undertaken to improve the quality of teaching and learning in schools. But, all too characteristically, they are activities seen as being undertaken for schools and teachers by people outside--by experts or authorities who are sometimes benign in their intentions, at other times less benign, who believe they know what the schools should be doing. Syllabi, guidelines or texts are written and then the task becomes one of persuading, cajoling, urging or teaching teachers to follow the directions being outlined.

Writing about curriculum development reflects these all-too-common starting points for thinking about curriculum change and development. And, inasmuch as such writing typically comes from people who were teachers (but aren't now), or from people who know what good teaching should be, a further distancing of 'voice' or perspective occurs. Not only is the curriculum a 'big' question but it is something that we know about and they need to be attending to. Needless to say, 'they' are teachers. Even when experts and authorities emphasize the need for 'partnership' or the role of teachers as the 'animators' of schooling, the emphasis often becomes a focus for the new kinds of in-service or curriculum planning which are needed if teachers are to liberate their potentials. Always, it seems, teachers need the help, guidance, direction, and leadership which others can provide.

All of us who think about teaching from vantage points outside the schools have come to live with such starting points and there is a sense in which they do reflect something in the world of schools. But those of us who were teachers also need to reflect on our own biographies and ask whether we really believe that dons and other experts or people in ministries had that much to say when they talked so earnestly about what we should be doing. They could help yes, but lead? What did they know about what it was like and what it could be like at the chalk-face I experienced every day? What did they know about where I wanted to go, what my needs were, and what worried me?

In this book Freema Elbaz confronts directly the ways in which teaching, curriculum development, and teacher growth and change are seen by scholars and policy-makers within education. By reporting in vivid detail an analysis of the insights and ideas of one teacher, Sarah, as they emerged in a series of long interviews she brings into full view the hopes, the concerns and the style of thought of many teachers who want not advancement but the opportunity to 'open windows' for their students. Sarah is clearly where the action is, her problems are clearly the problems of the schools, and her excitement is the real excitement of education. We have an account here of a woman who is moving her world and, as she does so, is growing and changing.

We welcome this book to the Curriculum Policy and Research Series as both a theoretically and methodologically exciting picture of what can and does happen behind the classroom door. It is, moreover, a symbol of what there is to be hopeful about in education. And there is more to this book than its description of the thoughts, hopes, and ideals of one person. Elbaz renders this description into words which can give us insights into the worlds of many teachers and, in so doing, offers a commentary on many of the basic issues confronting education in these times.

All too often, for example, educational research and teacher education are presented as if they were irrelevant luxuries that are of no use to "practitioners". But this was not so in Sarah's case: she sought out courses, she listened to discussions of research, she read professional journals and used all she could pick up from these sources in her work—but in her own way, at her own pace, and as she could fit them into her view of her world.

This aspect of this account is reassuring to those of us who are teachers of teachers. But there is another theme which emerges here which is disconcerting. We see here a teacher who was driven by forces that she could not handle to flee from class teaching, from her subject department, from the "academic top" of her school. There were, it seems, hostile pressures in these places which, at this point in her life at least, made it difficult to do the real work of teaching as Sarah understood it: to address the needs and privations of her students and to communicate in authentic ways. We cannot avoid wondering why this was so as we read this book and, as we pause to think about Sarah's reasoning, consider what she is saying about the institution of the school as she, and many others, experience it. What is there in the contemporary school that led Sarah away from its institutional life? In how many other places are teachers like her being pushed out of the classroom by forces they cannot handle? Why?

But while such questions as these emerge from this account they are not the heart of the matter being explored here. Indeed, they only come to mind because of the view we are given here of a creative teacher moving with verve and élan to create environments in which education could be a possibility for her students. The ways in which she approaches this task and works out its implications for her is the theme which is at the core of Elbaz' concerns. And as she develops this theme with Sarah's help, we are given a new view of the complexities of the teacher's work--and a new view of the ways in which teachers respond to their work of educating.

It is a privilege to read this book and, in so doing, share in a real conversation about the realities of teaching. It is a conversation which should serve to remind all of us that teachers and their hopes and their concerns are where the passion and the real questions are in education.

Ian Westbury
University of Illinois at
Urbana-Champaign

W.A. Reid
University of Birmingham

EDITORS

ACKNOWLEDGEMENTS

In carrying out this study I enjoyed the support and encouragement of many people, and it is a pleasure to be able to thank them in print. Michael Connelly, as the chairman of my dissertation commitee, provided the right mix of critical guidance and freedom; the intellectual environment at OISE was enhanced, for me, by the presence of people like Gila Hanna, Helen Hayes, David Hunt, and Douglas Roberts. More recently I have benefitted from the interest of colleagues who share similar purposes--Richard Butt, Jean Clandinin, Chris Clark, and, in the Département de pédagogie of the Université de Sherbrooke, Hélène Méhu, Danielle Raymond and the participants in the Curriculum seminar. The Université de Sherbrooke and the Fonds F.C.A.C. have provided financial assistance in the preparation of the manuscript.

"Sarah", the teacher of this study, gave willingly of her time and her self; I regret that research constraints impinged so heavily on the experience we shared. While I tried to present her fairly, I know that distortion is inevitable and can only hope that this account may nevertheless be of some use to her.

Ian Westbury has been a patient, constructive and always encouraging editor and I am greatly indebted to him.

Throughout this work, my family gave me constant and unfailing support; I love them all. My gratitude to Robert, for caring about every detail, every step of the way; to Maya and Shai for making it worthwhile; to my father, Charles Luwisch and my uncle, Irving Rubin, for help and concern. My mother, the late Bertha Rubin Luwisch, did not see the completion of this work, and this I regret deeply; it was she who gave me a model of practical knowledge worth striving toward.

Freema Luwisch Elbaz
Sherbrooke

Part One

STUDYING PRACTICAL KNOWLEDGE

Chapter 1

INTRODUCTION

This book is concerned with the practical knowledge of teachers. It makes the assumption that teachers hold a complex, practically-oriented set of understandings which they use actively to shape and direct the work of teaching. My task here will be to present this practical knowledge as I found it in a case study of one Canadian teacher, a high school teacher of English called Sarah.

I began this study in 1976, a time when there was great concern to involve teachers in local curriculum development. In North America, curriculum workers had rejected the extreme of 'teacher-proof curricula' to emphasize the necessity of involving teachers in the implementation of new programs. But these efforts did little to change the basic stance: the teacher's contribution was still viewed as dependent on the intentions of the curriculum developer. The teacher could at best be a facilitator, someone who had taken the trouble to understand the approach of the developer, to adapt it minimally to her own situation and to convey it faithfully to students.[1] Inevitably, such a view committed the curriculum developer to working, if not against the teacher, 'on' the teacher, to modify her behaviour. But there was little evidence for the success of such approaches; it appeared rather that teachers resent, and resist, efforts to change them.[2] Thus the option of intensified teacher involvement in curriculum development seemed to be an idea whose time had come. And the interesting work being done in Britain[3] by and with teachers helped to bolster the conviction that it was time to credit teachers with a knowledgeable, autonomous role in the planning of instruction.

My own experience, when I began the study, had taught me to have considerable respect for the special skills and personal qualities which are required of teachers, day after day, in carrying out their work. And although increasing lip-service was being paid to the idea of teacher autonomy in curriculum development, it seemed to me there was something wrong with the way the teacher's role was conceptualized, and with the image of the teacher which researchers in particular carried around. Too frequently the emphasis was on diagnosing teacher failings and on prescribing improvements, whereas I was interested in seeing and understanding the situation from the teacher's own perspective.

Thus I set out to explore the consequences of taking up a view of the teacher as an agent, with an active and autonomous role shaped by her classroom experience. My purpose was to illustrate and to conceptualize this role with an emphasis on the knowledge held and used by the teacher in her work.

I explored the notion of the teacher's 'practical knowledge' in a series of open-ended discussions with one teacher, Sarah. These discussions dealt with her involvement in the planning and development of an experimental course and with a variety of issues arising out of this work, including Sarah's attitudes to teaching and learning, her conception of her subject matter in the two areas in which she taught (English and Reading), her values, commitments and career plans as a teacher. The discussions were supplemented by two periods of observation in the classroom and in a Reading Centre. The series of discussions and observation reports provided data in terms of which the conception of practical knowledge could be elaborated as well as illustration and insight into how this knowledge is held.

Before proceeding to think about the case study, it would be useful for the reader to consider for a moment his or her own experience of teachers' knowledge. While the specific situations in which teachers work vary considerably from place to place, I believe that if we reflect on our everyday experience of the work teachers do, their knowledge and its use are manifest. In program planning and in instruction, we see teachers choosing among alternative materials, deciding how to adapt programs to the needs of particular classes, combining materials to make up new curriculum packages, writing units and complete programs, and putting these into use in the classroom. Materials often require further modification in the light of student response, or diverse uses to meet the needs of individual students. Sometimes carefully made plans are thrown out the window in order to respond to one of the fleeting opportunities that classroom life offers; this too is a judgment made by the teacher.

In carrying out this work, the teacher exhibits wide-ranging knowledge which grows as experience increases.[4] This knowledge encompasses firsthand experience of students' learning styles, interests, needs, strengths and difficulties, and a repertoire of instructional techniques and classroom management skills. The teacher knows the social structure of the school and what it requires, of teacher and student, for survival and for success; she knows the community of which the school is a part, and has a sense of what it will and will not accept. This experiential knowledge is informed by the teacher's theoretical knowledge of subject matter, and of areas such as child development, learning and social theory. All of these kinds of knowledge, as integrated by the individual teacher in terms of personal values and beliefs and as oriented to her practical situation, will be referred to here as 'practical knowledge'.

I have chosen to use the term 'practical knowledge' because it focuses attention on the action and decision-oriented nature of the teacher's situation, and construes her knowledge as a function, in part, of her response to that situation. Consider the case of a history teacher; her knowledge may be ordered partly according to the particular theory of history she espouses, partly in terms of the organization imposed by a preferred textbook, and partly in terms of her experience of matters such as which topics students find most interesting and relevant. A question which is of great historical interest may be subordinated to a less significant issue around which the teacher can more effectively organize student concerns. The teacher's daily functioning in the classroom, and especially her decisions concerning presentation of instructional material, reflect the practical cast of her knowledge.

Moreover, the notion of 'practical knowledge' provides the basis for a conceptualization which sees the teacher as possessing valuable resources which enable her to take an active role in shaping her environment and in determining the style and ends of her work. If the teacher has such resources she becomes someone to work <u>with</u> rather than <u>on</u>.

The importance of building on the teacher's strengths is often acknowledged, but less often made a priority in curriculum development. In developing a conceptualization which articulates and provides detailed understanding of teachers' practical knowledge, I hope to make possible a fuller use of the human resources which teachers bring to their work.

The inadequacy of existing conceptualization of the teacher and her role in curriculum development, and the need for reconceptualization along the lines suggested above, can perhaps best be understood by looking at the context within which the inadequate conceptualization has evolved. Let us consider this context from three perspectives: first, let us look at conceptions of the curriculum development process within which teachers are seen to operate; second, at the way teachers generally are perceived; and finally, at notions of the teacher's knowledge.

THE TEACHER IN CURRICULUM DEVELOPMENT

Models of curriculum development tend to be linear affairs, beginning somewhere in the realm of theory and proceeding to an outcome in the realm of practice. The Tyler rationale is certainly the most widely-known American formulation of the ideal curriculum development process.[5] This rationale and its many variants share similar starting points; whether one begins with a conception of subject matter, with a view of how children learn, or with a statement of a social need, one is, in effect, adopting a particular theretical viewpoint which will determine all subsequent curricular choices. Most patterns for curriculum development proceed toward similar outcomes as well--a prescribed way for students to behave. At each end of this progression we find one or more experts--the subject-matter specialist, or curriculum developer (or, sometimes, the psychologist) initiates the work, while the specialist in evaluation determines whether or not it has been accomplished. Often the evaluator has assumed a primary role, ensuring that developers plan the kind of programs which evaluators know how to assess. This in itself would not be problematic-- on the contrary, it is irresponsible for a developer to plan a program without some idea of how its worth may be determined. The problem, rather, has been that extremely limited conceptions of evaluation, confined to the measurement of restricted outputs, have come to dominate so much curriculum work.

The consequences of this situation for teachers are manifold. First of all they are largely excluded from the work of curriculum development. The pattern specifies that one party (the developer), usually prompted by a second party (the evaluator), writes objectives and prepares materials for a third party (the student) which, almost by the way, are to be enacted by a fourth party--the teacher. Of course there are variations: occasionally it is suggested that students be given a share in the formulation of their own objectives; sometimes teachers are consulted for their presumed knowledge of the needs, interests and abilities of students. But objectives are not written by teachers, for teachers, despite the fact that they are thinking, feeling, striving human beings who will have to live with the consequences of curricular prescriptions no less than will the learners. Thus, standard conceptualizations of the curriculum development process tend almost to dismiss the teacher as an active participant. He is seen not in terms of agency but as a facilitator, enactor or conveyor; in short, he is seen as an instrument.

Considering that teachers are the people whose task it is to translate theoretical notions into practice, and that classroom events are the sole "embodiments of the curriculum"[6], this view of the teacher's role in curriculum is seriously inadequate. A simplistic view of the process by which curricular prescriptions come to be embodied in classroom practice has one advantage of sorts for developers, however. If the teacher's task can be presented as a straightforward one, then whatever difficulties impede the implementation process can be attributed to the teacher's personal failings. This creates a paradoxical situation in which teachers' active role in the creation of new instructional arrangements is denied, but they are credited with a generous share of the responsibility for failure. The paradox is suggestive of a blind spot in the vision of curriculum specialists and developers; it would appear that they refuse to perceive that which is not in their power to control, the work of teachers.

It is, however, becoming increasingly difficult, in Westbury's words, "to see the classroom as a place in which goals can simply and directly order instruction because ends-means relationships are transparent."[7] There have, in recent years, been two types of critique of our habitual views of curriculum and the classroom. One critique concerns the practical viability of the linear conception of curriculum; the second critique is directed at the implicit values underlying the conception.

The first type of critique is best represented by Joseph Schwab[8], who has argued forcibly that the theoretically-derived conceptions of curriculum with which we have been operating lack both the power to generate serious discussion in the field and the power to order and regulate practice or bring about change. This critique is supported by a variety of phenomena--the contentious debate around the subject of behavioural objectives, for example, and the now well-documented failure of traditional curriculum research to reveal significant differences for one curricular treatment over another.[9] From his critique Schwab elaborated a conception of curriculum as practical, a view which does away with the artificial divorce of ends and means, and focusses attention on decision making, or deliberation. Working within this conception, Connelly's notion of the teacher as 'user-developer'[10] acknowledges the autonomous decision-making function of teachers in adopting, adapting and sometimes developing materials appropriate to their situations. This conception of curriculum development makes possible, and legitimates both a different style of curriculum development and a different form of curriculum research. Thus there is an increasing number of studies which serve to demonstrate that the locus of the teacher within the curriculum development process is one of great intricacy, calling forth from him a complex type of action and decision making which is simply ignored by curriculum studies focused solely on intended outcomes.[11]

The second type of critique of the linear view of curriculum has taken a variety of forms. Within the current of existential and humanist writing on curriculum, for example, it is argued that the curriculum is not merely a product but a lived experience in which the efforts of individuals to disclose meaning are critical.[12] The ethical thrust of such work is an important complement to an overly pragmatic view of curriculum. It is, however, important to try to understand why it has been so dificult, within curriculum, to deal with issues of value. In some cases we can see this as simply an influence of the behaviourist idiom, which inevitably restricts the formulation of evaluative issues.[13] But the behaviourist idiom, and the technological perspective on which it rests, are extremely pervasive in our society, and we must look to more fundamental social analyses to gain a critical view of the framework within which our industrial society permits us to view the processes of schooling.[14] However such analyses provide a critique of curriculum at a high level of abstraction. The implications of such critiques for practice are not immediately obvious, therefore, and within the curriculum field there is at present little consensus concerning viable practical alternatives to the technologically-oriented linear view of curriculum development. Thus it is by no means surprising that within the context of current thought on curriculum a more adequate view of the teacher's role has not been developed.[15] Let us now compare this situation with the views put forward in current research on teaching.

THE TEACHER

While conceptualizations of curriculum development and of the classroom are critical in determining the role played by the teacher in using curricula in classrooms, there is also much direct discussion of teachers and of teaching which bears on the way they are viewed and on the roles made available to them.
    Research on teaching, like classroom research, has generally viewed teachers in a fragmented way, in terms of isolated characteristics, and from a negative stance.[16] Thus "psychologists have usually approached the psychology of teachers in a negative fashion through Hawthorne effects, novelty effects, Rosenthal effects, halo effects, etc. These biasing effects smack of the 'paint by numbers' conception of teachers as automatic painting machines."[17] Such approaches reinforce the

view of the teacher as instrument; she is a cog in
the educational machine, and one which often seems
to fall below the quality-controlled standards of
the whole, at that. Thus suggestions--training in
competency-based teaching, for one--are offered for
improving the quality of the product.[18]   Part
of the problem of such research undoubtedly lies in
viewing the teacher and her work in isolation from
the substance of what she teaches, that which gives
much of its meaning and direction to her work. But
the main failing of these approaches is that they
view teachers as passive, dependent and often
unsuccessful participants in the educational enterprise; given such a view it is not to be expected
that much evidence of teachers' active and purpose-
ful role will be brought to light.

Examination of the social context of education
tells us that the research stance towards teachers
is consistent with the prevalent view of teachers
in our society: though not often publicly stated,
it is commonly held that teachers are inadequate to
their tasks, either by reason of ineffective training or of self-selection. ("Those who can, do;
those who can't, teach.") The negative assessment
of the teacher's abilities is so widespread, and
the reasons for it so apparent, that it hardly
seems worth discussing. But in fact this 'taken-
for-granted' situation is quite unique: I can
think of no other field of endeavour in which there
is a comparable gap between the value and importance attached to the work, and the level of ability generally attributed to those performing
it.[19]   The influence on teachers' self-
conception of so demeaning a social assessment
cannot be overestimated. It is likely to dampen
enthusiasm for independent and creative work, and
to ensure teachers' acceptance of a passive, instrumental role.

Fortunately, the limitations of such negative
and fragmented views of the teacher are now receiving attention in the research literature, and more
adequate approaches are being formulated .[20]
Sarason stresses "the need to adopt the set of
understanding each role, controlling the tendency
to criticize" and making a conscious effort to see
matters from the point of view of the persons under
study. Hunt reminds us that teachers are persons,
not mere objects of research.[21]   Research on
teaching is gradually becoming aware that a holis-
tic study of 'persons-in-relation', though it does

10

not operate from the usual canons of scientific objectivity and verifiability, need not lack in rigour and analytic power. It is on work such as this that the present study draws for its approach to the teacher.

THE TEACHER'S KNOWLEDGE

The single factor which seems to have the greatest power to carry forward our understanding of the teacher's role is the idea of teachers' knowledge. Teachers' thinking processes have been given some attention in recent research.[22] But teachers are not commonly seen to possess a body of knowledge and expertise appropriate to their work, and this tends to diminish their status in the eyes of laymen.

It is hardly surprising that teachers have developed no such articulated body of knowledge, if we consider the context of teaching. To begin with, teachers are trained in a setting which is rarely seen by them as serious or relevant to their future work; thus, whatever conceptual skills they might acquire during their training would tend to be compartmentalized, rather than applied to the understanding of teaching. In teaching itself, while teachers may often rehash and compare experiences, they in fact have little experience that is shared, and there are few opportunities for them to reflect on and attempt to articulate their experience in an organized way. Finally, the view of knowledge as 'empirical' and 'analytic', which prevails in educational thought, tends to place a relatively low value on experiential knowledge, and thus teachers themselves may be unaware of the value of their own knowledge. Certainly there is little encouragement for teachers to view themselves as originators of knowledge.

I believe that the view of teachers as lacking in knowledge is mistaken and misleading, and that it has maintained credibility, partly at least, because of the conceptions of curriculum development and of teaching through which teachers have been viewed. Once these conceptions are suspended, a very different picture of teachers' knowledge comes to the fore. Thus, for example, Reid, in summarizing a series of case studies which focus on the diversities of actual curriculum practice, points to "the teacher as one of the main sources of curriculum stability" due to "the existence among teachers of stable bodies of ideas about how and what to teach."[23] And Hunt, making the shift to view teachers as persons, comes to regard as primary the conceptions of students, teaching approaches and learning outcomes which shape their work. In both instances, a view of the teacher as holding and using knowledge emerges from study done under the aegis of conceptions of curriculum and of teaching which take account of the work actually done by teachers.

Several recent studies of the work teachers do have directed their attention to teachers' knowledge in one form or another. Bussis, Chittenden and Amarel, for example, have examined what they term 'teachers understandings'.[24] Using in-depth interviews with sixty teachers involved in 'open education', they probed the constructs relating to curriculum, child development and learning which teachers bring to their work, and examined the relationships among these constructs. However, these authers have not attempted a conceptualization of teachers' knowledge per se, and because their analysis draws many of its terms from the philosophy of 'open education' which the teachers they interviewed were trying to implement, they have not been concerned with knowledge of discipline subject matter which is an important element of the present study. Nor have they treated the socially-conditioned aspect of teachers' knowledge which will be discussed below.

A number of British researchers have also dealt with teachers' knowledge. Barnes, Keddie, and Esland,[25] share a concern with the socially-conditioned presuppositions manifested in the teacher's linguistic expression, which shape his interactions with pupils. Such work seems to me extremely important in so far as it helps both teachers and researchers to become aware of the implicit values and assumptions which shape our work. In Chapter 9, I will take up a similar perspective in order to reflect on the interview process in which Sarah and I engaged. However, in studying teachers' knowledge I chose deliberately not to adopt what might be termed a critical perspective. The main reason for this choice is that critical analyses of teaching often tend to cast the teacher once again in a passive role, as we are made aware of how teachers unwittingly serve to reproduce the inequitable social distribution of knowledge. Because of my concern to show that it is possible to view teachers as autonomous agents, holding and using knowledge, it seemed preferable to hold the critical perspective in abeyance (though certainly my own values and assumptions will be in evidence throughout the presentation and interpretation of data) and to try to present the teacher from a perspective that can reflect her own experiencing of her role and work.

In attempting to articulate the teacher's perspective, of course, it is inevitable that I as a researcher should bring to the task a perspective, or conceptual framework of my own. This perspective, derived from my own experience of curriculum work and of teaching as well as from theoretical sources, generated a number of working assumptions which guided the study. The most basic assumption, of course, is simply that practical knowledge exists and that a direct examination of the thinking of teachers at work will make apparent to us the nature, defining characteristics and criteria of this knowledge. Obviously this statement implies both a conceptual focus, or a particular way of speaking about teachers' knowledge, and a methodological commitment to a particular way of studying this knowledge. In the sections that follow these two aspects of the study will be discussed.

THE CONCEPTION OF PRACTICAL KNOWLEDGE

The conception of practical knowledge with which I worked in the study was not an abstract, theoretical notion, nor did it arise in a vacuum. As a researcher and a curriculum worker I had observed the work of teachers and this observation had been assimilated into my own experience of instruction. At a certain point my experience became problematic: the expectations placed on teachers did not match with the contribution they could realistically make in planning for instruction.[26] In my efforts to deal with this problem I developed a number of working assumptions which helped give shape to the notion of practical knowledge. These assumptions were influenced by a variety of theoretical formulations but they do not, in themselves, constitute a theoretical account of practical knowledge. They are simply a series of ideas which enabled me to work on the problem, and I present them here so that the reader can follow the process, can trace the development of some of the analytic categories to be used in looking at the data

and can, if he or she wishes, pursue some of these
directions in looking at his or her own practical
knowledge. My assumptions concerned the content of
practical knowledge, the way it is held or oriented, its structure, and its 'cognitive style'.
Each of these aspects will be reviewed, after which
the methodological considerations which followed
from this conceptual starting point will be
discussed.

The Content of Practical Knowledge

The assumption that practical knowledge is knowledge of something, that it has content, involves a basic choice. We might imagine that practical knowledge is strictly knowledge of how to do
things; indeed, this would seem the more obvious
position to take. But I feel it is important to
recognize that teachers do have knowledge of con-
tent--propositional knowledge of states of affairs,
beliefs, and the like--and that such knowledge is
usually undervalued only because it seems to compare poorly with the seemingly superior knowledge
possessed by specialists in the various fields. It
seems to me worth showing that teachers do, for
example, have psychological knowledge (albeit less
or different than the psychologist's) in order
subsequently to show what they do with this knowledge, the unique ways in which they hold and use
it.
    In talking about the content of teachers'
practical knowledge I chose to use five categories
which appear to reflect differences that are relevant to teachers (rather than academic distinctions
among disiplines of study): thus we will speak of
knowledge of self, of the milieu of teaching, of
subject matter, curiculum development, and
instruction.

The Orientations of Practical Knowledge

The term "orientation" is meant to reflect the way
that practical knowledge is held and used. I
identified five orientations each of which generated assumptions and questions about the teacher's
use of knowledge. The five are the orientation to
situations, the personal orientation, the social
orientation, the experiential orientation and the
theoretical orientation. The five orientations of

Sarah's knowledge will be discussed in Chapter 6; here the five aspects will be reviewed briefly.

Orientation to Situation. Observation of teachers' work, their discussions of it and their participation in pre-service and in-service training clearly demonstrate that teachers' knowledge is oriented to situations. Teachers in graduate programs in education as well as in pre-service training typically complain that courses structured in terms of the areas of academic specialization of faculty are irrelevant to their practical problems. We can understand from this complaint that teachers are aware of the need for .an integrated, practical orientation.

The orientation of teachers' knowledge to situations should not be understood to mean that the teacher will necessarily incorporate the most "practical", rather than theoretical, bits of knowledge from the various disciplines; the teacher's practical knowledge is not a compendium of practical advice from other fields, but a body of knowledge oriented to a particular practical context. Thus, for example, some of the most useful practical tools possessed by a psychologist--those concerning therapy--may be quite inappropriate for the teacher, whereas some of the theoretic knowledge of psychology may be applied very effectively by the teacher in her own situation.

Orientation to practice also determines the methods by which practical knowledge is sought. The teacher has no unique, specialized methods by which he extends his knowledge; he uses his skills of observation, comparison, trial and error, as well as whatever specialized research training he may have (though such training may well conflict with the needs of practice). Deliberative process is the main way in which practical knowledge is examined in terms of its adequacy to particular problems, but intuitive and reflective processes that focus on general issues, goals and beliefs, are likely to be equally important for some teachers.

This view of the teacher's knowledge as oriented to situations is influenced by a number of theoretical statements concerning the relation of theory and practice. Dewey's analysis[27], which emphasizes that all knowledge originates in felt problems, is perhaps the clearest statement of the interrelation of theory and practice. However, it is Schwab[28] who brought the issue of theory versus practice to the forefront of concern in the curriculum field, and the present study is in line with the thrust of his argument insofar as it sees the teacher's work as eminently practical and calling for conceptualization in practical terms. However, Schwab used as a major tool of his argument an analysis of the Aristotelian distinction between theory and practice, which the present study views as inadequate for a characterization of teaching practice, because teachers' knowledge is viewed as informed by theory rather than divorced from it.

Another important effort to eliminate the theory/practice distinction is found in the work of phenmenological sociology[29] which speaks of the knowledge which structures our unexamined reality and which makes possible both our everyday functioning and that specialized form of activity which constitutes the scientific enterprise. The teacher's practical knowledge can be viewed as a special case of the everyday knowledge which we all possess. Because the teaching situation has distinctive features which make it easier to define than everyday situations, the teacher's practical knowledge may be more accessible than other kinds of everyday knowledge. However, I am not particularly concerned with the teacher's knowledge as an instance of the more general phenomenon, but rather with the relation of the teacher's knowledge to his specific situation, tasks and purposes.

Practical Knowledge as Personal. The second group of assumptions concerns the personal character of the teacher's knowledge. Every encounter between teacher and student, or teacher and researcher, reveals the divergent points of view from which the two parties perceive their common situation, select different aspects of the situation to attend to as data, and place differing interpretations on the data. These points of view, and the interpretations which they produce, reflect a personal need to integrate, order and render meaningful one's experience. The role of purpose and personal meaning in shaping perception, point of view and interpretation is recognized and elaborated on by philosophic systems as diverse as the pragmatic, the existential and the phenomenological[30]; by philosophers of science[31], psychologists and educators.[32] Thus any study of the teacher's practical knowledge must seek out the particular perspective and point of view which shapes it, however implicitly.

The notion of the teacher's perspective is not to be understood narrowly. It encompasses not only intellectual belief, but also perception, feeling, values, purpose and commitment. This breadth of perspective which underlies knowledge is captured in psychological theories which emphasize the individual's "construct system".[33] Such theories show that the search for knowledge is motivated by the entire range of human feeling, need and desire, and by the perspectives, points of view, system of constructs, which are elaborated to deal with the world. To characterize knowledge in general, and teacher's practical knowledge in particular, in this way is to speak less of knowledge-as-product than of knowledge-as-process, the act or acts of creating knowledge. It is to emphasize the active, constructive and purposive nature of mind and of knowledge. This view seems particularly appropriate simply because, being practical, the teacher's knowledge is much more accessible to observation in use than in formally articulated or codified form.

It is also appropriate to emphasize the elements of purpose and commitment when speaking of practical knowledge. The teacher confronts a classroom full of waiting human beings; ultimately, the psychological sense of responsibility for what happens to these students in the course of the day devolves upon the teacher. In the practical context it is the teacher, not the learning theorist, who is the final authority on learning; the teacher, not the sociologist, who is the final authority on the social development of children; the teacher, not the psychologist or artist, who is the final authority on the creativity of children; the teacher, not the scientist, who is the final authority on the science kids learn. Whether or not such authority is actually granted him, the teacher is the only one in a practical position to discharge it. This situation gives rise to a two-sided personal commitment of the teacher to his knowledge: he is responsible for it, in the sense of having authority; and he has an enormous interst in the validity of his knowledge since the discharge of his responsibility depends on it.

In summary, then, to speak of the teacher's knowledge as personal is to operate within a framework which sees the teacher as the ultimate practical authority on what kids do in classrooms, and to view his practical knowledge as the result of his effort to assume that authority in a responsible and personally meaningful way.

Practical Knowledge as Social. It is acknowledged that practical knowledge, like any other ordering of experience, is socially conditioned. This aspect of the teacher's knowledge is reflected in the way she will, for example, automatically shape her subject matter to take account of ethnic or economic factors that influence students' (or their parents') expectations, interests, and sense of propriety. It is revealed in the kinds of expectations and limits teachers set for students of particular social backgrounds, However, while this kind of conditioning of the teacher's knowledge is pervasive and important, her social biases and preconceptions are in principle no less available to her awareness and no less suitable as subjects of deliberation and choice among alternatives than are other aspects of the teacher's practical knowledge. Thus, in this study I was less interested in detecting social bias in the teacher's knowledge than in observing the social nature of the deliberative process. I assume that practical knowledge will be manifested in any encounter between the teacher and other parties concerned with her work. In particular, the meeting between teacher and researcher is seen as having the potential to illuminate some of the boundaries and points of vulnerability of the teacher's knowledge. However, while the social dimension is unquestionably basic, it is not seen as taking priority over the other dimensions of the teacher's knowledge.

Practical Knowledge as Experiential. Implicit in the situational, personal and social orientations of the teacher's knowledge is its experiential base. This aspect of knowledge has been most directly and thoroughly examined in the writings of phenomenologists. For example, Schutz and Luckmann's The Structures of the Lifeworld takes up the task of describing the world of our everyday experiencing and the knowledge which gives shape to this world and by means of which we function in it. Schutz points out that the stock of knowledge is structured broadly in terms of different 'provinces of reality', each with its characteristic 'meaning-structure': the everyday life-world, the world of dreams, the world of science, the world of religious experience; these worlds can be distinguished in terms of the particular 'cognitive style' taken by the agent. The world of teaching seems to be an open one, overlapping the everyday world, yet it has a certain coherence and distinctiveness which are important to note.[34]

One of the factors which help to maintain the coherence of a given world consists in the suspension of all doubts concerning the existence and nature of objects in the world around us. In the world of teaching this suspension of doubt involves a particularly marked 'bracketing' of experience. For in teaching the assumption often seems to be made that the world of school is complete unto itself. Teachers are often cautioned not to become overly involved in students' emotional problems nor to project their own personal lives into the classroom; there are debates concerning the degree of moral or political influence which teachers may have over students; religious and sex education are often seen to be private matters; and all of these issues, it is assumed, can be eliminated from discussion of the curriculum and from classroom life without detriment to the integrity of what goes on in class. Often it is acknowledged that these matters inevitably creep in the back door through teaching style, manner of presentation and organization of clasroom life; and sometimes, teachers are encouraged to bring to awareness thir hidden presuppositions[35] but such reflective activity is always--and necessarily--seen as an adjunct to teaching. To reflect constantly on one's teaching acts while they are going on would be to destroy the coherence of teaching and perhaps render it impossible to continue. The nature of the teaching situation as practical seems to demand that this restricted world be taken as whole and complete. In order to characterize her world as the teacher experiences it, it will be necessary to delineate its boundaries and to determine their permeability. To what degree, for example, can the teacher afford to become involved emotionally with students? What happens when she begins to consider seriously the moral impact of her teaching, or its political implications?

The time perspective taken up by the teacher is another important dimension of her experience, which seems to be related to the bracketing procedure which makes of school life a totality. Thus three o'clock is the end of the day; students (and teachers) are tired--the violent display of energy with which they burst out of the school notwithstanding. The school week, the school year, have their particular rhythms which, once learned, are taken for granted. There are, however, very different time perspectives which can be taken up: the progression of days and weeks can be seen as essentially similar, a simple series of events, rhythmic or monotonous as the case may be, or as a dynamic series with progress and change--patterned and planned, or unexpected and chaotic.

Third, the tension of consciousness, the agent's level of interest or attentiveness, is an important aspect of the teacher's experience. Several writers, indeed, have spoken of the teacher's need to be aware of many phenomena simultaneously, and of the stress which results.[36] Finally, the form of spontaneity which is allowed within a given context is a factor which clearly differentiates different 'worlds' (compare the teacher's response to a discipline problem at school with the way she might react to the same behaviour manifested by a child at summer camp, or at home).

These dimensions of the teacher's experience are mutually related and mutually informing. Thus the teacher's time perspective tells us something about how she perceives herself (imprisoned in a lock-step of meaningless routines, or racing to keep up) and her students (alive and growing human beings, or mischief-makers forever playing the same tricks?) The tension of consciousness which she brings to her experience would seem related to the level and form of spontaneity possible for her: a change in the form of spontaneity seems to require some corresponding change in the tension of consciousness, as daydreaming depends upon relaxation, and creative activity requires a form of increased awareness, Finally the maintaining of the world of teaching as a coherent whole seems to depend on all the other factors--calling into question matters usually taken for granted will have the effect of altering the teacher's awareness, changing the forms of spontaneity available to her and her self-experience, and possibly even influencing the social and temporal dimensions of her experience. For example, altering teachers' self-experience and social perceptions by imposing on them curricular reform which treats them as students who must learn the developer's materials inevitably has the effect of restricting spontaneity and heightening tension of consciousness, crowding the time perspective so that teachers despair of accomplishing the work expected in the time available, and calling into question the very nature and meaning of their tasks.

The Theoretical Orientation. The notion of theoretical orientation refers to the fact that the teacher's knowledge is held in a particular relationship to the realm of theory. Teachers, like all members of society, are influenced by the forms of thought and discourse which go on around them; their academic training invariably deepens such influences and instils conceptions of theory, of valid knowledge, of research. If articulated directly, such conceptions would form part of the content of the teacher's knowledge. But when a view of what "theory" is operates indirectly to shape knowledge in various content areas, it is appropriate to speak of a theoretical orientation.

Sarah, as we will see, holds a view of theoretical knowledge as general, comprehensive and objective; she sees her own knowledge as subordinate to theory. It would perhaps be more correct to say that she holds an implicit theory of knowledge which informs her practical knowledge, or that her knowledge has an epistemological orientation. But in Sarah's case it is the idea of "theory" to which she relates, and to speak of an epistemological orientation would be to go somewhat beyond the data, so we will retain the term, theorerical orientation.

The Structure of Practical Knowledge.

Although the five orientations just outlined serve to order a view of the teacher's knowledge, it is also important to attend to the internal structure of her knowledge. Because the teacher's knowledge serves to guide her work and helps, in part, to generate a degree of consistency in her practice, it is reasonable to assume that her knowledge will be marked by some form of structure. Otherwise we would have to envision a long series of rules of thumb, or recipes--a sort of unwritten cookbook without table of contents or index, to which the teacher would refer mentally before deciding on a course of action. Such a jumbled mass of information, no matter how relevant to practice, could hardly guide teaching (and would surely not give rise to consistent practice) since the teacher would be unlikely to come up with the most appropriate recipe very often.

Thus I assumed the teacher's knowledge would be organized in a somewhat hierarchical manner, with varying levels of generality, and I also expected to find different types of ordering devices at each level. Three terms will be used to reflect this: "rules of practice", which are specific directives, "practical principles" which are at an intermediate level of generality, and "images" which are broad, metaphoric statements. The use of these terms to analyse the structure of Sarah's practical knowledge will be described in Chapter 7.

Cognitive Style

I believe that teachers exhibit a particular style in the way they hold and use their practical knowledge.The notion of "cognitive style" has generated a considerable body of literature in psychology, but despite an intent to rejoin the cognitive and affective domains, this work seems to me too narrow in scope to further our understanding of teachers' knowledge. The conception of "cognitive style" elaborated by Shutz[37], however, is most helpful in pointing to the quality which unifies an individual's "lived experience". I use the notion of cognitive style to indicate the features of unity and coherence which make it possible to describe someone's actions as having "style". Further, the notion of "cognitive style" enabled me to draw together the various strands of the analysis of Sarah's practical knowledge and to present them in a single account; this will be done in Chapter 8.

The set of terms just outlined is closely tied to the particular way in which the study was conducted; thus the nature of the methodological commitments made can help to clarify what practical knowledge might be.

METHODOLOGICAL ISSUES

The methodology of this study was determined by the notion of practical knowledge in several different respects. "Practical knowledge" is a conception which seeks to bridge gaps existing between areas of knowledge which particular points of view enjoin us to view as separate--theoretical and practical knowledge, the cognitive and the affective domains, knowledge viewed (empiric-analytically) as product and knowledge viewed (phenomenologically) as process. Similarly, the methodology of the study seeks to bridge methodological gaps between theoretic and practical method, between cognitive and affective modes of understanding, and between empiric-analytic and phenomenological styles of research. The bridge sought is in each case a practical one. The aim is to develop a method of studying teachers (and of conceiving their role and work) that takes account of both cognitive and affective considerations; that reflects their orientation to action and to experience, without ignoring the stable and invariant features of their work and their knowledge; and that acknowledges the importance of theory while firmly situated in practice.

It is the last consideration which is central to what follows. While there is much recent work on methodology in education and in the social sciences which argues for unification of cognitive and affective, and for rapprochement of empiric-analytic and phenomenological methods[38], the justification for the methodology elaborated here is first and foremost practical. It is because the teacher functions as a whole person that we seek to unite cognitive and affective. It is because of the dual need to account for, and help to order, the teacher's everyday experience in teaching, that empiric-analytic and phenomenological methods must be relied upon. And the need to elaborate a conception which can speak to the curriculum field and to those concerned with teaching necessitates that the methodology of the study be one which respects the canons and conventions of the field.

I chose to carry out a case study because, in the present state of our understanding of teachers' knowledge, it seemed that vivid and complete description of a single case was especially needed. I see the case study as a method that is particularly appropriate to attain an understanding of the teacher's knowledge from her own point of view. One guarantee of being able to account for the teacher's knowledge in a real way was the choice of a teacher who was committed to her work, able to articulate her point of view and interested in doing so. Furthermore, the teacher I chose was a friend whose work I found interesting, and this made it probable that we would establish a rapport easily and early on in the interviews.

I held a series of five informal interviews with Sarah, each about two hours long, and supplemented by two periods of observation in her classes. All the interviews were recorded and later transcribed. Following each interview the tape or transcript was studied, preliminary interpretations were made, and questions were formulated to guide the next interview. I gave copies of the transcripts to Sarah, usually prior to the following interview. At the end of the interview series (a period of about 18 months), I analyzed and interpreted the complete set of transcripts using the categories outlined above. When the analytic portion of the study was complete I gave it to Sarah and we held a final talk (which was taped but not transcribed).

Within this view of the case study, issues which might be problematic to the experimental tradition often become matters of interest to be pursued further. For example, the teacher's awareness of her knowledge, and her ability to articulate it (which might be viewed as obstacles to getting at the "facts" in an experimental study) are precisely the issues I hoped to observe and document in the interviews. Similarly, Sarah's willingness to cooperate and her feelings of comfort or discomfort in the interview situation served as clues to her practical knowledge. The reader who wishes to follow more closely the interpretive process can consult the Appendix, in which summaries of each interview, along with extensive citations from the transcripts, are provided.[39] In this way it becomes possible for the case study to meet rigourous criteria of validation.

The basic assumption which guided the interviews and the case study was the notion that the research subject is a person, who has feelings, values, needs and purposes which condition his or her participation in the research. Thus I undertook to disclose my purposes and interpretations to the teacher and to solicit her own purposes and interpretations. This proved to be much more difficult than I had anticipated: the notion of "objectivity" clung to the fringes of my awareness, as a strong situational constraint that subtly influenced me to favour a more detached style of interviewing. Despite this, the emotional climate during the interviews was largely positive and allowed a rapport to be established, and errors of interpretation to be clarified. As an example of this process, consider the following excerpt from the first interview. Sarah had been describing the Learning Course, an experimental course on which she was working, and had been explaining the careful structuring of skills that the Learning Course involved. She went on:

S. Well, I think I am more aloof and more structured and more demanding in the Grade 11 course, which is a regular, traditional literature course. And part of that is from whatever input I get from the Learning Course.

F. Do you think maybe it's in some way also a kind of reaction to having so much of the open kind of stuff in this course? The Learning Course. Would you somehow feel that, I don't know, that you weren't doing your job if you were having very open-ended, high risk, little evaluation and judgment in all of your courses?

S. We missed each other somewhere along the line, because my feeling about this course that we're talking about, the Learning Course, is that it is actually quite a tight course.

F. Yes, I'm sorry, you said that before, maybe I'm projecting my own...

S. And I don't want to give the impression that we sit and rap, and stuff like that, because we definitely don't.

F. Yes.

S. I think I do communicate a feeling that it's a special course for me, and that I consider them special kids. But the assignments I give, and the way I mark, are quite objectively there, and I don't have to have to take a lot of human considerations into my view of what they're doing.

The communication block that became apparent in this segment of the discussion helped me to become aware of my own bias against the notion of "content-free" learning skills, and helped me to realize how important it was to listen carefully during the interviews.

The Teacher--Sarah

Sarah is an English teacher who was about thirty years old and had had about ten years of experience at the time the study began. For several years she had taught English as a second language abroad, and had worked with disadvantaged students. She had received an Honours degree (which involved four years of study as opposed to the three years required for a general degree) in English from a large university whose English department was known for a classical approach and rigorous standards. Although she had never taken a regular teacher training program, she had been allowed, because of her experience abroad, to obtain certification through a series of summer courses. She was in her fifth year at her present position in a large, suburban high school in a middle-class neighbourhood in Toronto, Canada. While the school did not offer a vocational program it nevertheless took in students with a wide range of abilities; both "general" and "academic" programs were available, covering the span from grades ten to thirteen.[40] Sarah had taught English literature and writing workshops, often (but not exclusively) to the academically-oriented students of grade thirteen. Sarah and I had discussed her work, and I had seen her teach, so I knew her to be a committed and successful teacher. For the most part, what we discussed in the interviews was information I had not known before. During the previous year Sarah had worked with four other teachers on the development of the experimental course (mentioned above) known as the Learning Course. The course, which drew on material in language, communications, behavioural science, statistics and history, dealt with reading and information-getting skills, and was intended for Grade 10 students. I found the course particularly interesting because it seemed to bring to the surface Sarah's view of learning and her idea of the relationship between teaching and learning.

SUMMARY

I have sketched the intellectual context within which this study evolved and have indicated the main aspects of the conception of practical knowledge which will be used in the chapters to come to analyze the data. The brief overview of the methodology will, I hope allow the reader to follow the account. In Chapter 9, I will return to a consideration of methodological issues as I review what I have learned from this study about the shared participation of teachers and researchers in such work. In Chapter 2 the account begins with a description of the world of teaching within which Sarah carries on her work.

NOTES

1. With respect to the gender of pronouns, my solution to the dilemma here is to use both; female pronouns will predominate, however, just as women tend to predominate in the field of teaching.
2. Teacher response to innovation has been treated by many writers; see, for example, J. Goodlad and M. Klein, Behind the Classroom Door (Worthington, Ohio: Charles A. Jones, 1970); Michael Fullan, "Overview of the Innovative Process and the User," Interchange 3, Nos. 2-3 (1972), 1-46; Seymour B. Sarason, The Culture of the School and the Problem of Change (Boston: Allyn and Bacon, 1971); and L.M. Smith and P.M. Keith, Anatomy of Educational Innovation (New York: Wiley, 1971).
3. In the area of curriculum I have in mind, in particular, the work of the Humanities Curriculum Project--see Lawrence Stenhouse, "The Humanities Curriculum Project", Journal of Curriculum Studies I, No. 1 (1968); and the Ford Teaching Project--see John Elliott and Clem Adelman, "Innovation at the Classroom Level," Unit 28, Open University Course E203 (Milton Keynes: Open University Press, 1976), 43-92.

British sociologists of education have also focused on teachers as agents, specifically on the notion of classroom coping strategies. A recent effort to integrate some of this work is found in Andrew Pollard, "A Model of Classroom Coping Strategies," British Journal of Sociology of Education 3, No. 1 (1982), 19-37. Pollard seems to be working to overcome one limitation of earlier work which seemed at times to portray teachers as able to do little more than 'cope'.

4. I am not concerned here with how skilled teachers actually are in curriculum planning. In fact, having been given little training and few opportunities to take part in organized development efforts, they may indeed lack some of the necessary skills. But the considerable and varied knowledge brought to the task is surely evident.

5. Ralph W. Tyler, Basic Principles of Curriculum and Instruction (Chicago: University of Chicago Press, 1949).

6. Ian Westbury, "The Curriculum and the Frames of the Classroom," paper presented at the annual meeting of the American Educational Research Association, New York 1977.

7. Westbury, ibid, p. 2.

8. Joseph J. Schwab, "The Practical: A Language for Curriculum", School Review 78 (1969), p. 1-23.

9. See, for example, Decker F. Walker and Jon Schaffarzick, "Comparing Curricula," Review of Educational Research 44 (1974), 83-111.

10. F. Michael Connelly, "The Functions of Curriculum Development," Interchange 3, Nos. 2-3 (1972), 161-177.

11. The volume of case studies edited by W.A. Reid and Decker F. Walker, Case Studies in Curriculum Change (London and Boston: Routledge and Kegan Paul, 1975), provides a number of interesting examples, in particular the chapters by Hamilton and Shaw.

12. See Dwayne Huebner, "Curriculum as a Field of Study," in Helen F. Robinson, ed., Precedents and Promise in the Curriculum Field (New York: Basic Books, 1965); John S. Mann, "Curriculum Criticism", Curriculum Theory Network 2 (Winter 198-9), 2-14.

13. The issue of behaviourist language is treated by L.B. Daniels, "What is the Language of the Practical?", Curriculum Theory Network 4, No. 4 (1975), 237-261, and by Kenneth E. Strike, "On the

Expressive Potential of Behaviorist Language," _American Educational Research Journal_ 11 (1974), 103-120.

14. Two fundamental works are Michael F.D. Young, ed., _Knowledge and Control_ (London: Collier-Macmillan, 1976), and Michael Apple, _Ideology and Curriculum_ (London and Boston: Routledge and Kegan Paul, 1979).

15. See, however, Malcolm Skilbeck, "School-Based Curriculum Development," _Supporting Curriculum Development_, William Prescot and Ray Bolam, Open University Course E203, Unit 24-26 (Milton Keynes: The Open University Press, 1976), pp. 90-102.

16. A classic study of this kind is D.G. Ryans, _Characteristics of Teachers, their Description, Comparison and Appraisal_ (Washington, D.C.: American Council on Education, 1960).

17. David Hunt, "Teachers are Psychologists, too: On the Application of Psychology to Education," _Canadian Psychological Review_ 17, No.3 (July 1976), 210-218.

18. In a critical analysis of four behaviourally oriented teacher-training models, Apple points out that these models "attempt to use behaviorism to establish a sense of teacher responsibility and accountability;" but this is done in terms of goals determined by others in the system. See Michael Apple, "Behaviorism and Conservatism: The Educational Views in Four of the 'Systems' Models of Teacher Education," in Bruce Joyce and Marsha Weil, eds., _Perspectives for Reform in Teacher Education_ (Englewood Cliffs, N.J.: Prentice-Hall, 1972).

19. The notion of identifying and reexamining a portion of our "taken-for-granted' reality is drawn from the work of phenomenological sociologists and psychologists; specific references will be provided below.

20. A good indication of the range of recent work in this area is provided by P.L. Peterson and H.J. Walberg, _Research on Teaching_ (Berkeley, Calif.: McCutchan, 1979); see also Richard Shavelson and Paula Stern, "Research on Teachers' Pedagogical Thoughts, Judgments, Decisions and Behavior," _Review of Educational Research_ 51, No.4 (1981), 455-498.

21. Sarason, op. cit., p. 4. Hunt, op. cit.

22. See Christopher M. Clark and Robert J. Yinger, "Research on Teacher Thinking," _Curriculum_

Inquiry 7, No.4 (1977), 279-304.
     23. Reid and Walker, op. cit. Reid's formula-
tion is especially interesting because it shows
clearly how a shift in point of view moves us from
seeing the teacher as a reactionary figure who
obstructs change to regarding her as the source of
a necessary continuity and coherence in schooling,
without which rational change would be impossible.
     24. Anne M. Bussis, Edward A. Chittenden, and
Marianne Amarel, Beyond Surface Curriculum (Boul-
der: Westview Press, 1976).
     25. Douglas Barnes, From Communication to
Curriculum (Harmondsworth: Penguin Books, 1976);
Nell Keddie, "Classroom Knowledge," in Young, op.
cit.; G.M. Esland, "Teaching and Learning as the
Organization of Knowledge," in Young, op. cit..
     26. Thus far we have spoken mainly of the
underestimation of the teacher's role in curriculum
but there have been errors of the opposite kind as
well. On occasion teacher-based curriculum development has been enthusiastically espoused with
little thought given to the necessary preconditions
and, quite paradoxically, without consulting the
teachers who are to be involved. Typically teachers are less than pleased with what they see as
the imposition of extra work, and the conclusion is
drawn that teachers are not interested and prefer a
passive role. But this kind of situation fits the
linear model all too well--teacher curriculum development is seen as yet another product to be introduced into the system.
     27. John Dewey, Logic: The Theory of Inquiry
(New York; Henry Holt & Co., 1938).
     28. Schwab, op. cit.
     29. The work of Alfred Schutz, Collected Papers
Vols. I-III (The Hague: Martinus Nijhoff, 1962-73)
is particularly important; although his use of the
term "practical knowledge' is narrower and more
specific than mine, this seems to me a matter of
terminology rather than a serious conceptual difference. See also Alfred Schutz and Thomas Luckmann, The Structures of the Life-World (London:
Heinemann, 1974).
     30. See Dewey, op. cit.; Maurice Merleau-Ponty,
Phénoménologie de la perception (Paris: Gallimard,
1945).
     31. See Joseph J. Schwab, "What Do Scientists
Do?" Behavioral Science 5 (1960), 1-27; Thomas
Kuhn, The Structure of Scientific Revolutions
(Chicago: University of Chicago Press, 1962,
1970).

32. Earl C. Kelley, Education for what is Real (New York: Harper and Brothers, 1947); Sarason, op. cit.

33. For example G.A. Kelly, The Psychology of Personal Constructs (New York: Norton, 1955); A.A. Maslow, Toward a Psychology of Being (New York: Van Nostrand, 1962).

34. The terms used in the discussion which follows are drawn from Schutz and Luckmann, op. cit.

35. See for example C.A. Bowers, Cultural Literacy for Freedom (Eugene: Elan, 1974); Maxine Greene, Teacher as Stranger: Educational Philosophy for the Modern Age (Belmont Calif.: Wadsworth Publishing Co., 1973).

36. Robert Dreeben, "The School as a Workplace," Second Handbook of Research on Teaching, ed. R.M.W. Travers (Chicago: Rand McNally, 1973); Philip Jackson, Life in Classrooms (New-York: Holt, Rinehart & Winston, 1968).

37. Schutz, op.cit.

38. See Malcolm Parlett and David Hamilton, "Evaluation as Illumination: A New Approach to the Study of Innovatory Programs", Occasional Paper 9, Centre for Research in the Educational Sciences, University of Edinburgh, 1972; Stephen Wilson, "The Use of Ethnographic Techniques in Educational Research, "Review of Educational Research 47, No. 1 (1977), 245-265; Louis M. Smith, "An Evolving Logic of Participart Observation, Educational Ethnography, and Other Case Studies", in Review of Research in Education 6, ed. Lee S. Shulman, (Itasca, Ill.: F.E. Peacock, 1978); Liam Hudson, The Cult of the Fact (London: Jonathan Cape, 1972). In psychology, see for example, T.W. Wann, ed., Behaviorism and Phenomenology: Contrasting Bases for Modern Psychology (Chicago: University of Chicago, 1964); A. Giorgi, Psychology as a Human Science: A Phenomenologically Based Approach (New York: Harper and Row, 1970).

39. The complete interview transcriptions are found in the Appendix to my "The Teacher's 'Practical Knowledge': A Case Study," (Ph.D. dissertation, University of Toronto, 1980). All quotations from the interviews are taken from this source.

40. Grade 13 is currently required for university entrance in the Province of Ontario. A recent report of a task force on secondary education of the provincial ministry of education calls for the

abolition of grade thirteen, a move which many
consider long overdue.

Chapter 2

THE TEACHER'S EXPERIENTIAL WORLD

The world of an individual, and the life-experience
that unfolds within it, are marked by a certain
pattern and a degree of consistency, features which
enable us to understand the individual's experience. The purpose of this chapter is to describe
Sarah's experiential world. This world is twofold,
consisting of material objects, persons and events
on the one hand, and, on the other hand, thoughts,
feelings and purposes which shape the experiencing
subject's perception of those objects, persons and
events. Here Sarah's experiential world will be
presented in a provisional account that will serve
as a preliminary to the more analytic chapters to
follow. Her world is the basis for her practical
knowledge, the forum in which knowledge of teaching
is acquired, and an appreciation of her experienced
world will enable us to understand what knowledge
she holds and why. And conversely, the teacher's
world is itself shaped by her knowledge and reflects it; it is the context in which we can best
examine her knowledge in use.

In this chapter we will follow the chronology
of Sarah's work during the period of the study.
The account will centre on the several changes that
she made in her work, because these changes reveal
important aspects of her work situation, her ideas
and goals in teaching, and the way she experienced
the teaching setting in which she found herself.

ENGLISH TEACHING

When the interview series began, Sarah was an English teacher. She had come to her school as one
of the younger teachers on staff, and saw her work

as experimental, relevant to students' concerns, and exciting. She taught English literature, sometimes organized around 'themes', and writing workshops, primarily in the higher grades.

Sarah had been and was a regular participant in the professional development activities offered by her Board, and these had enabled her to pursue a variety of interests. She had long been concerned with communication and had attended a workshop in group work which developed her skills in this area. She sought practical experience through participation on school committees, and had been involved in some of the major decisions made during that period. Her interest in writing was focussed on "how to get kids to write using voices other than that very austere voice of literary criticism." She had done no in-service work in English literature, partly because she had felt no need for it, and partly because the trend in her Board had been to focus on broad professional development concerns such as personal growth, values clarification, and group dynamics, rather than on specific content areas.

Sarah had been teaching at her present job for about five years when the study began and, in her own assessment, she was starting to 'run dry'. This was reflected in Sarah's feelings about her work inside and outside the classroom. She was disappointed in the professional development activity she had completed. The various seminars, weekend workshops and the like had all fired her enthusiasm and given her something to work on, but always the enthusiasm faded once she was back in the classroom with no one to provide feedback or share the experimental challenge.

In her teaching, too, there were new problems. Sarah had begun to feel that students were not particularly interested in literature; many of them did not read for pleasure and were not enthusiastic about the materials she presented in class despite her efforts to make the work relevant to their concerns. Furthermore, she felt increasingly that students were not adequately equipped with the reading and writing skills needed to do the work she required of them in the upper grades. As a result, she was forced to lower her expectations, and often felt that her talents and energies were being wasted in the classroom; it seemed to her that classes were controlling her with their limited abilities and lukewarm responses.

Sarah also felt that her teaching was being controlled from outside in yet another respect. The English department to which she belonged was undergoing a shift in orientation. There had been a teachers' strike, followed by reports of student deficiencies in 'basic skills' and a series of ongoing attacks in the press against teachers, and "as a profession we felt completely emasculated". The head of her department had taken refuge in what Sarah saw as a 'narrowed vision'. There was heavy emphasis on 'back to basics' interpreted in terms of grammar and composition, structured by formal lists of requirements and marking schemes. The teachers in the English department were required to work on committees, set up in what Sarah felt was an authoritarian fashion, to elaborate on the program, but without considering in detail what students needed to learn, why and when, or how to develop the desired learnings. Sarah felt that this "finished products" approach was not productive, and that the punitiveness of marking systems did not raise standards. But her talk of "encouraging kids to write, and to feel that writing is a valid form of expression" fell on deaf ears. Sarah was unable to contribute to policy in her department; she felt alienated, threatened, and even guilty about continuing to teach in a relatively informal way.

Fortunately for Sarah's well-being, her sense of discomfort in the English department came upon her gradually, and became most conscious and acute only after she had made the decision to become a Reading teacher. But before this happened, Sarah became involved with a small group of teachers working on a new course, first called the "Thinking Course" and later renamed the "Learning Course".

THE "LEARNING COURSE"

The Learning Course had begun in the informal discussions of three teachers who had frequent contact with one another concerning school matters: Liz, an English teacher, had originated the notion of a Thinking Course based on the conviction that reading is a function of thinking. Liz, Dave (a vice-principal), and Sarah had discussed the idea extensively. Several other teachers joined in the planning (while Liz was transferred to another school) to form a group of five. All of them were concerned with fostering general learning skills to serve students in all subject matter areas. They also hoped that by working together they could create for themselves a community that would be effective in both developing materials and in professional development for themselves.

The Learning Course planners began by contacting about 25 teachers from various departments, who contributed ideas on skills and tasks that students should be able to carry out in their subjects but were unable to do. Later this larger group met in committees to suggest exercises in various categories outlined by the course planners. The group of five then collected all this information and divided up the topics among themselves; each took responsibility for planning one or two units.

The planning process, and the intensive team work it involved, was described by Sarah as a heavy experience. One of the members was highly experienced in group work and influenced the course content in this direction. But ironically, the work of the group itself suffered from problems, such as grudges and bad feelings, that to Sarah typified poor communication. The group members were well aware of these problems and even of various ways of dealing with them; yet the problems continued. Generally, the atmosphere in the planning group was open and supportive, but practical pressures seemed to prevent them from taking the time to deal with the dynamics of their own work.

The task of putting together the various components of the course was staightforward, though time-consuming. Sarah described her work on the communications unit as a simple matter of combining materials gathered from seminars and texts; she took as basic those topics which were repeated in several sources. For the Reading unit, she researched and developed an organization of various approaches to reading. She then sought help from the Reading teacher, and was given a kit which seemed to accomplish everything she had intended, so this was adopted for the unit. She also did some work for the Collecting and Classifying unit, which had been prepared by two other people; her background in English, she felt, enabled her to develop the section on essay writing.

But in contrast to the uncomplicated and direct way that Sarah perceived the content and development of the Learning Course, is her view of the role of the teacher in the course. While the overt content of the Learning Course consisted largely of specific kinds of reading and writing work (e.g. exercises in 'thinking fallacies', organization of information, note-taking), much more important to Sarah were those aspects of the course that depended heavily on the way it was taught. For example, the success of the course was contingent on the creation of an atmosphere in which good communication was fostered, in which students felt free to take risks, in which active listening to others and paraphrasing, and the open expression of concerns without fear of judgement, were encouraged. And Sarah also sought to develop in students an awareness of what they were learning, by summarizing for them what they had learned and giving them forecasts of what they would learn next.

Two comments are especially significant, regarding the way Sarah experienced her role as teacher. She said that in the Learning Course "I feel as if I am an ally of theirs, and what we're doing is working together to allow them to beat whatever system is outside." And she mentioned an expression the planning group had been using to describe their work in the course, "There's nowhere to hide in the Learning Course." By this they meant that while in their subject matter areas teachers could always justify failure in terms of students' lack of ability or the complexity of the subject matter, in the Learning Course the teacher's commitment was precisely to overcoming whatever barriers prevent kids from learning and to providing them with skills that would serve them regardless of subject matter.

Sarah's work on the Learning Course influenced, and was affected by, her other teaching duties in several ways. As a teacher of literature, she had become particularly sensitive to the "human side of the classroom", to linking up "what was happening in the literature to what was happening in the kid's own development." Her abilities to be tuned in to many things at once, and to intuit student needs, were seen by the others in the group as one of Sarah's special contributions to their work. For her part, she had gained a better understanding of how to plan a course in terms of skills she wanted students to practise. For example, in teaching a Writers' Workshop, instead of the completely spontaneous approach she had used previously, Sarah tried introducing material on sentence structure and paragraph construction at the beginning of the term, and found that this provided a critical vocabulary and skills students could practise, without detracting from the spontaneity that came later on. In her other courses Sarah felt that her concern with the skills she wanted to teach had made her more directed, less inclined to digress, even aloof. This, she thought, was the result of the interaction of the Learning Course experience with factors such as her age and the way students perceived her: at thirty she was calmer and more serious than she had been when she first came to the school.

The major issue which concerned Sarah throughout the period of her involvement with the Learning Course was evaluation. Sarah worried that the course was somewhat faddish, and that the materials had been collected haphazardly. Sarah felt that her students had been the victims of much educational experimentation over the years, and she was reluctant to make guinea pigs of them yet again. From the ample information kids gave her about their activities in other classes, she sensed the existence of a vicious circle: because kids could not read well enough, teachers avoided using textbooks and consequently students were not asked to practise the skills they might have acquired in the Learning Course. Since students in her school had individual timetables, there was no way Sarah could follow up on their progress, and little help had been forthcoming from such external agencies as the local school board or the provincial ministry. While she felt her work on the course had definitely been worth the effort, there was a nagging doubt as to whether a professionally-developed course might not already exist, complete with evaluation instruments to assess progress and ensure that the job was being done.

A second reason for Sarah's concern with evaluation was her sense that the group's work had fallen short of her own professional and academic standards. To illustrate this problem Sarah gave an example from a Grade 11 literature course in which she was teaching Othello. She had used a critic, Bradley, to develop an approach to the play. But Bradley was an authority she would have scorned while at university, and the way she used him in preparing to teach Othello was quite different from the careful research she had done as a student of English. The critic was available,

38

could give a kind of immediate insight into Shakespeare, and provided material she could easily
shape to the needs of her class. While these considerations were legitimate and highly relevant to
her practical tasks, Sarah expressed the persistent
feeling that there was a basic inadequacy in this
style of work. Such sketchy work might be justified in teaching Othello given the particular abilities and interests students brought to class, but
the Learning Course seemed to require a more thorough and systematic approach, which was not possible due to the time constraints under which the
group had worked.

THE READING CENTRE

Sarah's preoccupation with the quality of her work
was one of the factors which led to her decision to
move from teaching English to Reading. Sarah saw
this as a 'back-door' decision: her interest in
Reading grew out of her work on the Reading unit
for the Learning Course, but she saw Reading initially less as a special interest than as a means
of diversifying her own skills so that she could,
over the next few years, spend time "away from the
pressures of the classroom" without having to seek
promotion. A Reading Centre, staffed half-days by
one teacher, Ellen, already existed in her school;
the school wished to staff the Centre all day, and
Sarah was interested in the work Ellen had been
doing. She was offered the position, and signed up
to attend a course in Reading given by her Board.
This took place in the spring, shortly after the
first interview, when she was teaching the Learning
Course for the second time.
    During the next semester (when the second
interview took place) Sarah taught the Learning
Course to one class, and spent the rest of her time
in the Reading Center, a small, pleasant room where
she met with students who came for help in skills
such as reading, studying, spelling and essay writing. Meanwhile work on the Learning Course had
slowed. Two of the original five members of the
group were no longer involved, and a third was not
scheduled to teach the course until the following
semester. Sarah and Vivian were continuing to
teach, but each had expressed the wish to work
independently, rather than like "horses running on
the same track," as they had the previous year.
The two women had different styles, and opposing

views of the course; Sarah was uncomfortable with Vivian's approach, and assumed the reverse to be equally true. So their team work was limited to technical matters.

Most of Sarah's time thus became taken up with learning and reading skills, and her first comment about this was that "I feel that I'm coming from a different place... I'm not defending literature anymore, I'm not struggling with literature." With the barrier of English literature removed, Sarah felt more comfortable in her relationship with students:

> I'm giving a lot of concern and a lot of empathy, and it's feeling sincere to me, but the subject at hand is not the kid's stepmother or abortion or whatever it used to be in past years, but rather how the kid is coping with the demands being made in class.

In this new role, the notion of learning skills was important to Sarah as a way of talking about her work, though she was still concerned that it was a faddish notion. She felt it was important to see the notion of skills in terms of tasks students were asked to carry out that were unnecessarily difficult and mysterious for them, but that could be made concrete, structured and manageable.

Initially, Sarah was not very busy in the Reading Center, because she preferred waiting for students to come in with self-identified needs, rather than asking teachers to refer students. But after a slow start, Sarah became extremely busy. At first enthusiastic, she soon began to feel rushed and ill-equipped. A superintendent had pointed out to Sarah and Ellen, her colleague, that they could have far greater impact working with staff than working individually with students. As a result they had begun developing relationships with staff and promoting awareness of the services they could offer (such as aid in choosing texts, guest lectures on study techniques for different subjects, and short-term workshops in reading), in addition to continuing the work with individual students. Sarah described the tempo of her work as very busy, though not "breathless, the way teaching is"; she continued to feel great enthusiasm for it.

Meanwhile Sarah had acquired new resources to draw on in her work. She had begun a reading

40

course which introduced her to a 'humanistic' approach to reading; she became more concerned with conversation as an aspect of language ability, and she paid even more attention than previously to giving students a feeling of success and to sharing experience with them in class. In the reading course she had the help of a tutor (a reading teacher at another school) who was a ready source of books, references and advice. A set of publications in remedial work provided her with additional insights and techniques, and she had taken a short course in writing. She had been influenced by an approach which involved beginning with the student writing of his own experience, and moving from there in one of two directions: either toward more personal, symbolic, 'literary' work, or toward factual research. Sarah adapted this approach through devices such as asking students to finish a conversation in writing (with a hidden agreement that she'd respond to their work as expressively as they wrote).

Sarah's work with individual students, as she described it, seemed to me to be relaxed, spontaneous and open-ended. Despite her strong concern with fostering specific skills, she began with the student's problems, and followed wherever his interests led; she avoided forcing a particular diagnosis and program of remedial work on a student. One student was sent in with difficulties in an essay; Sarah felt she could do very little for him on a one-time basis and was not surprised when he did not return; but some time later, he came back to say he was dropping English and wanted to do intensive work at the Reading Centre in order to catch up and pass English next year.

Sarah encountered a variety of planning problems in her work. One involved setting up work programs in various areas for students to work on independently; Sarah stalled on this task, until her tutor made her aware that perhaps that style of work did not suit her, and that there were more manageable alternatives. Another issue was the setting up of a spelling workshop; here again the tutor helped, showing Sarah how in practice two conflicting approaches (spelling rules versus word lists) could be used together.

With so many new resources, Sarah was overcoming some of her earlier doubts about her work. In much of the work in Reading, she felt she was on new territory and could not go back to her own school experience, but she was accumulating new experience in the Reading Centre itself and her expertise was growing. Sarah felt that she was dealing with broad concerns, grounded in theory (as opposed to earlier work when she had picked up, and discarded, good ideas at random) though she had not had time to read and study seriously the relevant literature. Apart from the constant need to do public relations work for the Reading Centre, Sarah's major concerns were all interrelated, and focussed around the student as an individual with particular needs. She emphasized, for example, the importance of supporting the student in the content area so that later he would be willing to work on skills; the need to begin with something in print that interests the student; making use of the spoken voice of the student reading his work on tape; building up a fund of common experience between teacher and student; keeping students actively involved in reading; showing students that she herself is still working at improving her language skills.

By the time the interview sequence was completed, Sarah was working confidently in the Reading Centre. There was a repertoire of 'routines'-- lessons in topics such as memorization--that she could take a class through without preparation, and more important, she could conduct workshops in an improvised manner, beginning with the concerns of students and drawing on the preplanned materials as required. Her attention was turned to new issues: she was trying to extend her own skills while at the same time developing a more effective setting for her work through collaboration with a Geography teacher. And she was looking back, with increasing nostalgia, to the English classroom as a place where she could have greater access to students' personalities and also reveal more of herself in teaching. She had, in a sense, come almost full circle; just how close, or distant, she was from her starting point as an English teacher, the analysis of her practical knowledge which follows will attempt to establish.

Part Two

THE CONTENT OF PRACTICAL KNOWLEDGE

Chapter 3

KNOWLEDGE OF SELF AND MILIEU

In this chapter we begin the process of articulating Sarah's practical knowledge by attending to its content. Our task in the next three chapters is to set down the substance of her knowledge--what she knows. The content of Sarah's knowledge will be described in terms of five categories. In this chapter we will identify her knowledge of self as a teacher, and her knowledge of the milieu in which she works. Knowledge of subject matter will be treated in Chapter 4; Chapter 5 will deal with knowledge of instruction (i.e. of students and of the teaching-learning process), and finally knowledge of curriculum development. (The precise nature of this knowledge as practical-its orientation to specific situations, its experiential aspects, and its relation to theoretical knowledge-will be treated in Chapter 6.) Here, we will speak about Sarah's knowledge in conventional terms, as content, but we will also attend to features of content that reflect its practical nature. Thus, we will note the origins of Sarah's knowledge, whether it be drawn from theory or practice, and will indicate some of the transformations that theoretical knowledge undergoes in being made relevant for practice. For example, we will examine Sarah's knowledge of communications and group dynamics, and see how techniques derived from this area of theory are fitted into the body of her practical knowledge as subject matter, while the theory itself is applied only partially as pertaining to the curricular and instructional contexts.

We will also look at instances of development and change in the body of Sarah's practical knowledge, for development is one of the hallmarks of knowledge that is formed out of and in response to the exigencies of practice. For example, in Chapter 4 we will look at the view of learning which Sarah evolved in the course of her teaching. She began with a notion of 'thinking', but soon abandoned this as inappropriate given the constraints of time and knowledge she and her group had to work with; a view of 'learning' tied to the work students were asked to do in school soon developed as more suited to the demands of her situation.

A third aspect of practical knowledge viewed as content is the way that conflicting ideas may be held simultaneously, because they are relevant to different but non-competing aspects of practice, because the teacher uses the ideas at different times or because she reconciles them in some practice-relevant way. In order to attend to this aspect of practical knowledge, we will indicate, at times by inference, some of the guiding conceptions which underlie Sarah's views and the choices she appears to have made in espousing these views. As we shall see in Chapter 5, for example, English literature is seen sometimes as a discipline dealing with the inherent value of the literary object, and sometimes as a medium for the expression and clarification of the feelings and experiences of students and teachers.

After we have laid out the content of Sarah's knowledge and seen where it originated, how it developed and how it coheres as a body of knowledge, we will be in a position, in Chapters 6 and 7, to consider how Sarah holds this knowledge, how it functions as practical knowledge and the uses to which it is put.

KNOWLEDGE OF SELF

In this section we will look at the way in which the teacher's personal values and purposes relate to and inform her practical knowledge. For example, the first interview focused on the conflict Sarah was experiencing between her academic standards and the practical criteria which bear on her work. Other important questions concern the teacher's image of herself as teacher and professional, the way she views her place in the classroom and in the school, the kinds of authority and responsibility she assumes. All these matters have considerable influence on how she controls the knowledge she uses and presents to students.

Sarah's knowledge of herself in her role as a teacher has many facets, but three aspects seem to stand out. First, because Sarah takes herself and her potential contribution to teaching seriously, she looks upon herself as a resource to be used in the best way possible; she has knowledge of her own skills and abilitites. Second, Sarah sees herself in relation to others and has knowledge concerning her relationships with others. Third, Sarah views herself as a unique human being with needs, personality traits, talents and limitations, all of which necessarily influence her work as a teacher. It is interesting to note when each of these different views of self prevails, and with what consequences.

Self as Resource

Sarah had a strong sense of her own abilities as a teacher. She had confidence in her ability to tune in to the needs of students in the classroom, to predict problems, to make human contact with students and then to shape her subject matter to make it relevant to their concerns. Sarah's confidence in her teaching abilities was such that when she began encountering difficulties in teaching English, her analysis of the situation led her to the conclusion "that Grade 13 is certainly not the place for a good, energetic teacher to be," because the difficult academic work to be done in Grade 13 (the pre-university year) had not been adequately prepared for in earlier grades. Her desire to fill this gap led to the decision to become involved in development of the Learning Course. (We might expect a less confident teacher to have begun by doubting her own effectiveness and abilities in the classroom.)

But Sarah also viewed herself as able to contribute to decision making in her school. She had been active on school committees, and her inability to influence policy in the English department was a source of frustration to her.

Sarah's role in the Reading Centre is the best example of self as resource; her task was to serve as 'literacy advisor' to staff, as a resource person for teachers and students. She worked hard to expand her skills, and pushed herself to move ahead in new areas to increase her usefulness in this role.

Self in Relation to Others

Sarah's knowledge of herself in relation to others is a recurrent theme of the interviews. In the Learning Course, she was the one person who remained actively involved throughout, coordinating much of the work and informing the other teachers who came in to teach the course for a semester or two; though initially apprehensive, she assumed this role willingly. Sarah's attitude toward students reveals a similar concern for others. Sarah struggled with the impossibility of following up all her students, but nevertheless kept track of as many as possible. In the past she had been willing to become involved in students' personal problems, and although she saw herself doing less of this than formerly, her teaching style encouraged students to approach her. In work with individual students this is particularly apparent; she used a therapeutic notion, 'unqualified positive regard', emphasizing her sense of responsibility for the student as learner. But at the same time she finds it offensive when teachers take credit for their students' achievements:

> I really resent teachers talking about What Happened to Lloyd, or The Miracle of Marg. I find that very distasteful; I get very tense when teachers speak about their personal, individual victories, usually to demonstrate that a certain more general thing works. And well, I think I'll always despise that.

The strong language here expresses the strength of Sarah's resolve to protect students' right to their own accomplishments.

Self as Individual

Sarah has knowledge of herself as an individual: she often refers to particular quirks of her personality, to her age and to her attitudes and values. She sees these as inevitable features of her teaching to be accepted and taken advantage of where possible. Thus, for example, she became aware that she had been avoiding the task of setting up materials for students who came into the Centre to work independently. She realized that this involved an elaborate system of bookkeeping, and while she could get this started, she was unlikely to keep it going. Once she became aware of alternative ways of handling the problem, she found it easy to abandon this task as not feasible for her, and drew from the experience an important principle: to ground her work in the Centre on her strengths as a teacher, the things she likes to do.

Sarah's knowledge of her own needs as a teacher influenced the course of her career. After five years of teaching English she sought through the Reading Centre to develop

> ...some way of doing a different job without necessarily having to seek promotion, because in terms of my own...the way I am, I don't want to seek a promotion. My idea certainly was to start getting qualified in another field, so that by the time I'm 35, 36, 37, I could perhaps be away from the pressures of the classroom all day long.

But examination of the interviews suggests that Sarah's view of herself as an individual is the least prominent of the three views. With respect to the problem of setting up individual work programs, until she became aware of an alternative way of dealing with this problem, she was unable simply to say "I don't want to do this." She felt a responsibility to provide a certain ongoing service for students regardless of her own preferences and strengths.

The range of services Sarah performs in the Reading Centre is also telling. It appears that the type of work closest to her is the work with individual students, when she can operate in a leisurely and personal style. Yet she took on the task of meeting a whole range of needs within the school, and did so even when the work seemed almost futile. The option of refusing to work with students unless they make a commitment to come back for basic work after the emergency has passed was not one she considered. Nevertheless she had become aware of the danger of overextending herself, and was trying to curb her sense of responsibility toward students.

> If a student comes in and says, "This essay is due tomorrow, and I've only got 15 minutes,"

I spend 15 minutes, and if anyone's sweating,
it's definitely the kid. But I'm thinking of
one girl who, if I had told her to come at
11:30 at night, would have come with her
sleeping bag; and then I really wanted to give
her the impression that writing that essay was
an adventure for me too.

It appears that Sarah's views of self as
resource and self as responsible to others were
both equally central to her experience, and further
that the two perceptions are beginning to come
together at this point in her career. She was
becoming aware that "giving too much and challenging too little" detracts from the independence she
wanted to help students achieve, and also resulted
in inefficient use of her own resources. Her perception of self as individual, on the other hand,
came into play only when it did not conflict with
her focal perception of self as resource at the
service of others.

KNOWLEDGE OF THE MILIEU

Sarah's knowledge of the milieu in which her teaching was embedded is evidenced by statements which
express her belief about the milieu, and by the way
she structures her social experience in the school.
In what follows we will pay attention to the ways
that Sarah's beliefs about the milieu interact with
her actions in organizing her own social setting.
We will look first at the basic setting of the
classroom, then at Sarah's relations with other
teachers and with the administration of the school,
at her view of the political context of teaching
and finally at the kinds of setting she seemed to
devise for herself within the school.

The Classroom

Sarah did not dwell extensively on the classroom
milieu in the interviews, but she was aware of the
class, composed of teachers and students, as a
distinct unit. For example, she commented repeatedly that the Learning Course class had "a very
specific flavour, a very definite tone and a very
definite personality...a specific character." She
saw herself creating that specific character, and
did so in ways that clearly reflect her practical
knowledge. In the classroom students were expected

to take a businesslike attitude to the work at
hand. Complaining might be allowed in certain
situations, but largely as a vehicle for talking
about feelings, for learning to communicate. Sarah
might communicate her expectations either with a
statement ("I wasn't opening up discussion for
complaints.") or simply by getting to work; occasionally a short speech might be required. In
return for meeting her demands, Sarah treated
students with fairness and acceptance: her marking
system was as simple and as discourgaing to competition as she could make it; she accepted value
statements that emerged in class, and refrained
from judging students; she was open about her own
feelings and values when this was relevant to the
lesson.

All of these behaviours suggest, however, that
Sarah viewed the class milieu largely in terms of
interaction among individuals rather than in social
terms. She spoke, for example, of the way that
"the class controls the teacher" in terms of feedback and communication between two parties (teacher
and class). On another occasion she described the
"interesting new dynamic" of a class as influenced
by a particular student, previously very problematic, who had recently changed his attitude:

> He talks so much, and so positively, that I'm
> not getting a chance to get a sense from the
> other kids of what they think of a technique
> or whether they think they can use it. It's
> as if the class has changed personality becau-
> se he's quite strong, whether he's being nega-
> tive or positive.

The class dynamic here, as Sarah saw it, was essentially that of one student drowning out the rest.
It was "as if" the class personality had changed,
but only "as if". Sarah did not convey a sense of a
class personality; rather, the class here takes on
the personality of its most vocal member.

Relations with Teachers and Administration

Sarah was generally sympathetic to the teachers
with whom she worked. She was aware that many were
harrassed, and needed time to sit down and observe
their classes, for example. She was eager to work
with others, giving and receiving support and
encouragement, but was also aware of, and respec-

ted, the strong individualism of many teachers--herself included--and the constraints this placed on group effort. While she was very accepting of diverse approaches, Sarah was not uncritical of other teachers; she was suspicious of a certain kind of charismatic teaching, and strongly indignant when teachers took credit for student accomplishments, as we have noted. The overall impression is that Sarah had generally good relationships with many teachers in the school, but she firmly rejected a limited number of teaching styles that conflicted with her basic values.

Sarah's relations with the administration reveal a similar pattern: she was comfortable with principals and supervisors, even in the Reading Centre situation where she felt herself "on trial for the future." But her experience in the English department stands out as a case of extreme conflict; Sarah could not accept the approach and the managerial style of the department head.

The situations in which Sarah did, and did not, get along with other staff members suggests that her successful social adaptation to and role in the school is a product of personal tolerance combined with a rather detached attitude. Sarah built relationships with individuals within the school, and her participation in the organizational world of the school (e.g. membership on committees) rested on individual relationships, rather than on a strong sense of organizational dynamics.

The Political Milieu

Sarah is aware of the larger political dimension of her role as a teacher but does not appear to act on this knowledge. She discussed a teachers' strike which had been unpopular with the public; a series of attacks had been made on the teaching profession in the press, and teachers as a profession had felt emasculated. This, Sarah felt, had directly affected both curriculum planning and classroom behaviour. She is, however, less aware of influences in the opposite direction, that is, of her own work in the classroom as a political act. For example, she shrinks from the obligation to determine, by her evaluation, which students will go on to university. She views this process as 'phony' rather than as an act with very significant consequences, both personal and political. Here again, then, she sees the larger milieu in terms of herself rather than seeing herself and her work in political terms.

Creation of Social Settings

Sarah's school was a large one, and although she didn't complain of this, we have suggested that despite her strongly expressed desire for community her general posture in the school was one of detachment. We note, however, that many of her activities can be seen as efforts to create within the school smaller and more congenial social settings for her work. Participation in the Learning Course is one example; likewise, the switch to Reading enabled her to be away from the pressures of the classroom, and to work closely with a colleague she respected. She kept her classroom open at lunchhour so students who wanted a quiet place to eat and study could use it. She did not actively criticize the school's basic arrangements, but acknowledged that she preferred working with students, as she did in the Reading Centre, where she was not required to pass or fail students nor to play a role in determining their academic fate.

In the English staffroom, a place she avoided because of conflicts with the department head, Sarah nevertheless took responsibility for setting up tea facilities in her own personal way (herb tea was one of the kinds offered); perhaps this made her feel more comfortable in that room when she had to be there. This trivial incident is almost a paradigm of the way that Sarah deals with a situation that is socially uncomfortable for her: she becomes more involved, takes on responsibility, and shapes the setting or creates a new one that is more congenial for her.

However, Sarah's efforts to create small, congenial settings inevitably involved an element of conflict with the world outside (i.e. the school at large). Other teachers were suspicious and challenging of her work on the Learning Course. The Reading Centre had to work to develop rapport with teachers and to establish credibility by a variety of public relations devices, and Sarah had a feeling of being on trial. The classroom posture of informality, openness and emphasis on student needs and experiences, to which she was deeply committed, had placed her in opposition to the prevailing attitude in the English department before she moved to the Reading Centre.

These situations reflect the picture of a teacher with strong convictions which are more or less at variance with those of other teachers and which engender conflict with the school system. Her response was not to work against the 'system'. She has moved in and out of involvement with the school's decision-making bodies, sometimes working to effect change in the school itself, but more often striving to create for herself the kind of alternative and marginal settings within the school which reflect her own values and at the same time fit into and serve the prevailing structure and goals of the school. This position is consistent with Sarah's knowledge of self, it rests on her views of self as an individual and self as responsible for others. Further, the settings she created are those in which she could work out her concerns most effectively. We now turn to an examination of Sarah's knowledge of subject matter since this knowledge served as the medium within which her milieu was shaped and her sense of self expressed.

Chapter 4

SUBJECT MATTER KNOWLEDGE

This chapter will provide an inventory of the subject matter knowledge on which Sarah drew for the
content of her teaching. The teacher's subject
matter knowledge, no less than other areas of her
knowledge, is practical knowledge, shaped by and
for the practical situation. To demonstrate this,
we will look at the conceptions which underlie the
different facets of content, the ways in which content from different subject matter areas is selected and combined, and at how this content changed
as Sarah used it in teaching.
    During the period covered by the interviews,
Sarah took on several different but overlapping
subject-matter designations: she was an English
teacher, a Learning teacher, and a Reading teacher.
We will consider first her view of subject matter
in English literature; next we will examine the
conceptions of learning and of study skills which
she first began to develop as part of the Learning
Course, and then her views of reading and writing
as these developed throughout her work. Finally we
will look at the interrelations among these areas
and see to what extent they hang together as a
coherent subject matter for teaching.

SUBJECT MATTER IN ENGLISH

Sarah herself remarked that "teaching English is
such a diffuse thing"; it is not surprising that
her conception of the subject matter of English is
equally diffuse. One statement seems to capture
the various elements present in her conception.
Speaking of students, she stated that "I did feel
an obligation to open them up a bit to an appreciation of literature." This sentence reflects two

conceptions of literature. There is a view of English literature as an academic discipline to which Sarah has an obligation; and there is a view of English literature centred on the experience of the student who is to be 'opened up'. Both views coexist, carrying shifting weight within Sarah's subject matter for English.

Sarah's view of English literature as a discipline to which she owes academic allegiance, and which imposes critical standards, is detailed but also subject to conflict. As a student, Sarah adhered to what she saw as rigorous standards involving, for example, the setting up of thorough and complex bibliographies. Given her respect for the concept of ambiguity and her scorn of the simplistic 19th Century morality of A.C. Bradley, we might guess that Sarah held some notion of the value of alternative interpretations of literature; at any rate, she seemed to view literature as an investigative discipline. But she also had a sense of the value of the literary text as an object, and she refused to allow the standards of the discipline to be stretched too far. She felt that it should not be reduced to a discussion of contemporary psychological or political issues. For example, she mentioned Othello taken as a point of departure for talking about jealousy, or women's liberation: "That's quite exciting for the kids but it's not studying Othello." She insisted, too, that students be taught something more than just the plot of the novel or the play; but what is not clear. Presumably this dilemma is one which she resolved from class to class, rather than generally.

The aesthetic dimension of English literature is less clearly developed. Sarah spoke of reading for pleasure, of the love and excitement generated by literature and of appreciation. The only specific literary quality she cited as calling forth any of these responses is ambiguity. So although one suspects Sarah could be quite specific about the literary qualities of a particular text, her statements do not reveal an articulate general conception of literary quality or value. Here again, Sarah's very muteness may be an indication of the practical cast of her knowledge. She does not have a clearly articulated general conception of literary value, nor of literature as a discipline, precisely because she must continually mediate between her academic conceptions and the need to engage students in literary activity.

Sarah's view of literature as a medium for dealing with values and experiences had a personal side as well. She was aware that "so many of our attitudes toward money, and life, and age, and growing older, and marriage, and not being married, come out in teaching an English class," and she welcomed the opportunity which the English class-room so well provides, to express herself and to come to know students. After a year's absence from English teaching, her nostalgia was strongly ex-pressed: "I would like more of a window onto the kids and what they're thinking, and I think I myself would like my window to be more open. And I guess I'm itchy for that, for English as a medium."

Clearly the second approach, English litera-ture as a medium for dealing with values and ex-periences, is the controlling one in Sarah's view of her subject matter. Although in the first interview she expressed considerable doubt about the compromising of her academic standards, the conflict between English as discipline and English as medium did not seem to be a serious one for her. (Rather, Sarah used the Othello example metapho-rically, to express her conflicts vis-à-vis the academic generally, but especially with respect to the non-rigorous way the Learning Course had been developed and evaluated.) Her primary concern in English was with the possibilities offered by a literary text for engaging students' interests and for offering them a vehicle through which to reflect on and enrich their own experience. Within this context, Sarah apparently had little diffi-culty making her peace with the discipline of English, 'shaping' the literary material in a way that could meet the needs of students without violating the integrity of the text. She encoun-tered difficulty only when students expressed no interest in the text and forced her into the pos-ture of "defending literature." Thus to work only with the view of English as discipline was unaccep-table to Sarah. But she apparently found it en-tirely possible to hold simultaneously two diverse views of English literature, and to mediate between them only in practice, in terms of priorities determined by another dimension of her practical knowledge--for example, her conception of students and their needs.

It may be that the severity of the potential conflict was attenuated by the fact that the two views had different origins, and were therefore called into play under different circumstances. The view of English as discipline was drawn from Sarah's academic experience and from her study of literary theory, while the view of English as medium of expression, though it may have been shaped by theory, was probably developed and refined in the course of Sarah's teaching experience. The latter view was given more articulation and clearly took priority, while Sarah's notion of English as discipline remained vague and was kept at a distance from her everyday concerns. Sarah herself pointed out that her conflict relating to academic standards was not part of her everyday experience but arose in the context of the academically tinged interview setting.

LEARNING AND STUDY SKILLS AS SUBJECT MATTER

The area of subject matter concerned with learning and study skills is difficult to define because of the constant and inevitable overlap between the subject matter itself, the actual skills being taught, and the view of learning which Sarah espouses and which guides her teaching. The latter topic will be considered in the next chapter, but will be anticipated here in order to make clear the organization of the 'skills' subject matter. We will examine first the actual skills content and its sources, and then the view which Sarah takes of this area of her knowledge.

Although it is difficult to classify the skills Sarah saw herself teaching, we can identify (somewhat arbitrarily) study skills, skills of research and organization, and skills of group work and communication. (Most of these skills involve reading and writing, which will be examined shortly; here we are concerned with reading and writing only insofar as they involve specific, directly teachable skills.)

The study skills derive from several basic sources. One early source is Sarah's own repertoire of successful techniques, dating from high school and university. In working on the Learning Course Sarah drew heavily on these skills, but with misgivings. She felt there was no external justification, other than her own past successes, for passing on these particular techniques. As time went on, Sarah acquired many new techniques from colleagues and from the educational literature, for example: teaching students to recognize thinking fallacies; methods of reading such as 'inventory' and previewing; and a typology of four basic ways that information is organized (listing, illustration, cause-effect, comparison-contrast).

An example of the way Sarah's skill repertoire grew is found in the discussion of memory. The fourth interview presented an example of a mnemonic device taught in isolation at the end of a lesson. In the fifth interview, Sarah described a complete lesson on memory which she and her colleague had developed; it included psychological background information, advice about selection of materials and time management, and mnemonic techniques, followed by general discussion. Time management also became a topic in discussion of general study skills. Sarah pointed out that she had included this topic in her repertoire before she was entirely sure of herself, "as a way of forcing myself to move ahead in certain areas." Her sources for these techniques were texts in reading and psychology.

In the area of research and organization, Sarah taught skills such as note-taking, paragraph-writing, the notion of classification, use of the library and preparation of bibliographies. Here again she drew on her own school experience, on the conventional wisdom of education, and on her study of essay writing and research, reading and writing.

The third area, that of communication and group skills, derived from Sarah's direct study and experience in this field and involved a number of basic ideas which she tried to teach, to embody in her interaction with students and to enable them to practise. In identifying these basic ideas, Sarah emphasized the conclusions which theoreticians had reached, and the specific techniques they had developed, rather than the underlying theoretical notions about the nature of human communication or of group functioning. For example, she held that work in groups involved the two basic functions of 'task' (accomplishing the work of the group) and 'maintenance' (keeping good feeling going in the group), and that these required the use of communicative techniques such as active listening and paraphrasing. Because Sarah believed that communication is a difficult task which necessitates taking risks, much of her work in teaching these skills consisted in creating an atmosphere in which students would feel free to risk expressing themselves openly. But there was also some direct teaching and practising of group skills.

The evolution of Sarah's conception of skills is most interesting. When work began on the Learning Course it was called the "Thinking Course." After some time the group concluded that their knowledge of 'thinking' was inadequate but that they did know about 'learning', which they ultimately interpreted in a limited way to mean "coping with the work demands made of the students in this school." Sarah attached the 'learning skills' label to this notion with "great relief, because finally I had a way of talking about what I did." The vague label gradually took on definite meaning for Sarah, in terms of "the kind of things that I know kids are asked to do during their four years," tasks that were mysterious to students but could be made concrete and structured, could be taught.

Initially Sarah used the 'learning skills' label to refer to a collection of down-to-earth skills, independent of one another and of any overarching theoretical position on learning or thinking, though when she spoke generally about learning skills, her conception seemed to be of a unified, monolithic body of skills. She held that learning skills (like the recognition of thinking fallacies) are general and applicable to all subject matter, and felt that skills such as paragraph writing, note-taking and research serve as necessary prerequisites to further learning.

Sometimes she spoke as though skills could be learned quite straightforwardly, transmitted like facts from teacher to student: "It's almost like a mission that I have to equip them with certain writing skills before they get out of Grade 11. And it speeds me up, and I don't digress so much, and I have to be much stricter about assignments." Skills are independent of the motivation of the learner or researcher and should be learned and used by all students, apparently regardless of ability or cognitive style. At one point, for example, Sarah argued that there could be no excuses for her failure to teach skills.

This conception underwent important modifications toward the end of the interview series, however. Sarah realized that many of the skills included in the Learning Course had an academic orientation (and as a result the course was subsequently offered on a higher grade level). She appeared to have taken note of my suggestion that different subject matters require different skills and was perhaps trying to test this out in seeking to work with teachers in subject areas far from her own. She still appeared to hold that learning skills are valid across all disciplines, but in fact she did not express this belief in terms of subject matter. Rather, she pointed out that it was not the subject matter teacher, but herself, whose job it was to help students acquire skills. If she was unsure about the universal applicability of learning skills, a very practical instructional concern enabled her to hold to her view nonetheless.

More important, Sarah was reminded that people learn in diverse ways, and the traditional skills are helpful to certain students only; furthermore, she was exposed to research which suggested that even the learning of these skills is facilitated by affective change. So her view of skills had to be modified to take account of individual differences and the relationship of cognitive and affective in learning.

Sarah saw the skills and techniques she taught as applicable to a range of real situations and materials. She was aware that this application is not obvious and must be made clear to students, but she seemed to see it as a matter to be stated or explained rather than learned through experience. A related aspect of skill learning with which Sarah was concerned is "reflexivity", the student's awareness of the skills he is acquiring. Sarah had not articulated a possible relationship between the reflexivity of skills and the possibility of transferring the skills to other situations, but there are indications that she viewed skills increasingly as requiring the awareness and understanding of students, as the personal and even idiosyncratic property of individuals, rather than as a monolithic body of fixed and organized techniques.

Despite the fact that Sarah abandoned the pretentious aim of teaching "thinking" early on, in favour of a notion of learning skills that was grounded in practical need and that evolved to conform to her understanding of practice, a form of theoretical bias nevertheless colours her conception of skills. Her purpose, ostensibly, was to provide students with "coping skills", to teach them whatever they needed to know in order to get along in the school system, and to meet the demands of teachers. This purpose was an eminently practical one that grew, we have seen, out of Sarah's assessment of both student needs and her own (and other teachers') abilities. But there is evidence that she never entirely abandoned the notion of "learning", though she saw it as a theoretical notion beyond the scope of her work. For example, Sarah disparaged the idea students sometimes had that a typed essay was better than a handwritten one. Indeed students' assumption that typing actually improves the quality of a piece of writing is absurdly mistaken; but it is striking that a teacher concerned with coping skills did not consider it worthwhile to pass on and explain the conventional wisdom that a typed essay will make a better impression on the reader and will, in all probability, be awarded a higher mark. Sarah does indeed recognize that getting passing grades is an important aspect of coping. But it is never enough for her, and at bottom she remains concerned to teach students something that sounds very much like 'learning skills', rather than simply 'coping skills'.

READING AND WRITING AS SUBJECT MATTER

Beyond the reading and writing skills outlined above, Sarah had a view of language and language teaching throughout her career as an English teacher. Many of her early ideas undoubtedly stayed with her, confirmed over time by experience and by encounters with theory. She commented that "I was aware a long time ago that talk was important in the classroom;" thus an idea she had had for several years gained in validity for her after being formulated in a course she took. But her awareness of a problem in the way reading and writing were taught in her school started Sarah on a process in which she tried to shape a new subject matter for teaching.

The first step was Sarah's realization that "the kind of work that we were demanding in terms of reading comprehension and writing from Grade 13 had no basis for it in the way that we were reading, or grading the courses up to Grade 13." This awareness led to involvement in the Learning Course, and then to work in the Reading Centre. Sarah began to articulate her ideas on reading as she prepared the Reading unit of the Learning Course. These ideas were strengthened by the support of a colleague, who had come to similar conclusions, and by a set of materials which implemented precisely the approach Sarah had formulated on her own.

The conception of reading and writing which Sarah developed reflects her concerns with language, on the one hand, and with skills, on the other. She brought to the Reading Centre a broad, humanistic view of language, evident in statements like the following:

> It's something that really appealed to me as a teacher of English, that words do capture experience, and even one's own words transcribed on a page still have a life in them.

> Language is everywhere, it isn't only in the essay that the kid writes. I'm delighted to see two kids chatting during a class, which would never have happened before.

> I always assumed that there was something wrong in having the only thing the kids wrote being literary criticism. It seemed to me that kids have to write from a more personal side of their personality. I looked for practical ideas on how to get kids to write using voices other than that very austere voice of literary criticism.

Sarah took an in-service course in reading in which many of her ideas were confirmed. For example, she encountered the view that students should begin by writing about something drawn from their own experience, and in their own voice; from this starting point the teacher could guide the student "either toward the direction of much more personal, symbolic writing and poetry, or to doing an essay with a much more informational and formal organization."[1] This approach combined Sarah's sense of language as a human function with her concern for skills.

While skill learning continued to be important to Sarah, it clearly became subordinated to, and was viewed in terms of, her broader view of language, language use, and instruction. Thus, she pointed out that "one cannot expect organization, good grammar and punctuation and good sentence structure, and mark the kid, dammit, for all those things, on the basis of a half-hour try." Instead, she felt that one should work on several different kinds of writing, and "only one of those streams of writing is the type that gets refined and polished and corrected." Thus Sarah gave a variety of writing assignments (some very structured, others more expressive) in the Learning Course and in the Reading Centre. In marking student work, she responded "as expressively as they write."

Another context in which reading and writing skills were seen as subordinate to other concerns was in remedial work. Sarah's first priority was to have the student feel comfortable, and to gain his commitment to work on skills. Thus, "often before we can get to work with a kid on his reading we have to prop him up in content areas; when he feels sucess there, he might want to come back to work on catch-up skills."

Sarah had a wide repertoire of specific techniques (many of them outlined above) for working on 'catch-up' skills. In the Learning Course, isolated skills sometimes acquired independent status as items to be learned: for example a reading technique called "Inventory" which was taught in the second of the two lessons I observed. In the Reading Centre work, however, Sarah's approach to reading gradually shaped her use of techniques to teach skills. In beginning work with a new student, for example,

> At the beginning of the year I would start by giving a spelling test which didn't tell me anything. I might isolate that the kid didn't know how to double the final consonant, but I felt foolish starting there. What I did was find something that interested them that was in print, talk about it for a while and ask them to write something. Then I would look at it and ask them to tape it. And then I'd ask them to listen to the tape, and begin making punctuation. The final part of that process is for the kid to take dictation from his own voice.

In this routine Sarah was guided by the notion of beginning with the interest of the student; she emphasized reading aloud because "the human voice punctuates very effectively" and because reading aloud is "the only window you have on how the kid

reads." She tried to keep the student active in
reading, and to build up "a bank account of common
experiences" between herself and the student
through discussion of matters that concerned them
both. All the reading skills content was coloured
by Sarah's particular slant; the skills she taught
could well be defined as tools for human communication rather than simply reading and writing
skills.

Summary

We have dealt with three areas of subject matter
knowledge in turn; but the coherence among the
areas, and the continuity of their development must
be noted.
　　Sarah's sense of her subject matter in English
combined two quite disparate views of literature:
one was the view of English as an academic discipline based on a valuing of the inherent aesthetic
qualities of the literary work as object; the other
was a view of English as a medium for the expression and clarification of experience, feeling and
value. Intellectually Sarah seemed able to keep
the two views compartmentalized well enough to hold
both simultaneously. But practically the balance
was shaken by the situation in Sarah's school during
the period of the interviews: her application of
the view of literature as medium of expression was
threatened by her department's 'back-to-basics'
stance--according to which her work seemed too
radical--while the limited skills and lack of interest of her students created a situation in which
even her informal and student-centred approach did
not engage student interest and felt to her like
'defending literature'. Thus pulled in opposite
directions, her position became untenable and she
looked for a way out. Not surprisingly, she chose
to focus on the central problem which had been
raised in her English teaching: that of skills and
skill learning.
　　In Sarah's Learning Course work she began the
task of developing a new, eclectic subject matter.
Despite the criticisms that could be, and were,
brought against the course, and despite Sarah's own
misgivings, the course had great cohesion. Its
content paralleled Sarah's English subject matter
insofar as it combined two diverse conceptions of
the subject matter (not unlike the two conceptions
of literature). In some instances, learning skills

were viewed as fixed, generally applicable techniques to be mastered by all; in other cases (and
this latter view came to predominate) learning
skills were seen as the property of individuals,
varied and changing in use, dependent on the style
and affective makeup of those using them.

Sarah's view of skills underwent further modification in the Reading Centre. As she developed
the conception of language as a mode of human communication, new ways of teaching reading and writing and of operating in the classroom were generated and Sarah integrated the two views of skill
indicated above. She developed a detailed subject
matter for teaching, which took into account both
students for whom traditional skills work and the
"zillions of people who attack problems in different ways," and who might "appreciate that that's a
valid method, but they would never use it."
Sarah's new subject matter comprised a conception
of language as a human function, a catalogue of
skills in reading and writing as modes of language
use that are sufficiently general to be taught, yet
acknowledgedly individual and personal, and a style
of teaching that enabled her to embody her view in
classroom activity.

The development of this new subject matter in
Reading finally brought Sarah back almost full
circle to her starting point in English, at least
to the aspect of literature she formulated as
"English as a medium for getting to talk about
different values and experiences." By the end of
the interview sequence the learning skills content
she had elaborated and which had excited her because of the direct contact with students that it
made possible, had begun to seem somewhat barren.
It did not offer "a window onto the kids and what
they're thinking," nor did it allow Sarah enough
personal expression. Thus the subject matter of
English literature, which had been a 'place to
hide' initially, was transformed into a 'window"
onto self and students at the end of the process of
developing an alternative subject matter in reading. The imagery of 'hiding place' and 'window'
will be examined more fully in later chapters; here
we note the process by which two aspects of subject
matter content interact and modify one another. As
a result of exploring (through development of materials and in instruction) the notion of learning
skills and communication as subject matter, Sarah
became aware that one must communicate something,

and her attention thus turned back to literary content. No doubt if she does return to teaching English she will do so somewhat differently, with a view of subject matter influenced by the skills content to which she has devoted so much of her time and interest.

NOTES

1. These notions were drawn from the work of James Britton; see, for example, his "What's the Use? A Schematic Account of Language Functions," Birmingham Educational Review 23, No. 3 (June 1971),pp. 205-219.

Chapter 5

KNOWLEDGE OF CURRICULUM AND INSTRUCTION

Thus far we have looked at the content of Sarah's knowledge in three areas: we have examined her knowledge of self, of the milieu of teaching, and of her subject matter. While in each of these areas the content of Sarah's knowledge underwent significant changes over time, we were dealing nevertheless with knowledge of the (relatively) static--persons, social settings, bodies of thought. We now turn to knowledge that can be viewed only in turns of process--Sarah's knowledge of the curriculum development process and finally, her knowledge of instruction. We will look at each in turn.

KNOWLEDGE OF CURRICULUM

Sarah had experienced curriculum development processes in several forms: she had participated intensively in development of the Learning Course over a period of about a year and a half; she was involved in program planning in the English department; and she had worked on the curriculum of the Reading Centre. Each of these tasks contributed in a different way to the development of her practical knowledge of the curriculum process. Although Sarah's experience of curriculum development in the English department came first, we will begin with the Learning Course experience, because it was the most extensive and deliberate. We shall survey both the development process and the underlying approach to curriculum development found in the experience. We will then look at Sarah's experiences in English and Reading to see whether a consistent view of curriculum development can be found to inhere in her practical knowledge.

Development of the Learning Course

As Sarah reported it, development of the Learning Course began with informal discussion to conceptualize the problem to be tackled. The talk centred on perceived problems in student' reading and writing skills, joined to the view that "reading is a function of thinking". But the theoretical stance changed focus as the planning committee collected information from teachers about student needs in reading and study skills. This information was sorted into common-sense categories which the planners then divided among themselves and on which they worked individually to prepare units. Sarah was responsible for the units in Reading and in Communications.

For the Reading unit, Sarah did research, considered and organized the various approaches she felt were important, and then, wearily, confronted the task of preparing materials. Fortunately, she was presented with a kit which "did everything that I wanted to do beautifully," and which she decided to adopt for the Reading unit.

The Communications unit grew out of Sarah's participation in seminars and workshops. She simply put together materials she had collected from various sources, and from courses and workshops she had attended. "When I found that the different courses were repeating the same kinds of things, I figured that they were probably very basic." During the first two semesters of teaching the Learning Course, the units were refined, by the group and by each of the planners individually in his own classes.

Phases in the Development Process

We can identify five phases in the group's work:

1. They began by identifying and conceptualizing a problem.
2. Then they went on to gather information on student needs.
3. Next the planners formulated categories for their work (course unit titles).
4. They then elaborated these into units consisting of lesson plans and materials in varying degrees of detail.
5. Finally they evaluated the results of

their work and refined the product.

Though the stages overlapped, and constantly informed one another, we will examine them in turn.

Conceptualization of Problem. The Learning Course
committee began its conceptualization from the
theoretical position that reading is a function of
thinking. Although the shift in focus from 'thinking' to 'learning' and then to 'coping with
school' was described by Sarah as "copping out", it
illustrates a sure sense of the practical. These
teachers felt that while their knowledge of thinking, and even of learning, was inadequate, they
could do something to equip students with "strategies for succeeding in the particular politics of
our school." This assessment of their own capabi-
lities and possibilities, then, guided their conceptualization of the problem.

Determining Student Needs. Concurrent with conceptualization of the problem was the stage of determining student needs. As an English teacher, Sarah
felt she had to "constantly be tuned in to so many
things" and her special ability to "smell out the
needs of the kids quickly, and kind of predict
problems" was recognized by her colleagues. Furthermore, the area of 'needs' received input from a
large number of teachers. So Sarah's confidence in
this phase of the work was very strong, and (as in
the first phase) this sense of her own abilities
gave her practical knowledge a firm base.

Organization. The third phase, organizing the
projected course into categories, was described by
Sarah with a degree of doubt. She suggested that
some of the units were shaped around current fads
and jargon:

> We got all these "Why can't the kids do..."
> statements, and someone, I think it was Liz,
> organized those into various categories, quite
> jargoned, you know --words like strategies,
> hypothesizing,... and then we divided into
> groups. Let's say there would be a group on
> problem -solving, and they would bring up all
> kinds of suggestions for exercises, and write
> them. We got reports from most of those com-
> mittees, and then we met, shuffled all those
> things around and came up, basically, with the

classification you see. We called reading "Coping with Print", because we thought just calling it reading would turn the kids off. "Collecting and classifying information" I guess would be research and essay writing, but we wanted to make it sound broader than that.

In other respects, however, Sarah illustrated the practical knowledge she had developed in her ordering of the units of the Learning Course. Thus, initially one member of the group held that "everything has to come first; " as Sarah saw it, "the kids are new in the school and they have to learn to cope right away." To overcome this difficulty Sarah had suggested a 'spiral' arrangement in which the course began with a brief taste of each area and then returned to the topics in more detail. Later she concluded that this notion was pretentious:

> As I see it now, there's no particular rationale for any order, at all. I think what's a better rationale is the rhythm of the school year: you don't want to do very heavy, demanding stuff the week before a holiday, or at the end of June. Nor do you want to start with very 'soft' stuff, like communications, group dynamics, at the beginning where the kids are doing no writing.

Thus Sarah was aware of the notion of spiral curriculum. But she was more clearly aware of the many ways such an arrangement is likely to be sabotaged (by holidays or other disruptions), or to be self-defeating because it interferes with the more basic purpose of the teacher to create an appropriate classroom atmosphere.

Development of Materials. In elaborating materials, Sarah drew heavily on her own experience (e.g. her conception of Reading, specific directions and methods she had used for teaching essay-writing, the study skills and techniques that worked for her in high school) as well as on readily available sources (such as the current literature on communications). Sarah had strong reservations about some of this work. She spoke of the group's "naiveté in believing that we're actually accomplishing something by adding one more ditto exercise to the file, or finding one more short article on a topic."

> So much of the stuff depends on haphazard con-
> tacts that we had, and I sometimes get the
> impression that there's a whole vast area of
> material that's behind some closed door.
> Somewhere, I have the feeling that there's
> this terrific package of overheads, and films,
> and snazzy exercises and, you know, evaluating
> instruments, that are so much better calibra-
> ted and better presented than what we did."

And she felt uneasy about passing on to students
her own particular study habits and techniques, the
effectiveness of which she could not guarantee or
even explain.

But again, despite areas of doubt, Sarah's
sense of this aspect of curriculum development was
enhanced by her experience in planning instructional units for the Learning Course. Two examples
can be cited. First, Sarah felt she had derived
from the Learning Course an understanding of how to
structure instructional units "strictly in terms of
objectives or skills that I'd like the kids to
practise." This approach quickly became an important element in her practical knowledge, as evidenced by application to a Writers' Workshop. Sarah
had been accustomed to giving students considerable
freedom in writing, but found that this made it
difficult, later, to bring critical tools to bear
on their work. She decided to begin with careful
teaching of skills (sentence structure, paragraph
development, and the like) through limited and
clearly-defined assignments, and to let spontaneity
develop later on.

> As a result we've developed a critical vocabu-
> lary of sorts; they're able to criticize their
> own work, and they're able to evaluate other
> prose, and I think that I'm seeing some im-
> provement. They're practising specific skills
> of varying sentence structure. But all of
> that came from the notion that whatever I
> expected from the kids, I had to give them
> first. I couldn't criticize the paragraph
> development until I had given them dogged
> exercises in paragraph development.

The second example is related to the first.
In working with individual students in a variety of

subject areas, Sarah had become aware of the extent to which they were assigned tasks with unclear and conflicting purposes. For example, a student might come in with an essay on <u>Hamlet</u>: "I try to work with them, but I feel a sense of futility. If the purpose is to learn to write an essay, they could be doing it on a topic they choose, and if the purpose is to appreciate literature, then don't ask them to write a literary essay."

Both these insights were integrated into Sarah's practical knowledge of curriculum development, and was applied later in her work in the Reading Centre. It is important to note that both ideas, differently phrased, could well have been obtained from a study of learning theory. But because they were derived from Sarah's experience in the classroom and in planning, these principles were used not in a linear and 'theoretical' way but practically and deliberatively, in combination with other principles. Thus in the example of the Writers' Workshop, Sarah had in mind at least two other important purposes: she was concerned not to sacrifice the spontaneity she had achieved in previous courses, but was also working toward a 'critical vocabulary', i.e. integration and awareness on the part of students of the skills they are acquiring. In the second example, too, Sarah weighed competing purposes against one another and was aware, in the context of practice, that she must choose between them: teach essay-writing, or literary appreciation, but do not overburden a lesson with both aims at once: they require different treatment.

Evaluation. The final stage, evaluation, was carried out in an informal and unsystematic way which caused Sarah much concern. The research department of the local Board had failed to supply a promised model for evaluating the units. Sarah had relied on conversations with students about their schoolwork to see whether they were making use of skills and insights acquired in the course. One persistent and disturbing impression she had was that teachers were conducting classes in ways that minimized the need for students to use the troublesome reading and writing skills, so they were given few opportunities to practise what they might have learned. Furthermore, Sarah felt that students' judgments were not always reliable, and the logistics of systematically following up all the students stymied her. So evaluation was a major stumbling block for Sarah, on two levels: she lacked appropriate evaluative techniques ("I have no inkling about how we could judge whether the course was successful,") and further, she was unsure about "what constitutes success."

The five stages just described constitute the outline of Sarah's view of the process of curriculum development. Before going on to compare this view with Sarah's experiences of development in English and in the Reading Centre, we should examine one aspect of curriculum development that was most important for Sarah in the Learning Course work: curriculum development as group process.

Curriculum Development as Group Process

The desire for a sense of community through group work was one of the major motives behind Sarah's participation in the Learning Course development. As I mentioned earlier, initially she found the group process a "very, very heavy experience" but, implicity, a necessary and valuable one. However, she was concerned that the knowledge of group process which the planners held, which they taught to students and used in their teaching was not brought to bear on the functioning of their own group. Sarah described this situation with keen awareness of the irony:

> The course had a very heavy emphasis on group dynamics and communication, a very heavy 'socializing' content, and one of the things that we kept harping on was the idea of a group having two functions, a task function and a maintenance function. After preaching so much, you'd think that some of that would have rubbed off on our little group of five. It turned out that we were all harbouring these separate, different burdens of grudges, and feelings of inadequacy and jealousy, that we never had time to expose to each other because we were always so busy with the task of "What are we going to teach tomorrow?"

Thus Sarah was aware that group skills need to be practised as well as preached, and that this requires time. But somehow, even after a single, cathartic group session brought this home to them, neither she nor any of the other members of the group acted on this knowledge.

Although the atmosphere in which the group worked was a positive one (Sarah spoke of community, of enthusiasm, of freedom to admit failure, and of the group's growing credibility in the school), it seemed to lose momentum after a year of teaching the course: two of the original five members left (for reasons unrelated to the course itself), and the group virtually ceased to exist. Sarah, who had taken on the role of coordinator, was the only one to go on teaching the course continuously, for a total of five semesters. In the second year, when she and Vivian were teaching the course, they discussed their working relationship and concluded that "We didn't want to feel again like horses, all running on the same track at the same speed, doing the same work." They planned to meet regularly to discuss their experiences, but even this loose arrangement dissolved, apparently because they had very different and conflicting views of the course. It seemed that once Sarah and the other teachers in the group had succeeded in putting together a viable course, each teacher reasserted an individual need to work independently and to give the course a personal stamp. The personal orientation of the teacher's knowledge will be discussed in the next chapter; here, we emphasize the fact that the scope and content of Sarah's curriculum knowledge is bounded by a need that stems from the situation of the teacher.

Another instance of the members' needs for individual expression is found in Sarah's statement concerning the decision to move the Learning Course from Grade 10 to Grades 11-12: "I feel very strongly that everyone who invested time on this Learning Course should have a say there." This is an important group decision concerning the level at which the course should be taught; Sarah's statement stresses not the knowledge and experience which the group members can bring to this decision but rather their rights, as individuals who had invested time and effort in the project, to have a share in determining the 'fate', as it were, of their creation. It is as though the individuals had acquired property rights over the results of their work, and Sarah's concern was to safeguard these rights.

Thus, the first two interviews trace a process in which Sarah moved from a strong sense of shared purpose with the Learning Course group to an equally strong need for autonomy in refining the product of that group effort. Thereafter, although Sarah occasionally sought help from others in further developing aspects of the course, she tended to see it increasingly as her own creation: "It's as if I've created this monster, because it's largely mine. There has been some very valuable input, but I think most of it is mine."

Each of the examples cited contributes to a single impression: it appears that Sarah's knowledge of group process is, with respect to curriculum development, subservient to her concern with the classroom. The group process was of value in beginning work on a new course, but inconvenient once the teachers had become comfortable with the materials. Thus Sarah's knowledge of group process is, in effect, not practical knowledge, at least not for curriculum development. It does not come to be applied because the need to apply it is only a temporary one (for the duration of the planning effort) and it is not viewed as relevant to the goal of functioning well in the classroom.

Curriculum Development in English

Sarah's experience of program planning in the English department, though thoroughly negative, had given her useful exposure to a different mode of curriculum work. The department had taken what to Sarah was a rigid and narrow approach, returning to the 'basics' of grammar and composition interpreted in a highly structured way. Committees had been formed to set up criteria for the following year in various courses and grade levels. Sarah felt severely alienated by the authoritarian style of the committees and by the substance of their discussions. Their procedure was to state formal requirements, "giving a list of the finished products of what we want kids to do," and to follow this up with the elaboration of essentially punitive marking schemes. Sarah argued that setting down objectives and marking systems was insufficient; "we have to teach the kids some things before we mark the kids on them." Further, in the context of discussions centred on concerns stemming mainly from the subject matter of English (e.g. survey of poetry, Shakespeare, the formal essay), Sarah injected concerns relating to the student and his needs: for example, at what grade level should topics best be taught; how can students be encouraged to write; what benefit do students derive from Shakespeare when they treat it as a foreign language to be learned by rote.

It is evident that Sarah's experience in the English department had brought into focus two important ideas about curriculum development. First, she regarded 'subject matter' and 'student' as equally important areas of concern for curriculum development. Second, she was quite clear about the limitations of an approach to development that begins with specification of objectives, and moves prematurely to evaluation without paying careful attention to instruction. Both these ideas, we have seen, were articulated in terms of her classroom experience. She knew what it felt like to teach Shakespeare in Grade 10; she knew what it meant to take a directive like "Teach essay writing" and apply it in the classroom. Thus her experience in the English department had contributed to her understanding of curriculum development to a degree that far outstripped the importance of the experience itself.

Curriculum Development in the Reading Centre

Initially Sarah spent much of her time in the Reading Centre planning and preparing. She developed workshops, lessons on various topics to give on invitation from teachers, exercises, and units of work for individual students. Gradually, she began to realize that she was taking on too much, and that there might be other ways of handling the situation. By her second year this realizations was developing into a new style of work, as reflected in the way that an Effective Reading Workshop was conducted:

> Rather than taking out the file, which has all kinds of xeroxes of material that the kids couldn't care less about, why not start where the kids were and with the things they were concerned with? I think the kids bring with them the materials that they really need to work on. And it's a matter, on the one hand, of my listening, and on the other hand, of having confidence that I can deal with things at the moment.

Although this particular workshop came about by chance on the suggestion of a substitute teacher, it is clear that Sarah would not have adopted the method so readily unless it were congenial to her teaching style and skills. In fact, it seems to have been a particularly happy accident for Sarah given her commitment to allowing students to formulate their own needs, and the limited time she could devote to preparation.

Summary

We have seen that Sarah's practical knowledge of curriculum grew directly out of her school experience. Though she had not studied curriculum theory directly, she was familiar with and frequently made reference to ideas that are current in the literature. However, she did so in her own terms, giving her own assessment of the idea--often a rejection. For example, she had entertained the notion of 'spiral curriculum' but easily put this idea aside in favour of a more homespun organization based on the structure of the school year. Similarly she had arrived through her experience at a notion of the organization of instruction that could well have come from learning theory. She had acquired a sound knowledge of the use of objectives in planning: she was aware that objectives had to be clear and non-conflicting, and that one had to teach, and make provision for the learning of, the objective. She was equally clear (particularly from her experience in the English department) about the limits of this knowledge for planning. She saw that the objectives which organize instruction must be chosen with a view to the value for the student of what one is setting out to teach, and must be elaborated in terms of the means available for teaching them; as a result objectives might have to be changed, traded off against one another, set aside temporarily or indefinitely. Thus Sarah had a clear understanding of the limitations of the 'objectives' approach to curriculum development; this knowledge was personal, and quite distinct from the prescriptions of conventional theories.

Another instance of the practical derivation of Sarah's knowledge of curriculum is seen in the way her knowledge of group process fitted into her curriculum knowledge. The knowledge of groups was not seen by Sarah as bearing on her central purpose, to work well in the classroom. Effective group work and a sense of community had been important factors in launching the Learning Course project, but once the task was in hand, the knowledge of group process became irrelevant, and was held in abeyance.

Sarah's general approach to curriculum development is a commonsense view likewise derived from practice. The five-stage sequence we have imposed on her account bears a strong resemblance to the Tyler rationale[1], but there is no evidence that Sarah was influenced by such notions nor even that she paid particular attention to the curriculum development process. When she expressed doubts about the development work, these doubts invariably concerned particular issues (e.g. streaming, how to evaluate results, the validity of the approach taken in particular units) rather than the way the work had been done. Paradoxically, when she did reflect on the curriculum development process, it was in connection with the knowledge of group dynamics which was <u>not</u> applied to the work. She could easily formulate guidelines about maintaining communication among members of the planning group, getting together for open-ended sessions and so forth, but these guidelines were not followed ("I learned that you must practise that ... it's not significantly better now, by the way.") so we cannot consider them to be a part of her practical knowledge.

The intuitive, commonsense and practical nature of Sarah's approach to curriculum development leads us to apply to it Schwab's view of curriculum.[2] In fact Sarah and her group did begin with the identification of a practical problem (students' deficiencies in reading and writing skills). They did quickly attempt to work out alternative practical implications of their ideas: a large group of contributing teachers met early on to thrash out ideas and write exercises. The conception of the problem with which they began changed repeatedly in the course of their work, and was strongly influenced by means available as well as ends espoused:

> We weren't doing anything about thinking because we didn't know anything about thinking. But we probably could do something quite minimal in the sense of getting the kids to cope with the demands that are made of them.

Indeed Sarah was rather apologetic about the

messy and sometimes haphazard nature of the group's work, as suggested by the embarrassed laughter which accompanied the above comment. If she had articulated a view of what curriculum development should be like, it would likely have been closer to a neat and orderly process à la Tyler (as he is commonly, though probably mistakenly, understood) than to a Schwabian view of curriculum as practical.[3] However, the interviews suggest that while Sarah gave little thought to the development process, she did function with a sure sense of both the tasks involved and the practical realities to which curriculum work must respond (in particular time constraints, limitations of knowledge, the need to function in the classroom, group pressures, and the expectations of school personnel) as well as of the inevitable messiness of the process itself.

With respect to the specific tasks involved in curriculum development, we note that for the most part Sarah's view of these was derived from her own experience. The phase of conceptualizing the Learning Course was really an outgrowth of ongoing informal discussions among several teachers; though this undoubtedly involved much give and take, there was no deliberate effort to examine and choose from among alternative conceptualizations. Assessing the needs of students was done partly by survey but, especially in this area, Sarah relied heavily on her intuitive grasp of student needs and on her unquestioned ways of formulating these. In developing the specific goals of the course and planning the instructional units, Sarah and her group relied on a range of prepared instructional materials from which they chose suitable items, and on which they modelled lessons using articles and other materials collected for current interest or relevance to students.

Interestingly, it is in the area of evaluation that Sarah's practical knowledge faltered. Here again she relied on commonsense methods, such as talking to students about their work in other classes, but this rightly did not satisfy Sarah. She bemoaned the lack of "precisely-calibrated instruments" for evaluating the course. Finally her inability to evaluate the Learning Course was an important factor in Sarah's disillusionment with it. It is surprising that she did not apply her ingenuity about classroom techniques in this area to develop classroom methods of assessing the effects of the Learning Course. She might have collected reading matter, tests and exercises from various subject areas, and used these in diverse ways, asking students to identify the skills involved and testing them in ways that required increasingly independent use of their skills. There were lessons in which Sarah used reading matter from other courses (e.g. the lesson on Inventory technique) to teach a particular skill, but no detailed evaluative techniques were built in beyond her general and vague assessment of how students performed.

This gap in Sarah's practical knowledge of curriculum suggests a form of theoretical bias: Sarah regarded evaluation as an area of expertise, amenable to the use of precisely-calibrated instruments. Awareness of her ignorance (perhaps compounded by memory of the heavy-handed procedures the English department had developed) made her reluctant to rely on the rough-and-ready evaluation methods she might herself develop, and seemed to paralyze Sarah's resourcefulness in this area.

In the Reading Centre, Sarah went on to develop a style of work which tended to focus on her strengths and minimize areas of weakness. The improvised workshop format allowed Sarah to rely on her natural abilities in needs assessment and in choosing and devising instructional techniques to meet the needs identified. Furthermore, because students selected themselves and participated in formulating their own needs in relation to school coursework, the problem of evaluation was partly circumvented. If Sarah taught a particular reading skill, she knew it was relevant, and used, at least for the material the student brought, and on which he learned the skill; and he likely also saw the skill work for another student's material. For Sarah this apparently solved the problem of evaluation, and in an interesting way: she put aside the question of how student learning is to be evaluated, and reshaped her teaching context so that the question (at least in that form) would not arise. This is a type of solution to a practical problem which recurs in Sarah's experience, as we shall see.

Early on, Sarah had described the Learning Course work as a 'copping out' process, from "thinking" to "learning" to "coping with school". This process reached its final stage in the Reading Centre with Sarah's focus on problems and materials presented by students. We can see this sequence as a resumé of her curriculum development experience, beginning from a theoretical base (the notion of "thinking"), moving to a school-relevant but still theoretical starting point ("learning"), then formulating a practical aim ("coping with school") and finally reformulating this purpose in specific terms that begin with the student's concerns rather than working towards them. For Sarah as a teacher based in the reality of school and its demands, this represents an appropriate role in the curriculum development process, and one in which her knowledge is firmly grounded, as her own expression of confidence attests:

> I'm prepared, at this point, to have much more confidence in that kind of process than in a process of planning and looking for materials. It's a matter, on the one hand, of my listening, and on the other hand, of having confidence that I can deal with things at the moment they arise.

An important element bolstering Sarah's confidence in this type of development process was her knowledge of instruction, since this knowledge allowed her to work effectively within the open-ended curricular framework she had created. We turn then to an examination of this knowledge.

INSTRUCTIONAL KNOWLEDGE

Sarah's practical knowledge of instruction is considerable. Aspects of it have already been alluded to, but it warrants separate elaboration. Sarah has a view of learning and knowledge of teaching generally and of her own teaching style in particalar. She has views on how instruction should be organized, on the kind of interaction with students she wants to promote, and on the evaluation of student learning. I will outline each of these aspects of her knowledge of instruction, and the coherence of this knowledge will be assessed.

Learning

Sarah's 'learning theory' is a simple and appealing one. It is expressed directly in statements about learning, and indirectly in statements about students and teaching. Sarah did not use a term such as 'learning theory' in referring to her knowledge, and in fact insisted that she did not know anything about learning. But the transcripts reveal the outline of a view of learning, and its elaboration not as theory but in terms of practical knowledge about students and instruction.

Sarah holds that learning is an activity that is tied to, and must be relevant to, life. Students learn best when they see the implications of what they are learning for their lives. This belief is reflected in Sarah's emphasis on the usefulness of learning skills, the possibility of students expressing their personalities through writing, and the similarity between what one is reading about in a fictional work and what is happening in one's own development. The relation of learning to life also entails that learning is developmental, dependent upon 'levels of maturity' --a broad term, not clearly defined by Sarah but involving emotional as well as cognitive factors. And learning is also an individual process. Sarah came to believe that formalized study skills work for some, but not all learners; for many others, the learning process is a messy one which admits of little intervention by teachers but whose meanderings must nevertheless be respected.

Two central issues in Sarah's view of learning are struggle and success. Together they fuel the learning process. The need to struggle ensures motivation to learn, while a feeling of success and accomplishment provides the reason to continue. In most cases, Sarah saw the need for success as taking precedence, perhaps because much of her work was remedial. But she was no less aware of the need to challenge students to work to overcome deficiencies. She had found that "being shaken up" was an important, though unpleasant, part of the learning process as she had experienced it. The need to balance struggle and success meant that learning had to be strucutred for students; otherwise, they might perceive as insurmountable tasks which, properly ordered, they could easily master, such as essay writing.

A final aspect of Sarah's view of learning is the notion of reflexivity. Learning, she held, is enhanced when the learner is aware of what is happening to him, and when he is active in controlling his learning. In summary, then, Sarah viewed learning as an orderly, even rhythmic process, tied to development by struggle and success, in which the

learner as an individual is active, aware and
involved.

Students

The most obvious feature of Sarah's view of students is her great sympathy and liking for them.
The following comments are typical:

> The Grade 10's have a kind of enthusiasm and a
> naive, open-eyed attitude which reinforces my
> own openness.

> It's sad to see kids being bored by a reading
> assignment in Catcher in the Rye. But again,
> they're assigned a book to read with the
> threat of a content test over their heads, and
> then they are asked to comment on it on the
> basis of that first reading which was done
> under a gun.

> A kid came in, forced to come in by an English
> teacher. He was really frustrated, and just
> never came back. I figured he was being frus-
> trated by his teacher, and frustrated by me,
> and he just escaped.

> Eddy is a very fair, honest, fun-loving, swin-
> ging kid; he's almost archetypal. I'm very
> fond of him. I hope that he'll stick around
> the school, and maybe get into an academic
> stream where there's more challenge for him.

Sarah's view of students reflects, and gives
substance to, the view of learning just outlined.
With the exception of the notion of individual
variability in styles of learning, most of the
features of Sarah's view of learning are found in
the first interview. But her view of students
in the initial interviews was a negative one,
whereas her conception of learning is positive.
Sarah's concern for students is expressed in a
deficiency-oriented way: students lack necessary
skills, are unable to cope with demands made on
them in school, are unaware of the learning process
in which they are engaged. She commented, for
example, that kids "very rarely see what they're
learning; they don't see that till much later."
And when they do play an active role it is not in
the autonomous direction of their own learning but

in the (almost unconscious) manipulation of the teacher: "the class controls the teacher" by their unenthusiastic response to the materials she presents.

The view of students in terms of privation is most obvious in the early interviews when Sarah's conception of learning centred on skills as fixed and universally applicable techniques for learning (and, perhaps not incidentally, when she was unhappy about her work in the English department). As her work assignment, and her notion of learning, changed, there were subtle shifts in her view of students. The 'humanistic' orientation which she adopted emphasized the student's need for a feeling of success, and the teaching aim of "trying to make the kid happy to walk into the classroom." This formulation still stresses privation: Sarah's task, as she saw it, was to make of the student something other than what he was. But as a result of "looking at the kid much more positively than he's been looked at before," not only the student came to see himself and perceive the problem in a different light; Sarah did too.

Thus, for example, when in the fourth interview Sarah described her work with students on essay writing, her description was marked by an equal number of active verbs for student and for teacher behaviour, as the following excerpt shows:

> The kids <u>chose</u> topics from a list which had been <u>prepared</u> by the librarian and myself, based on what the kids seemed most interested in, paperbacks that kids <u>were requesting</u>. They <u>spent</u> a week in the <u>library</u> with the teaching librarian there, and she took them through a series of steps. They were tested, and then they <u>set up</u> a trial bibliography, which had them <u>investigating</u>..they <u>started</u> note-taking, and I was quite stringent, and supervised..the kids <u>were objecting</u> quite strongly to a lack of time, and they <u>said</u> that they <u>wanted</u> more time to take notes.

By the end of the interview sequence Sarah's view of students had caught up with her view of learning; she stressed the importance of students identifying their own needs, being in control of their own learning. When students are not in control, this may be the fault of teachers, Sarah hinted:

The kid who's 'brought' by the teacher doesn't have much faith in the whole process. And it probably isn't a very successful encounter.

There are many more pauses and silent times, in my dealing with a kid, while they search for something. I would like to think that; I know that at times when my defences are a bit low, I'll retreat to that other thing.

Teaching

Sarah's knowledge of the teaching process involves a number of basic beliefs about the act of teaching, detailed knowledge of the means of organizing instruction and of ways of interacting with students, and of the evaluation of the results of teaching. This knowledge reflects the particular style of teaching Sarah is attempting to embody in the classroom and, as we shall see, facilitates the practical work of teaching.

Beliefs about Teaching. One basic belief about teaching which underlies Sarah's comments about her work is the idea that teaching is a chaotic activity. There is a multiplicity of events, stimuli to which the teacher must pay attention not just serially but simultaneously. There are aims which conflict, and tasks which cannot be ordered because "everything has to come first." And one of the "occupational hazards" of teaching is a lack of time to reflect on one's work. Further, the teacher is subject to pressures which interfere with her ability to plan and carry out instructional goals. Often, "the class controls the teacher" by the nature of their response to her teaching and to the materials she presents. And sometimes the teacher finds herself, as Sarah did, swimming against the current of department policy.

For the student too the classroom can be a confusing environment; as Sarah perceives it, teachers make demands but fail to clarify these adequately or to teach students how to meet them: "The task of writing an essay, the task of making notes, things that appeared to me very concrete and structured were actually full of mystery for the kids." Students are reduced to guessing what goes on in the teacher's head, often relying on what Sarah considers mistaken clues (such as the idea that a typed essay is better than a handwritten one).

Nevertheless, Sarah does believe there are worthwhile functions she can carry out within the class setting. First, she can 'demystify' the confusing structure of demands made on students: she can teach them to write essays, take notes, answer examination questions. Second, and probably more important for Sarah, she can institute a valuable form of human relations among the members of the class:

> What the kids learn from the human experience of being in the classroom and the way an adult reacts to them and helps to create an environment where they react to each other... that's where I've put my money about learning. I'm not really sure how much learning goes on in the so-called assignments kids do, but I think that a lot of important, sometimes spectacular and sometimes really destructive things happen in the classroom, and I suspect that that's what the kid leaves high school with.

We note that the task of transmitting subject matter knowledge is peripheral in Sarah's view of teaching. She dismissed the "big pitcher pouring into little pitcher" image of teaching, but did not have an alternative view of subject matter teaching. Clearly, in teaching reading, writing, or learning skills she was "not working with pure subjects." But even when she taught English, the main alternatives of which she was aware were the use of literature as a medium for getting at other things, and "defending literature"--a posture Sarah understandably rejected. Thus there is perfect consistency between her view of teaching as an interpersonal encounter in which the teacher provides some service or 'how to' knowledge, and the particular stock of subject matter knowledge she holds.

The Organization of Instruction

Ordering of Materials. Sarah had a number of basic notions about how instruction can be organized. Several ideas learned from her experience in developing the Learning Course quickly became part of Sarah's knowledge of instruction: for example, the notion of making provisions for students to learn the particular tasks one is teaching, before testing them; and the idea that objectives must be taught for separately so as not to conflict and cancel one another out. These are practical principles Sarah made use of not only in work on the Learning Course but also later in teaching reading and writing skills. The application of these principles, however, is conditioned by Sarah's view of her subject matter. We have seen that her view of skills as requiring self-awareness on the part of the learner, and as applicable to varied subject matters, was not thoroughly worked out. As a result her application of instructional principles to skill learning was sometimes ambiguous. At times Sarah might plan a lesson so carefully that the skill was learned in a routine way, with little room for student awareness; at other times she seemed to abandon students, providing little help in transferring the skill to other situations.

Thus, in explaining to me the lesson I was to observe as part of the fourth interview, Sarah said "I try to present these techniques as something that hopefully can carry over, if they wish it to carry over, into their studying for other courses." When I asked how she would do this, she replied, "I suppose by a statement, at the beginning." In that same lesson, she allowed students to come to an understanding of how to use the Inventory techniques, and was pleased that they seemed, individually, to make sense of this. But she did not ask them to talk about whether they saw it as helpful, nor try to press home the usefulness of the technique, or to suggest different situations and ways in which they might use it.

Another notion that should work to organize instruction is Sarah's statement in the first interview that students can't be taught to function in groups. Interestingly, this idea is in direct contradiction to the presumed intent of much of the Learning Course material and the knowledge of communications and group work cited earlier. It illustrates the inconsistencies of practical knowledge. Unfortunately this inconsistency was not pursued in the interviews so we can only speculate. Sarah may have been expressing the skeptical edge of her knowledge: she accepted the views of communication and group work, even used them in teaching, but retained doubts about how far they could be applied in the class setting. In effect she may have been drawing a line between her subject matter knowledge and her instructional knowledge, saying, "Here is a bit of subject matter knowledge that appears to apply to instruction but I find it inapplicable." Perhaps it is a further implication of her belief that whatever is deliberately taught in class is ultimately less likely to have lasting impact than the 'hidden curriculum'.

Quantity and variety. In planning for instruction Sarah appeared to make use of the two notions of quantity and variety. In the Reading Centre she was "gradually learning to set up some activities that they do all of the time when they come in, so that I don't have to be sitting intensely with them every minute." Her aim was "to get to a point where I can just reach over to a shelf and take down a workbook." She had developed a series of different kinds of writing work, types of exercise on which she could improvise to produce appropriate assignments for different situations. Some of the exercises were planned so they could be used by the student in various ways and to which, in turn, Sarah could respond in keeping with the student's need.

Sarah's attention to quantity and variety of materials made for flexibility in teaching. However, quantity and variety sometimes worked to fill in gaps where Sarah was unsure of her subject matter. Thus, in teaching the Learning Course for the third or fourth time (a period of disillusionment when she was not working actively on the course), she spoke of going into lessons without a detailed lesson plan, but with a range of extra materials to cover a number of situations that might arise. Here, having extra materials may have enabled Sarah to avoid thinking through the lesson carefully, identifying clearly and ordering her goals. Instead, she taught a variety of different techniques, as many as would fit into the lesson.

Spontaneity. The notion of spontaneity refers to the particular ways in which the teacher participates in and shapes classroom life. It is hard for a teacher to be really passive in the classroom and survive, but some teachers rely heavily on established routines, conventional subject matter and stereotyped patterns of teacher-pupil relations, while others are constantly at work giving form to the subject matter taught and to the activities of the classroom. One dimension of spontaneity is that of change or novelty: Sarah gives much evidence of searching for new ideas and techniques, and of willingness to change not only her classroom work but her career orientation within teaching.

The notion of spontaneity, as opposed to simply impulsive behaviour, also involves two opposing factors. The first is the ability to release control, to receive stimuli from outside, and to respond to a situation or to a person. Thus Sarah spoke of making room for 'chance, mood and time of day' to influence her work, and of her ability to smell out student needs and act on them. The other factor is the ability to control the spontaneous event, to use the special energies which it releases to move learners in a direction intended by the teacher.

Sarah was well aware that spontaneity had to be weighed against structure, and that structure sometimes took precedence, as the following example of her teaching in a Writers' Workshop illustrates:

> I began giving the kids a very free hand in doing autobiographical sketches. But I could not go back at that point to talking about sentence structure and rhetorical devices, because I had locked myself into this more spontaneous approach. What I did this time is figure that if the kids are going to be spontaneous they can wait a month. I gave them very limited assignments, and told them very definitely what I would be looking for. As a result we developed a critical vocabulary of sorts. And one can't work it the other way, at least I don't think I would want to work it the other way, beginning with spontaneity and then reining in.

Thus Sarah had developed a principle of instruction according to which spontaneity, and responsiveness to student needs, had to be tempered by direction and control.

At times Sarah experienced difficulty in mediating between the two aspects. The 'nonsense words' presentation illustrates this difficulty. On the occasion in question, Sarah came into class in what she described as a 'hyper' mood. To catch students' attention in a rather unexciting lesson on different types of reading, she asked them to suggest three nonsense words, which she used as labels for the three types of reading. Towards the end of the lesson, when she gave them the correct terms for the types of reading, some students had difficulty letting go of the nonsense words. This fact, combined with the pleasant and cooperative atmosphere, indicated that the device had been sucessful. But I raised the question whether this kind of device was not a bit of 'mystification' which set up a barrier between Sarah and her students. Sarah reflected that while involved in this style of teaching she was aware that some students were baffled, but the momentum of the lesson led her to ignore them. Typically, "the hyperness on my part often leaves before the activity is over, and those things don't get finished well."

An opposite type of situation occured in the second observation session. This time, the 'hyper' mood took place during planning, when Sarah did the Inventory exercise herself, and found it strikingly effective in helping her to read a difficult text. She hoped to convey this feeling to the class, but soon realized she could not reproduce her experience for them. She contented herself with going around the class to work with individual students, but her own reduced expectations led to a kind of flatness in the lesson. Afterwards she was disappointed, despite a feeling that the point of the exercise had come across to individual students.

Both these examples sustain the impression that for Sarah, responsiveness often interfered with control. She seemed to view the dramatic event, like the 'nonsense words' presentation or the Inventory exercise, as an 'all or nothing' effort to shape the class activity. When it became evident that students were not reacting in the way she had hoped, or her own mood faded, the momentum of the lesson was lost. She did not backtrack to consider what the spontaneity was meant to accomplish, and whether she could fulfil her purpose in different ways. Rather, she reduced her expectations and narrowed her purpose to suit the response she was getting from students. Interestingly, Sarah had described her English teaching in just such terms: "I was reducing my demands in many ways" and "the class controls the teacher: if consistently a class registers very lukewarm responses, eventually that kind of feedback becomes very, very debilitating."

On another occasion Sarah related an episode in which one student influenced the reading choices of another. The first student, Joe, had become interested in James Dean and had read several books about the actor. Then,

He found out that James Dean had acted in East of Eden, so he picked out that book to read. He was there one day when Mary was there, and I was telling him that that seemed to me to be the way that readers, people who read a lot, chose their books, and we called it 'chaining'. And I showed him how one interest had chained onto another, because what he said was that now he wanted to read all of Steinbeck's books.

So Mary, this other girl who last year was practically illiterate, was sitting there and listening. I could tell that she was very impressed, and also very frustrated; she's at a stage where she really doesn't know phonics very well, and she has to sound out every word. It takes her, oh, maybe ten minutes to read a page of easy adolescent fiction. She was sitting there and listening pretty carefully.

Anyway, last week, she was waiting for me. She had written on a piece of foolscap, 'Margaret Mead', and she said, "I want to read the book called Margaret Mead." I said I didn't think there was a book called Margaret Mead, that Margaret Mead was an anthropologist--Mary knew what an anthropologist was because she's taking a course in ancient history--who had written several books, and then Mary said, I want to read that book (laughter), so I said, "Why do you want to read it?" And she said, "Well, I'm reading another book about a girl who reads Margaret Mead, so I thought that I would read Margaret Mead too."

So I got scared, because Mary is building her confidence very slowly, but she's still reading at about a Grade 4 level, and I thought that if I showed her Coming of Age in Samoa or something like that, she would get very frightened. So we went to the library, and I used it as an opportunity for her to handle the stuff in the card catalogue and locate books on the shelves. Anyway it turned out, really luckily, there was a children's book that supposedly had been written by Margaret Mead. It had big print and colourful pictures, and we were going through that a bit at a time, looking at a paragraph and asking questions about it and building some vocabulary, predicting what would come next, and using a lot of the skills that appear in a programmed workbook, but here it's doing something on her interest. She got that from Joe, the idea of one book recommending another book.

This example reflects great responsiveness to the student, and short-range control of the activity (using the chance to practise library skills and reading skills). But there is no evidence of longer-range planning and control. Sarah took the risk of destroying the student's hard-won confidence; the fact that they found a suitable book by Margaret Mead was recognized by Sarah as mere luck. Furthermore, the interest in Mead was, in a sense, superficial: Mary's interest was not in Margaret Mead so much as in identifying herself as a reader, and in expressing the new identity which she was developing as a result of her growing ability to read. Had Sarah discussed her interest with Mary, she might have found a safer, but equally satisfying, channel along which to pursue it. While it may be unreasonable to demand this degree of foresight and control, the example is nonetheless suggestive of Sarah's difficulty in exploiting the spontaneous event.

There are, however, examples which show Sarah exercising clear and confident control of her lessons. This is particularly evident in her description of remedial work with individual students; for example:

When dealing with a kid for remedial help in reading, we have a chat, and in the chat I try to pull out interests that the kid has, or strengths. Whereas in the past I might have said, god, I've spent half an hour and the kid hasn't learned anything, I feel very easy about that, and I try to say things to make the kid feel easy about it.

By the fifth interview Sarah had developed a style of planning in which her starting point was the materials and problems students brought to workshops: "I guess I had enough faith that they would be concerned with the things that were preplanned." These statements reflect Sarah's ability to respond to student needs and to improvise classroom activities and learning experiences. But more significantly, they rest on her confidence in the subject matter knowledge brought to the lesson: in remedial work, her approach was prescribed by a definite view of language learning which generated specific kinds of assignments as well as a style of working with students. In teaching workshops, too, Sarah had both carefully worked out materials and a flexible mode of using them. These situations contrast with the earlier examples in which, for various reasons, Sarah was unsure of her subject matter knowledge. We have indicated the ambivalent nature of her subject matter in English, and have shown how this created a particularly difficult situation for her at the time of the first interview. We have also seen that her conception of skills and skill learning was not without contradictions. Sarah herself was unsure of her knowledge in this area; she spoke of "the huge distance between what learning is, and what these isolated strategies that we're working on are." Bearing these considerations in mind, it is my contention that the equilibrium of Sarah's teaching depends on the extent to which she has a clear sense of her subject matter. She can maintain control of the direction of a lesson, and make use of the spontaneity, only when her immediate goal for the lesson fits into a firmly-held, broad view of the subject matter being taught.

This is not to say that spontaneity necessitates subject matter that is comprehensive or complete in a theoretical sense. Rather, what is required is a 'subject matter for teaching' that is adequate to the lesson in question. Thus, in the Writers' Workshop example, Sarah's subject matter consisted of a series of techniques for writing and analyzing writing, combined with a view of how writing can be learned; furthermore the subject matter was, by definition, of great interest to students who had signed up for the Workshop. This combination of a conception of the subject matter, a view of how to teach it, and motivation on the part of students is in no way theoretically significant, but it allowed Sarah to master the opposition of spontaneity and control. Similarly, in the Reading Centre, the skills subject matter was integrated into Sarah's general approach to reading, and she had no difficulty in showing students the usefulness of the skills she taught in dealing with their problems.

However, in both the "nonsense words" lesson

and the Inventory lesson Sarah taught specific, isolated reading techniques. In both cases she encuntered the problem of the applicability of the skills in question, and this problem arose because her view of skills was not yet fully worked out. She needed the device of nonsense words to attract students' attention because the subject matter did not respond to any felt need of theirs; this reflects her intuitive understanding of the affective dimension of learning, but it was not until later that she articulated this.

Interaction with Students

As we have seen, Sarah's ability to bring about a specific form of interaction with students is an important aspect of her practical knowledge of instruction. Sarah's main concern was with making contact with students, communicating with them; to this end she drew on the knowledge of communication and group process outlined above. Her knowledge of student needs and interests enabled her to shape learning materials that were relevant to students, to initiate remedial work around their interest, and to create with individual students a "bank account of common experience" which became the focal point of their interaction. And we have seen that Sarah had knowledge of self which enabled her to fulfil her goal of communicating openly with students. So this aspect of Sarah's practical knowledge of instruction draws on and integrates elements from her knowledge in all the other areas.

Evaluation

We noted earlier that the evaluation of her curriculum development work was a major problem for Sarah. In the instructional context, however, evaluation is straightforward.

> There are four marks. They can get Excellent, Good, Pass or Fail, and I give most of them Good. A Good is anywhere from 66 to 80, and there's not much competition. It's not a course for kids who are really concerned about marks. What they tried to do last time was to go from a Good to an Excellent; they're motivated to do that. And one fails if one skips class and doesn't hand in assignments; it's

very clear and clean.

This position on evaluation reflects Sarah's views of students, and of learning. Her position respects the student's need to know where he stands, to be protected from excessive competition, to be allowed to work to learn rather than to attain marks, in short to be in control of this own learning. On the other hand, this stance also reflects Sarah's concern with objectivity in learning: the student should be taught specific skills in a clear, unambiguous way and should subsequently be tested in an equally clear and unambiguous way on his learning of just these skills. It would appear from all that Sarah says about her relationships with students that she is successful in achieving a delicate balance between the two views of evaluation, but one suspects that this is accomplished by the way she implements the marking scheme rather than by the scheme itself (e.g. by her willingness to correct papers in detail, explain marks, allow students to rewrite papers, and so forth).

Summary

We have looked at Sarah's knowledge of instruction in some detail. While there may be minor conflicts here, as in other areas of her knowledge, what emerges most strongly from this account is a sense of the coherence of Sarah's views. Clearly, Sarah knows what she wants to accompish in teaching, and her purposes make sense in the light of her understanding of students and of the teaching-learning situation. Further, her knowledge of instruction is tied to Sarah's knowledge in each of the other areas. Her view of herself complements her picture of students, and both together make possible the kind of instructional interaction she envisions. Students and teacher are all seen primarily as individuals who (along with a few others) make up the milieu as she sees it--a loose collection with only weak ties to larger political structures. The curriculum development process is one whose primary purpose for Sarah is to create the instructional framework within which her knowledge of teaching and learning can best be deployed. Sarah's subject matter knowledge, as we have seen, was undergoing change throughout the interview period; always, however, this knowledge was closely tied to her knowledge of instruction. She made subject matter choices in the light of her understanding of students and, conversely, her success in the use of particular instructional strategies often depended on the level of coherence and completeness of her subject matter.

It will be the task of Part Three to examine these interrelationships and, more generally, to consider the various ways in which Sarah's practical knowledge is held and used. That, of course, is the major focus of this study. But it is important to bring to that examination a sense of the scope and coherence of Sarah's content knowledge.

NOTES

1. Ralph Tyler, Basic Principles of Curriculum and Instruction. (Chicago: University of Chicago Press, 1949).

2. Joseph J. Schwab, "The Practical: A Language for Curriculum," School Review 78 (1979), pp.1-23

3. Despite superficial differences, the approaches of Tyler and Schwab are similar in many of their presuppositions. Tyler, in fact, has endorsed the process of deliberation outlined by Schwab as an appropriate method of moving through his five stages. See his article, "Specific Approaches to Curriculum Development," in J. Schaffarzick and D.H. Hampson, eds., Strategies for Curriculum Development (Berkeley, Calif.: McCutchan, 1975), 17-33.

Part Three

HOW PRACTICAL KNOWLEDGE IS HELD AND USED

Chapter 6

THE ORIENTATIONS OF PRACTICAL KNOWLEDGE

Part Two examined the content of Sarah's practical knowledge. Despite an emphasis on its origins and development, we viewed this knowledge there as essentially static. We were concerned to map the terrain of Sarah's knowledge, to identify different areas of content and to determine their relationships. But, using Sarah's imagery, the purpose of a map is to allow us to get somewhere. Because Sarah's knowledge is held actively, she can move her ideas from intellectual space out into the classroom to affect practice. In Part Three our concern is to show Sarah's knowledge as held, as related to the world of practice, and as used to shape classroom life. We will begin by looking at how Sarah's knowledge is oriented.

The term 'orientation' is used to indicate the way that practical knowledge is held in active relation to the world of practice. We will be looking here at five aspects of this orientation. First, knowledge is oriented to the practical situation the teacher encounters (situational orientation); it is formulated in response to these situations—the classroom, the school, the curriculum group. Second, practical knowledge is oriented to the self or owner of knowledge, who is aware of holding it and sees it as applying, in some measure, to him or herself. Furthermore this knowledge is used to express the self, to give meaning to experiences and to realize purposes. The term 'personal orientation' will be used to refer to these aspects of the holding of practical knowledge. Third, practical knowledge has a social orientation. It is shaped by social constraints and is used to structure the social reality of the knower. Fourth, practical knowledge is held in the context of the particular experiences through which it was acquired, and is experientially oriented in that it reflects and gives shape to the knower's experience.

A final way in which practical knowledge is oriented, paradoxically enough, is to theory. The theoretical orientation, in a sense, conditions all the others, determining the contours of practical knowledge. The way the knower conceives (implicitly or explicitly) theory and practice and the relations between them determines both how he acquires and uses practical knowledge and how he attains theoretical knowledge and exploits it for practical ends. This chapter will discuss the five orientations of practical knowledge in turn, beginning with the theoretical orientation because it is seen as conditioning the others, and moving on to the situational, personal, social and finally the experiential orientation.

THEORETICAL ORIENTATION

Sarah's conception of theory, practice, and the relation between them was not a topic discussed in the interviews. It may be that she had no explicit views on the subject, but her conception can be inferred from a variety of statements she made, and from the way she works. We can begin by noting that Sarah did not appear to be concerned with the explanatory value of theory or its predictive power. Nor did she emphasize the power of theory to solve problems. When talking about theory generally or about a particular theoretical notion, Sarah used terms such as 'view', 'map', and 'orientation'; and she used them in common-sense ways, as the following statements illustrate:

> In the overall, more general and more theoretical view, I felt quite fumbling. If you think in terms of flying high enough to look down at something and recognize it, but not high enough, not able to rise even higher and get a broader view, or to see how that particular thing fits into the larger map.

> I think I have absorbed part of the orientation to writing and I can, with that in mind, think of practical things to do.

Thus theory is seen as something broad, general,

comprehensive. It stands above practice, and can serve as a guide to practice. The imagery of height suggests that Sarah places theory in a position of superiority to practice, and this is borne out. Sarah recalls, for example, the standards of her university work, which "was much more thorough, and I did investigate, I did set up complex bibliographies. I was quite ethical about not taking shortcuts." Sarah's respect for the rigour of theory sometimes generated a diffidence concerning her own work. She insisted that she was generally confident in the classroom and this self- deprecation was largely a product of the interview situation, and I am inclined to accept this assessment.

Nevertheless, theoretic knowledge seems to play the role of setting limits on Sarah's work. Thus, the entire focus and definition of the Learning Course was determined by the group's view and knowledge of theory:

> It started out being called a "Thinking Course", and the evolution from "Thinking" to "Learning", I think is a very interesting one, because in a sense it's a huge evolution of copping out.

> We realized that we weren't doing anything about thinking because we didn't know anything about thinking. But we probably could do something quite minimal in the sense of getting the kids to cope with demands that are made of them. It's much more modest, but I feel more in control of that, because none of us really had any theoretical knowledge of 'thinking', or even of what 'learning' is.

The fact that 'thinking' and 'learning' are theoretical terms bearing particular meanings within a body of literature seems to place these notions out of bounds for Sarah and her group. (In Chapter 5 we noted a similar attitude to the notion of evaluation). Indeed, the notions of 'thinking' and 'learning' are virtually reified. Sarah speaks several times of "what 'learning' is", and of "the huge distance between what learning is, and what these isolated strategies that we're working on are." But we note that this 'huge distance' is a creation of the Learning Course group's attitude to theory no less than it is a product of the nature of theory in the area. The study of thinking and

learning is distinguished chiefly by a prolifera-
tion of theoretical views and considerable disag-
reement concerning the applications of those views
(often formulated in contexts dissimilar in varying
degrees to that of the classroom) for educational
practice. In such a situation intelligent, experienced and motivated teachers are probably as competent as anyone else to exploit the formulations
and empirical findings of research into thinking
and learning. But the Learning Course group, and
Sarah among them, appears to believe that there
exists some unequivocal and clearly applicable
theory with which they, unfortunately, are not
equipped to deal (perhaps simply because of a lack
of time to master the theory, perhaps because they
lack the critical abilities to identify the 'right
theory').

We noted earlier that, despite disclaimers,
the notion of 'coping skills' on which the Learning
Course was centred always retained within it a concern for 'learning'. Yet Sarah's view of theory
effectively cut her off from all knowledge of thinking and learning beyond what she acquired through
practice (or, later, as a by-product of her work on
reading, communications or skills). In the light
of this, we can see Sarah's disillusionment with
the Learning Course as a result, in part, of her
view of theory. Because the relevant theory was
seen as somehow beyond her abilities and therefore
unavailable, Sarah had no means to critically
assess and rework the course materials outside of
the group planning situation. And the group
itself, denying their concern with learning, had
only their own interaction and the immediate
results of their teaching to work with. It is thus
not surprising that they foundered on the evaluation of the course: classroom-based evaluation was
seen as not professional, therefore inadequate, and
the theory which might have provided concepts from
which to build critical guidelines was likewise not
admitted to their consideration.

Underlying this situation, one suspects, may
be the influence of Sarah's education in English
literature. According to one view to which she was
probably exposed, literary scholarship consists in
a far-ranging and detailed knowledge of the literary corpus. The literary work is seen, in this
view, as a finished product bearing aesthetic
value; its significance is fixed and can be exhaus-
ted. The critical standards which inform literary

knowledge are taken as pregiven and immanent in the structure of the literary works themselves. The chief method of acquiring literary knowledge is analysis based on close examination of the works. The product of this scholarship, it is held, is objective understanding about the literary work.[1]

In retrospect we note similarities between Sarah's view of literature and this conception--in particular the notion of literary work as aesthetic object, amenable to conclusive study ("That's not studying Othello.") But as noted in Chapter 4, Sarah's view of her literary subject matter is a complex one in which 'traditional' components play a minor role, presumably because the governing considerations are practical. Yet the underlying conception of theory as the complete, careful and exhaustive study of fixed objects, leading to objective truth about them, is apparently a tenacious view which has remained a part of Sarah's practical knowledge despite its inconsistency with her emphasis on process in other areas of her knowledge (e.g. her instructional knowledge) and despite its obvious practical disadvantages.

The influence of this view explains in part the appeal which the notion of universal 'learning skills' still held for Sarah, as well as her diffidence in the face of theories bearing on learning and her difficulties with evaluation. Not having the extensive knowledge her literary training taught her to demand of herself, she would be reluctant to deal with theory in psychology: how could she assess the multiplicity of views? What standards would she choose? Similarly, by what criteria could she evaluate her curriculum development work when she had no professional knowledge of evaluative techniques? Thus Sarah found herself in a bind with respect to standards, unable to accept their relativity:

> Did I like the Tactics because I had invested so much time on the approach that Tactics takes? Had I taken a different approach, I might have been attracted to another.

> I remember distinctly going to the professional library one day, and, let's say, stacking up with eleven articles.... It was hot and I was hungry, so I left having read six. What if the pile had been upside down,

and I had read the six in the other direction?
Would it have changed my thinking on that
particular thing?

Further, she seemed to retain the view that the
univocal theory, the completely relevant body of
knowledge, exists somewhere unknown to her:

I sometimes get the impression that there's a
whole vast area of material that is behind
some closed door, and we don't quite know how
to get to the door.

There are some indications of change in
Sarah's view of theory, however. Most notably, she
began to realize that learning skills are not the
monolithic, universally applicable tools she had
imagined. Another indication is found in the way
that Sarah used theory, as we shall see shortly.

In general we can say that Sarah viewed theory
as rather remote from her work in the classroom.
However, she valued reflection and the process of
testing out "my own ideas against other people's
ideas" in discussion and committee work, and did
grant that theory is important and useful for practice. How, then, did she see the relation of theory to practice?

There are several instances in which Sarah
made explicit and deliberate use of formal knowledge. She used texts on communications in preparing a unit for the Learning Course. She sought
material on memory for a lesson she developed in
the Reading Centre. She studied 'time management'
and adapted some insights on this topic for use in
a lesson on study techniques. All of these instances, however, seem to involve the adaptation of
practice-oriented material from other, more general
contexts, to her specific classroom context. The
work Sarah consulted on communications was a compendium of exercises rather than a theoretical analysis of human communication; the material on memory was drawn from a text in reading, not a psychological study; and 'time management' is a practical
rather than a theoretic notion.

It would appear, then, that when Sarah set out
to do a deliberate job of researching and applying
a piece of knowledge she chose, not the theoretical
study which she felt was at a great distance from
her concerns, but a 'theory of practice' or a practical application that she could more easily adapt

to her purposes. This is not to suggest that Sarah never dealt with theory; rather she had her own way of treating theory.

Speaking of a reading course she took over a summer, Sarah commented that "I absorbed a lot of things that didn't seem to be very practical, but I seem to be working them out in what I'm doing now." This statement is paradigmatic of Sarah's mode of dealing with theory. She made deliberate efforts to expose herself to new ideas, and was initially very receptive to these. Then followed a period in which Sarah did nothing (at least did nothing overt); at times she actually appeared to be avoiding the new idea, and the demands which it made of her. In the second interview she spoke of "some new ideas about language that I've been exposed to through lectures, but haven't had a chance to do much reading about yet." Similar comments were made about the theories she drew on in the Reading Centre work, and recent investigations into study skills. Another example is the notion of classification: Sarah was initially quite excited about the implications of some comments I made in the second interview, but as time went on she found herself reluctant to work on this area, and she went so far as to avoid teaching the lesson the next time she taught the course.

Finally, however, Sarah acted to incorporate the new ideas into her work. Sometimes the application was direct and almost systematic, as with the orientation to reading that Sarah derived from her summer courses. Sarah's approach is not to analyze the theory and apply it point by point; rather, she 'absorbs' the theory and, when she feels comfortable with it, elaborates its practical implications in a detailed way. This is reflected in her explanation of the humanistic approach to reading that she had adopted. She mentioned her acquisition of a new set of vocabulary and gave as an example the Rogerian phrase "unqualified positive regard". When I questioned this I was given, not a definition or an explanation in terms of the relevant theory, but a totally practical, descriptive acount of the type of work with students that this notion dictates:

> Unqualified positive regard, and I don't like the sound of it, but it... I think it's obvious that when dealing remedially with kids with a whole history of failure, maybe you can

institute a change through having the kid see
himself and perceive the problem in a different light, and that often is achieved by
looking at the kid much more positively than
he's been looked at before.

A similar example is one in which Sarah
"picked up a guidance journal in which there was an
article about the latest investigations about study
skills." Sarah found the information there "devastating" to her previous work, because it suggested
that formalized study skills work only for some
learners, and that affective considerations are
crucial. Yet despite the fact that--once again--
she had difficulty in finding time to read thoroughly all the relevant material, she made use of
the new knowledge almost immediately. She described at length her new approach:

> I don't force things on a kid. I don't say,
> "Here's the technique." I do a lot of talk-
> ing. I do a lot of non-directed talk-
> ing...paraphrasing, to make sure that I've
> understood, and also so that the kid can hear
> it played back. With a couple of kids, I've
> never seen their essay.

It seems likely that in this case Sarah was able to
incorporate the new theoretic knowledge and to
adapt her teaching so quickly because the less formal, affectively-oriented approach was quite in
keeping with her teaching style.

In another instance, Sarah allowed a new idea
to percolate for some time and her eventual use of
it was indirect. From my comments on the notion of
classification Sarah took the very general message
that "the discipline of science is something that a
scientist understands, and it should be taught by a
science teacher." Sarah was unable to rework the
lesson on classification which had occasioned my
somewhat critical comments. But the idea motivated
her ("that thought has been haunting me a lot") to
seek contact with teachers of math and physics, and
to try to develop through discussions with them a
point of entry into their classes as well as a personal understanding of their work. She went even
further and tried to set up a collaborative project
with a geography teacher concerning the literacy of
his students. Sarah had other reasons for engaging
in these activities, of course; they were part of

108

the definition of her job. But it is evident that in exploring "a discipline that's quite foreign to me, to become aware of some of the literacy problems the kids have in relation to that particular subject" Sarah is working on the notion, to which she was initially quite opposed, that different disciplines involve different kinds of thinking and require different skills.

The last example can serve as an anchor for our summary of Sarah's orientation to theory and her view of the theory-practice relation. When the interview series began, Sarah seemed to view theory as a general, all-encompassing body of knowledge ordered according to pre-existing criteria. Thus there could exist universal learning skills which governed the search for knowledge and the acquisition of existing knowledge alike. To make use of theory one had to attain the necessary critical standards; without these Sarah was sceptical about what she could accomplish. This view, however, was a difficult one to maintain for a practitioner committed to improving her work through increased knowledge. And so Sarah gradually developed a more appropriate orientation to theory. She began to accept the multiplicity and relativity of the theories from which she had to work: "What I'm doing now is a bit broader, and grounded in some theories that are at least popular nowadays." She was increasingly willing to work from theory, taking the risks of choosing the appropriate theory and establishing her own criteria, rather than confining herself to collecting bits of practical advice:

> When I tried to do professional reading, it was very often for a technique to use--one very isolated idea that would perhaps provide some interest to the kids.

> What I did a few months ago was to contact some people at the university who are combining these two things in workshops for kids-- anxiety reduction and study skills--and I got hold of the articles that they were working from, 40-50 page articles, and when I get some time I'm going to try to look at it and try to get some teamwork going with the guidance department.

We have seen how Sarah's view of theory go-

verned her receptiveness to new knowledge, and her
ability to make use of theoretical formulations
that bear on her work. On the other hand, we have
also suggested that the practitioner's need to
extend her knowledge contributed to bring about
changes in her orientation. These points direct us
to the remaining orientations of Sarah's knowledge,
to see how they shaped her knowledge and influenced
her use of it, as well as how Sarah's view of
theory interacts with the remaining orientations.
For what we have termed the 'practitioner's need'
here is in fact treated in the remainder of this
chapter, analyzed into its components--the situational, personal, social and experiential orientations.

SITUATIONAL ORIENTATION

In Part Two, we spoke of Sarah's practical knowledge as derived from the variety of situations in
which she found herself. Thus, for example, we
showed how her view of English literature was
shaped around her classroom experience of English
teaching, dictating which literary works spoke to
students' concerns and how they could best be presented. Our task in the present section is to show
how the practical knowledge Sarah holds is directed
to her situation. These two ways of looking at
practical knowledge are complementary, and constitute two aspects of a dialectical process in which
practical knowledge arises out of a situation and
responds to new or changed situations by continued
growth.
    In line with Dewey's[2] usage, the term 'situ-
ation' is used here to refer to that interaction of
objective conditions with internal factors which
constitutes experience. In this section we will
consider three situations which Sarah encounters in
her work: the situation of the teacher in the
classroom, in the school, and in the curriculum
planning group. An important aspect of each of
these situations is, of course, Sarah's perception
of the situation of the student in class and in the
school; her sensitivity to student needs is an
important internal factor, while the actual constraints under which students are placed are central to the objective conditions in all the situations.

The Teacher in the Classroom.

The classroom situation is defined by Sarah in terms of the need for the teacher "to constantly be tuned in to so many things". Though she sees this need as a distinguishing mark of the condition of the English teacher, it is apparent that Sarah is concerned about "the pressures of the classroom" in all facets of her work. The multiform, sometimes chaotic, nature of the classroom is both an objective factor and an internal one, a function of the way Sarah perceives her role. Objectively, the complexity of Sarah's situation is compounded by several matters. Students .are on individual time tables, meaning that she cannot count on their having any common base of knowledge or skills. They have been 'processed' through a long series of educational innovations in the course of their school careers, giving them a passing (if shallow) acquaintance with many of the approaches the teacher tries out, a generally blasé attitude, and a lack of what Sarah considers basic skills.

Sarah's response to these conditions contributes to the complexity of the situation, for she brings to it two goals equally pressing for her, not necessarily conflicting but by no means always convergent. She wants to teach students the basic skills they lack in reading, writing, and generally coping with school (or, in the case of English, a basic sense of the discipline and an appreciation of literary works). And she wants no less to make emotional contact with students, to be aware of their feelings and respond to them with her own person.

That the way Sarah holds and uses her knowledge constitutes a response to her classroom situation can be demonstrated by many and varied examples. The approach Sarah developed to curriculum development has the effect of rendering more manageable the situation in a remedial group: she has to deal only with those problems students bring to the class or workshop. This approach, too, economically combines her two goals of teaching skills and making direct (though not necessarily emotional) contact with students.

Sarah's use of her communications knowledge offers a more striking example. This generated materials (a specific Learning Course unit) but more importantly, it ordered classroom activity and interaction throughout the Learning Course (and to a lesser extent in the Reading Centre as well).

Knowledge of communications informed Sarah's efforts to establish a kind of atmosphere which make the Learning Course a place where kids can take more risks than in other classes. "I certainly try very hard to listen very actively to the kids, to paraphrase, to encourage them to paraphrase, and at most times to allow them to express their concerns and to discuss their concerns without judging them."

However, Sarah put specific limitations on the use of this knowledge. She had reservations about the 'values clarification' unit (a separate unit, but nonetheless derived from the 'communications' area):

> I had a class that was problematic. The kids weren't streamed, but I think I got a very slow bunch, and they were rowdy, and I was very, very paranoid about starting the Values Clarification unit, because they would have to put on name tags and kind of reveal things to each other.

> Vivian has gotten much farther into the affective side of the course. She did some Values Clarification work, and changed her style radically, at least in my perception. And I'm not really comfortable with what she's doing.

Too much disclosure, it appears, is disconcerting to Sarah--not, one senses, because she is emotionally shaken by it but rather because it distracts the class from its goals, and particularly from the business of acquiring skills, as the following excerpt indicates:

> What they start to do is, "Why do we have to do memory work? Why do we have to do Shakespeare?" And I try to use all the Communication things... And that's dangerous, because you have to tread a fine line between their gossiping and complaining about teachers, and feeling that they can do that, and my wanting to talk about problems of coping with school.

Open communication, then, is not an end in itself but a means of helping students to cope better with school. In order to further this purpose Sarah is quite willing to curtail the applications of her communications knowledge.

The suspension of this knowledge with respect to the work of the Learning Course group offers a further example of Sarah's orienting of her communications knowledge toward specific goals:

> Everything in the human side of me said, I should show him that I can risk expressing my own doubts. But I didn't, because it was only ten minutes till the class, and I couldn't allow myself that luxury, because we still had to get over a few points.

Sarah's knowledge of instruction also works to make the classroom situation more manageable. The notion of specific isolated learning skills is simple to understand, has an immediate appeal for students and gives them something concrete to work towards. It is thus useful in organizing the work of a class. By contrast, Sarah's idea that learning necessarily involves frustration is a notion that would obviously be difficult to 'sell' to a class and indeed, it is of little worth in a situation already taxed to the utmost by students' sense of confusion concerning the school's demands. The notion of frustration, or challenge, comes into play only in the much simpler and less pressured situation of one-to-one remedial work, where indeed it serves to increase the complexity and generate a little of the tension needed for effective teaching and learning. For example, in working with a student who came in strongly motivated to work on her essay:

> I really wanted to give her the impression that writing that essay was an adventure for me too. And what I did was to play very dumb: I don't think she knows to this day that I've ever read the book, or that I've ever taught the book, and both things are true. And I pulled a lot out of her before I made any suggestion about revamping what she had written.

Thus the teaching situation determines which aspects of her instructional knowledge Sarah will call upon. When the situations requires simplification, Sarah relies on her knowledge of skills to give lessons a clear focus. She uses her understanding of communications to aid her in this task by engaging students' attention and interest (but cuts off the interpersonal exchange when the point of the lesson is in danger of being obscured). On those occasions when the classroom situation can be handled easily enough, Sarah calls forth a broader view of learning as requiring some frustration and challenge, and uses it to shape a more dynamic classroom situation.

Of course, Sarah is not always successful in managing the complexity of the classroom situation. One kind of reason, as was noted in Part Two, is the nature of her knowledge. Conflicts or ambiguities within the content of knowledge may prevent Sarah from formulating a clear view of the purpose of a lesson. Another kind of reason may lie in the way Sarah uses her knowledge. For example, in the lesson on the 'inventory' technique around which the fourth interview was conducted, it may be that too pat a notion of reading skills, too univocally employed, had the effect of flattening out the lesson, and reducing the complexity of the situation more than was called for. In any event this example gives us a final instance of the way that Sarah typically uses her knowledge to focus on specific classroom purposes, thus reducing the complexity of a situation which otherwise would be unmanageable for her.

The Teacher in the School

Sarah's school situation is marked by a need to give an account of what she is doing, to explain; and a need to account for her work, to evaluate its worth. These needs characterize the situation with respect to both internal and external factors. Objectively, Sarah is repeatedly in situations where her work is new (the Learning Course, the Reading Centre) or different from what prevails around her (the English Department). She is called upon to explain her views on English teaching to unsympathetic colleagues; she must explain the intent of the Learning Course to a suspicious staff; she has to do public relations for the Reading Centre in order to attract a clientele of teachers and students. And in all of these settings Sarah is required to justify what she is doing as well, not only to allay hostility but to ensure the continuation of her job. The objective factors are matched quite precisely by Sarah's own inner needs: she wants to be able to articulate, to herself and others, what she is doing, and she wants to be assured of both its effectiveness and its value.

In the second interview Sarah commented that "I remember adopting the word, 'learning skills', with great relief, because finally I had a way of talking about what I did." She noted immediately that this notion was qualified, for her, by being cast in terms of "the kinds of things that I know kids are asked to do during their four years." Nevertheless, the use of a term like 'skills', implying specific, useful, teachable behaviours which can be evaluated easily and precisely is undoubtedly as compelling to a teacher in Sarah's situation as it can be misleading. Sarah taught many things that can (without benefit of extensive analysis) be construed as skills--useful tools for reading, writing and learning which could be applied by students in other situations. Few of those would be counted as skills in the sense of bike-riding or swimming, something that once learned cannot be forgotten. Paradoxically, though, at least some of her students would have acquired a general skill in reading or writing that indeed, once learned, is learned forever. We are misled, however, in thinking that this general skill can really be broken down into specific skills taught by Sarah in some particular order and combination. It is this false impression which underlies Sarah's idea that there must be some clear and straightforward way of evaluating what she is doing. But this notion, we have seen, was instrumental in directing the acquisition of Sarah's knowledge. It is equally central to the way she used her knowledge. Given the press of objective factors on Sarah to account for her work, and her own need to do so, combined with the very real difficulties in evaluating the Learning Course and subsequent work in the Reading Centre, we are not surprised to find Sarah using her knowledge to short-circuit the problem of evaluation. One example of this, already noted, is her development of a style of curriculum development in which evaluation is not the final stage of a process of materials preparation. Instead, because students bring their own concerns, the teacher need evaluate only her effectiveness in solving the immediate problem.

A second example of how Sarah orients her knowledge to the school around her is found in the way she continually balances two approaches to her work. The skills orientation is important to Sarah because it gives her a concrete and easily justified definition of her work (as well as generating specific content to be taught). When pressed, however, she admits that she puts her money on "what the kids learn from the human experience of being in the classroom." The latter approach, even in periods when it enjoys greater popularity than it did in Sarah's school during the interviews, is always difficult to justify in terms of results since its effects are long-term, ambiguous and hard to specify. In a sense, then, Sarah is merely being prudent by not investing all her energies in a single approach. This is not to deny that she genuinely believes both approaches have something to offer, but merely to indicate that her eclecticism makes it easier for Sarah to account for her work to her colleagues at school.

The Teacher in the Curriculum Development Group

One might expect that because curriculum development was a voluntary activity, the group situation would be less problematic than the classroom and school situations sometimes were for Sarah. However, she described the group experience as 'heavy', citing problems of communication as a source of difficulty. The group's refusal to act on their knowledge of communications was, in effect, a way of ordering their priorities and of asserting that the group situation was temporary and work on the group's inner problems was not warranted. Paradoxicaly, though, it may be that just this denial of the importance of communications, despite the knowledge held by the group, intensified their difficulties: the fact that they were aware of the need to air grievances, to express feelings, to support one another, may have made the group members more sensitive to the lack of these interpersonal niceties than a naively task-oriented group would have been. In short, it seems likely that one cannot simply legislate one's knowledge to be inapplicable at will.

Aside from its emotional and interpersonal colouring, another important aspect of the curriculum development situation was the need for a diverse group of individuals to focus collectively on an area relatively new to all of them and viewed differently by each. A striking way in which the group members oriented their knowledge to this challenging situation is found in the progression (described by Sarah as 'copping out') in the definition of the course from 'thinking' to 'learning' to 'coping with school'. We have already indicated how a particular conception of theory appears to have influenced this process. Here we note that 'thinking' and 'learning' are terms proper to the disciplines of psychology and philosophy. Had the planning group been willing to deal with theory, they would immediately have become involved in a dispute as to which of the many conceptions offered by these disciplines was most useful for their work. The notion of 'coping with school', however, is not only one with which they all felt comfortable, but it is a notion to which each could contribute in a personal way from his or her own background and experience. So this redefinition of the focus of the Learning Course had the effect of facilitating the group's cooperative effort which otherwise might have foundered in contentiousness.

Summary

In this section we have shown how Sarah oriented her knowledge to the various situations in which she worked, in an effort to render these situations more manageable. Thus she sought and used conceptions of subject matter (learning skills) and of instruction (communications) which made it easier for her to interact with students in a goal-directed way, to justify her teaching to herself and to other teachers, and to work in a group with teachers from different areas. We have seen that Sarah was not always successful in this effort. Our intent, however, was not to pass judgment but rather to highlight the ongoing nature of the activity of using knowledge; the orientation of Sarah's knowledge to her situation is no less fixed than are the situations she encounters daily.
    We have shown how Sarah's knowledge is oriented outward, to theory and to the various situations of schooling. The next section will consider the final, and most encompassing aspect of this outward focus--the social orientation.

SOCIAL ORIENTATION

One way of illustrating the social orientation of Sarah's knowledge might be to bring examples of how her use of knowledge reflects and reinforces her social views and social class status. Thus we could point out an intellectual and academic bias in Sarah's knowledge. For example, the Learning

Course was originally intended to provide basic learning skills appropriate for all students and all disciplines. But when the planning group realized that much of the material (e.g. essay writing and research) was relevant to academically-oriented work, their response was to raise the grade level at which the course would be offered. This would inevitably have the effect of attracting students bound for university, rather than the broader cross-section of students who took the course previously. In short, rather than remaining true to their goal of providing all students with basic skills, the planners finally directed the course to those least in need of it, the predominantly middle-class students whose likelihood of attaining higher education was greater even before they took the Learning Course.

We could also indicate the resurfacing of an academic bias in Sarah's use of her knowledge of English literature. When she began work on the Learning Course Sarah felt that literary knowledge often served as a barrier between herself and students; her knowledge was something to hide behind when she failed to evoke a desired response in students. Later, however, Sarah reasserted the view that the literary work could also serve as a medium for contact between herself and students, a contact which she craved. She would be returning to teach an English course which "involves democratizing the classroom and having the kids work in groups." Yet she nevertheless felt misgivings about teaching "the general-level, non-academic course, which usually gets kids who are non-readers or very poor readers, and they have trouble with writing." Thus, despite her interest in and commitment to teaching less advantaged students, teaching literature still means something different, and special, to Sarah when she is working with bright, motivated, academically-oriented students.

Once made, however, these comments do not take us very far, and for two reasons. First, we cannot claim to have unearthed a hidden truth about Sarah's underlying values. She is quite clear about her valuing of the academic, and is open about the conflict she experiences between middle-class values and social consciousness. Second, showing how Sarah's use of knowledge reflects social class distinctions gives us no sense of how things come to be that way, nor of how they might be otherwise. It provides an understanding of

Sarah's knowledge that is both superficial and static.

Thus we will try to show how Sarah uses her knowledge actively to shape a social world. Many of the details of this use of knowledge have already been noted. We indicated Sarah's unhappiness with the authoritarian and conservative style of the English department, and her unwillingness to be a part of the "phoney structure in which you're being perceived as the one who judges, the one who passes and the one who gets the other person into University." In the Learning Course, we recall, she saw herself as working on the side of students, helping them to get along within the school system, interpreting its demands and providing the skills needed to meet these demands. What enabled Sarah to do this, of course, was the fact that she had insight into the school system, understanding of the motiviations of teachers and of the purposes of assigned work, and skills which could be turned to mastery of schoolwork. All this is the knowledge Sarah worked to develop into a form suitable for teaching from the time she began her involvement with the Learning Course and throughout her work in the Reading Centre.

Thus, we can see that Sarah acquired knowledge with a view to creating a particular environment. It was a setting in which she could be on the side of students because what she taught was not some intellectual property to be transferred, but rather something which they learned to do. Her skills subject matter required ultimately that students evaluate themselves; it was not something for which she needed to assign marks (except very loosely in the Learning Course). At the same time this subject matter reduced the likelihood of conflict with the school system; after all, Sarah was serving the interests of all teachers by helping students to fulfil their requirements. Sarah's need to justify her own subject matter was reduced greatly, but at the same time she was set apart from other teachers. She was not one of those who made demands on students in her own right; she merely interpreted the demands of others. She could be neutral vis-à-vis the worth of the school system as it is, and this perhaps allayed her own inner conflicts. If hardly a radical, she hadn't quite sold out to the system, either, for she continued to uphold her own values with respect to the way she treated students as individuals. Thus as Sarah worked to develop a subject matter for teaching skills in reading, writing, and learning, she simultaneously established a social framework--smaller and more congenial than the school as a whole, apart from yet serving the school--in which she as an individual could be comfortable teaching this subject matter.

In what way does this view of the social orientation of Sarah's knowledge differ from the one sketched earlier? The main difference is that we view Sarah as orienting her knowledge to serve a social purpose that is her own, because it is consistent with her values, beliefs, attitudes, in short with the sum of her practical knowledge. It is not a mere reflection of social structure over which the individual has little control. I do not know whether or to what extent, Sarah is aware of the social use she makes of her knowledge, but this is of little importance. The crucial point is that this is a use of knowledge over which the teacher does, in principle, have control. She can do otherwise. She might decide, for example, to make a more substantive commitment for or against the system of organized schooling. She might choose to work directly within her school for a more open style of interpersonal relations that allows students and teachers to confront the barriers that the system inevitably erects among them. Recognizing the great difficulty of adopting a position that is at once inside and detached from the system might well enable Sarah to accomplish the feat with even greater aplomb that she has already displayed, insofar as she becomes aware of the specific arrangements on which her position rests. In short, an understanding of the social use of her knowledge can only open up possibilities for the teacher, enabling her to examine her purposes in a new light and giving her greater freedom to control her teaching and to act in ways that are more effective in realizing her purposes.

In the remaining sections of this chapter, we will consider the orientations of Sarah's knowledge inward--the personal orientation and the experiential orientation.

PERSONAL ORIENTATION

In this section I want to consider the ways in which Sarah uses her practical knowledge to give meaning to her work. That is, how does Sarah's use of knowledge reflect her values and enable her to achieve purposes that are in line with those values?

The first point that requires consideration here is the extent to which Sarah is aware of her own knowledge. Elsewhere we have noted cases in which Sarah's use of her knowledge (for example, its social orientation) was independent of her awareness; in those instances we inferred the use from Sarah's statements and behaviour. But it would be a contradiction in terms to speak of Sarah's using knowledge to render her work meaningful if she was not herself aware of the meaning in question. So we must begin by noting what should already be apparent: with some interesting exceptions, Sarah is generally well aware of the knowledge she holds and of how it functions.

Thus, Sarah perceives a difference between the practically-oriented thinking done "in gear" while at school, and the more reflective thinking that occurs in study. She is aware too of body language and of tacit knowledge that cannot easily be expressed. She realizes that some aspects of her school experience can be known only tacitly, never to be captured fully in words. Nevertheless she tries, and succeeds rather well in giving vivid, personal descriptions of her work and in telling how she feels about it. She is often critical (though accepting) of her own work and of her limited knowledge. For example, she comment on "the huge distance between what learning is, and what these isolated strategies are;" on her "fumbling" in the effort to frame a general, theoretical view of her work; on the "brazen" task the Learning Course planners took on and their eventual "copping out". Clearly, Sarah wants to understand her own functioning as a teacher, and makes efforts to do so.

We can best assess the extent to which Sarah is able to use her knowledge to make her teaching personally meaningful if we look at the values she revealed during the interviews. Two values which emerge as central to her work are interpersonal contact, and responsibility. We have discussed Sarah's wish for "a window onto the kids and what they're thinking." She values "the human experience of being in the classroom" both for its own sake and as the kind of learning students are most likely to retain after their schooling is completed. At the same time she is not content merely to

121

go with the flow of interpersonal encounter. Teaching, to Sarah, is an undertaking to give something to students. Her sense of responsibility towards them is a topic which concerns Sarah greatly, as she tries to sort out how much she must give and how much to challenge students, to what extent she must fill the needs of others and to what extent she should take account of her own limitations, abilities and preferences.

Sarah uses her knowledge to structure her teaching in accordance with these values in a variety of ways. Two images, that of "a place to hide" and the notion of a "window onto students", allow us to perceive this structuring clearly. Both images relate to the teaching of English literature. At the beginning of the interview series, Sarah used the phrase "no place to hide" to contrast her English teaching with the Learning Course teaching. In English she felt that she had been able to hide behind the literary subject matter whenever the going was rough. Failure to teach a particular piece of literature as she intended could always be explained away with reference to the subject matter: it was too sophisticated, or it required previous experience or a degree of sensitivity which students lacked. In the Learning Course, however, no such hiding was possible. Sarah's goal was to teach skills that had been defined as universal; if she failed in teaching them, it could be her fault alone. By the end of the interview series, and from her vantage point as a Reading teacher, Sarah took a different view of the discipline of English and of English teaching. English was no longer a barrier between teacher and students; it was now (at least potentially) a window allowing each to view the other and make contact.

How, in the light of these comments, did Sarah use her knowledge to reflect and embody her values? Sarah's situation in the English department afforded her little contact with students; they seemed uninterested in what she had to offer, and the sugar-coating of an informal teaching style had become difficult to maintain. Her formerly easy relationships with students were hard to sustain in this setting. She felt out of touch and alienated; she found she could "hear my own voice a lot of the time." Sarah also felt that she was not fulfilling her responsibilities to students. Their inabilities in basic skills forced her to lower her own expectations, and thus she was teaching them neither the literature she was supposed to teach nor the skills they needed to learn it. Sarah's work was doing little to realize the purposes she held as important. Thus we can see her involvement with the Learning Course and her subsequent work as a Reading teacher as deliberate and persistent efforts to develop a subject matter for teaching that would be in line with her goals and values.

Sarah conceived of a subject matter comprised of skills, which would put no barriers between herself and students. In learning to communicate, she had to take risks, as they did. As a teacher, she saw as problematic many of the same things they did. In learning to write, she too was "still working at language." Furthermore, the image of "no place to hide" tells us that the teacher does not stand behind a received tradition. Her skills were things she could do--read, write, study. Sarah was aware that students perceived many of these tasks as being "full of mystery". Significantly, she did not view her role as that of initiating them into the mysteries; this stance allows the teacher to maintain a distance from students, as the 'mystery' is revealed to be always a degree more complex than what the student has attained. Rather, Sarah felt that the tasks to be learned were in fact "very concrete and structured", and that students simply had to be shown how to do them. In this stance there is little gap between teacher and student; even if one performs better, by dint of greater experience, still both are doing the same thing. Thus Sarah's skills subject matter and her instructional stance alike were conceived in a way that effectively gave her close contact with students. Her knowledge of the milieu also contributed to the creation of settings in which this kind of contact could take place. As she expressed it, "Lately I've felt that I'm giving a lot of concern and a lot of empathy, and it's feeling sincere to me, but the subject at hand is not the kid's stepmother or abortion, but rather how the kids is coping with the demands being made on him in the classroom."

This comment also relates to the other of Sarah's major values, responsibility. Her concern for the welfare of students pervades all her statements. We recall that her involvement with skills was motivated by what she saw as student need (though she also expressed strong personal interest

123

in language and in writing). The image of "no place to hide" captures most clearly Sarah's desire to take full responsibility for her subject matter knowledge. She has shaped a subject matter for teaching such that its failure to appeal to students and meet their needs cannot be blamed on any of its features nor on any person but herself. Sarah's instructional knowledge, in particular her resolution of the conflict between the need to give and the need to challenge students, reflects her efforts to work in a manner that is fully responsible, not robbing students of their own need to learn independently nor taking undue credit for their accomplishments but clearly sorting out the respective roles of teacher and student and assuming her own responsibilities while enabling students to better fulfil theirs.

We have seen how the way Sarah develops and uses her knowledge of reading and learning skills, of instruction and of the school milieu enables her to give expression to the values of interpersonal contact and responsibility. Underlying the entire sequence caught by the interviews is a third value, discussed only briefly and in passing but evidently of great importance to Sarah: the value of development, change, growth. It is surely clear that Sarah uses her knowledge to transform her work situation into a setting for constant experimentation, learning and growth. She is always working at the outer limit of her knowledge, searching for new, more effective and more personally satisfying ways of carrying out her teaching task. The entire developmental process of work on the Learning Course, in the Reading Centre, and finally the look back to English literature, exemplifies Sarah's realization of the value of growth and development.

EXPERIENTIAL ORIENTATION

In this section we will consider the ways that Sarah's holding and use of practical knowledge give form to her experience. The orientation of knowledge to experience can best be seen by considering general patterns rather than detail. Thus we will be looking holistically at the impact of Sarah's knowledge on her experience.

We have already noted a dichotomy which pervades Sarah's knowledge in all areas, between a formal, discipline-oriented view of knowledge as

124

objective product, and a process-oriented view of knowledge. This was evident in Sarah's view of English, which balanced carefully a conception of the literary work as aesthetic object against a conception of literature as a medium for the expression of feelings and values. Sarah's notion of skills similarly contained elements of both views, encompassing both the view of skills as formal techniques, structures inherent in knowledge itself, and the view of skills as personal coping tools that are affectively toned and perhaps coloured by the disciplines in which they are used. Finally, Sarah's humanistic view of reading and writing was sometimes opposed by the formalistic view of reading and writing as skills.

Over the course of the interviews the process-oriented type of conception tended to become dominant in all areas. Sarah's view of skills, particularly, underwent change in this respect. The change is reflected in two general aspects of Sarah's experience--her conceptions of time and of intellectual space.

Time Perspective

Though being busy is an obvious constant of Sarah's work, the interviews reveal two different time perspectives which shape her experience. The first perspective, apparent from the first interview, is one which sees time as a commodity, almost a form of currency. Thus the time Sarah 'spent' working on the Learning Course was "an investment in my own development;" and she was concerned about problems in the development of the course in "areas that I can't afford time for." Sarah's commitment to efficiency in the use of her time structured her experience into a crowded and intense sequence of activities. She was always focussed on what would come next, as in her task as coordinator of the Learning Course, and in her constant concern to have materials prepared on time and to bring extra work to class for students who finish early. Her school day was ordered by the rhythm of "rushing from one thing to another...in a hurly-burly of a lesson and a discussion with a kid after a lesson, and catching a kid I want to speak to before the next lesson begins."

When she moved to the Reading Centre, however, a second and radically different time perspective began to operate in Sarah's work. She slowed down:

"I'm walking into the lesson much more slowly, and I'm probably breathing a lot more slowly as I walk up to the front of the room." Though still fully occupied, Sarah took time to plan and reflect, to move about the school and observe. In remedial work, she began by getting to know the student through informal discussion (rather than a questionnaire, for example, to zero in quickly on problems), to let him know something about her, to build up a "bank account of common experience." Students sometimes perceived this approach as time wasted, and had to be reassured, but Sarah herself was quite comfortable with it. She now viewed time as a kind of setting or frame within which certain kinds of interaction between persons takes place. It takes time for two individuals to get to know one another, but time is not thereby transformed into a commodity: we do not necessarily know one another better the more time we spend. In the course of the interviews the second time perspective became increasingly dominant, though Sarah retained some of the concerns which attach to the first (for example her efforts to be prepared and to use her time efficiently).

Space Perspective

Sarah's experience of intellectual space is structured similarly to her time perspective. We can characterize this experience once again by reference to the two images cited earlier. The notion of "no place to hide" reflects an experience of intellectual space as somehow threatening, unless hiding-places are found. Sarah had already moved away from this view (indeed, it seems unlikely she ever experienced it in such an extreme form) at the beginning of the interviews, but it is nevertheless significant that she characterized her sense of space in terms of enclosure. By the end of the interview sequence, Sarah was speaking rather of "windows": "I would like more of a window onto the kids and what they're thinking, and I think I myself would like my window to be more open." Thus her intellectual space had changed considerably: it was still structured, but its dominant feature was now the openings it afforded onto the space of others. We will consider the implications of these two images in the next two chapters; here we are concerned to indicate the transitions in Sarah's experience of time and space as these parallel the development of her knowledge.

But we need not confine ourselves to viewing the change in Sarah's experience as a move from one extreme position to another. We can also detect a move toward integration. This move becomes apparent if we look at Sarah's experience in terms of "tension of consciousness."[3]

Tension of Consciousness

The notion of tension of consciousness refers to the level of attentiveness which the individual brings to his experience, as reflected in the range and number of different considerations which are held in attention in the course of a given activity.

Two examples illustrate the extremes of tension of consciousness in Sarah's work. In teaching English, Sarah had many areas of concern and seemed to experience difficulty in coordinating these. Her concern for literature gave her an "obligation to open them up a bit to an appreciation of literature," while her perception of student interests and needs told her that students were not interested in the materials, did not read for pleasure and lacked many of the basic skills needed to deal with literature. The English department, further, was making demands which seemed to fit neither her own view of literature nor the needs of students as she saw them. And in this situation her own need to relate interpersonally with students could be met only after school and between classes as she made herself available to listen to students' personal problems. Her tension of consciousness in this context is characterized by her comment, "It made me shaky in the classroom," and by her use of the phrase "defending literature".

We can contrast this situation with Sarah's work in the Reading Centre. She herself referred to the difference in terms of tension: "I am busy, but it's not a breathlessness, the way teaching is." It is true that classroom teaching requires greater attentiveness than does individual or small-group teaching, but Sarah was so busy, and had so many different tasks to fulfil in the Reading Centre that the mere reduction in time spent in classroom teaching does not seem sufficient to explain her altered experience.

However, in the Reading Centre it was easier for Sarah to hold in simultaneous awareness the different considerations which had a bearing on her work. The subject matter—reading and writing skills—answered directly to students' needs, as Sarah perceived then, and even Sarah's personal need to express her feelings found an immediate outlet in her concern for how students were coping with school. There was thus a merging of concerns, so that a number of considerations could be held in focus on the same 'channel' of awareness. This integration of her concerns was reflected in a reduction of the tension of consciousness to a level Sarah found comfortable.

The reduction of Sarah's tension of consciousness on the experiential level also reflects an integration of her concerns in other areas already examined. We have already noted how Sarah's view of curriculum developed into an approach that took account of her situation and needs as a classroom teacher. Her conception of theory also appeared to change as it became possible for Sarah to make use of theoretical knowledge of learning which she had previously been reluctant to consider, thus acquiring a view of skills that accorded better with her own classroom experience. And she seems to have arrived at a position from which she may be able to make a new use of her knowledge of English literature (though the final interview only hints at this). It is not difficult to see how an integration of concerns on the level of practical knowledge makes possible a more comfortable "tension of consciousness" on the experiential level and conversely how the development and integration of practical knowledge is facilitated by the existence of an optimal level of tension of consciousness.

SUMMARY

In this chapter we have shown how Sarah holds and uses the practical knowledge the content of which was outlined in Part Two. We have seen that Sarah's knowledge is held in a rather complex relationship to theory; her view of theory had tended to block the accessibility of all but the most practical formulations of theoretical notions, but this orientation changed over the interview period, making her more receptive to theory. We have also seen how Sarah held her knowledge in a way that enabled her to deal effectively with her situation as teacher in the classroom, in the school and in the curriculum planning group. Her knowledge was also oriented socially in an important way: Sarah used her knowledge to shape a social context in which she could work comfortably. These three dimensions--the theoretical, situational, and social--constitute the various ways that Sarah's knowledge is oriented outward, to the world of practice.

Her knowledge is also oriented inward. Thus we showed how she used her knowledge to create personal meaning and to express her values. Finally we looked at the way in which Sarah's knowledge shaped the structure of her experience.

In examining the latter dimension, the experiential orientation, we provided a description of Sarah's experience, and suggested something of the style of her teaching. This account can serve as an interim summary of Sarah's practical knowledge in use, which may assist the reader in holding in mind the variety of detail amassed in this chapter. It is an occupational hazard of phenomenological research that a considerable mass of data must be assembled and grappled with before central themes will deign to emerge. In the next chapter, we will step back from the data to consider the way that Sarah's knowledge is structured, before going on to a more comprehensive, concluding view of her knowledge in Chapter 8.

NOTES

1.   This account of literary theory is not a caricature. The "New Criticism", in which Sarah had been trained at university, proposed just such close, objective reading of poetry. And in a critique of traditional French literary theory, Serge Doubrovsky, in Pourquoi la nouvelle critique (Paris: Mercure de France, 1966), attacked the view that, "There is a truth about the work, with which everyone can come to agreement. Relying in particular on the certainties of language, on the implications of psychological coherence, on the imperatives of the structure of the genre, the patient and modest researcher will be able to elicit evidence that establishes, in a sense, zones of objectivity from which he can--very carefully-- make efforts at interpretation." (My translation.)

2.   John   Dewey,   Experience   and   Education,
(Kappa Detta Pi, 1938; reprinted New York: Collier
Books, 1963), p. 42.

3.   The term 'tension of consciousness' is
used by Alfred Schutz and Thomas Luckmann, The
Structures of the Life-World, (London: Heinemann,
1974).

Chapter 7

THE STRUCTURE OF PRACTICAL KNOWLEDGE

Thus far we have dealt with the content of Sarah's
knowledge and with the various ways in which it is
oriented. In this chapter we will look at practical knowledge, as knowledge--the way it is structured, the kinds of generalizations it affords, the
ways in which it is related to the practical context on which it bears. It is easy enough to define practical knowledge negatively, in terms of
qualities it would seem to lack: it should not, we
expect, be ordered in terms of the rigorous logic
and propositional structure of theoretical knowledge: being idiosyncratic and unique to the individual teacher, it would seem to lack generalizability; and unlike theoretical knowledge which stands
at a distance from the world, practical knowledge
has a close relationship to its objects, the practical situations in which it is shaped and applied.
What is more important, however, and more difficult, is to describe the teacher's knowledge in
positive terms, with reference to those of its
specific, regular features which enable teachers to
deal effectively with practice.

Because practical knowledge is individual and
attuned to the teacher's unique purposes, as we
have seen from Sarah's example, it may seem that it
would lack in generalizability. Schwab[1], for
example, has argued that a practical decision is
specific to its situation and cannot be applied to
future cases. This may be true enough if we focus
narrowly on the outcome of deliberation, the decision, but it misleads us concerning the nature and
function of practical knowledge. Such knowledge is
not enshrined in the bare decisions which are the
outcome of deliberative process (as theoretical
knowledge may be thought to be contained in the

knowledge claims which are its final step). Rather, we must consider practical knowledge in use; this is why we have looked at all the vague and messy tentative formulations, rough generalizations and segments of formal theory brought to bear in the course of Sarah's deliberation and planning.

In analyzing this knowlege to identify its structure we are at first inclined to look for such features as clarity and determinateness in the terms used, and coherence or lack of contradiction among the various parts. These are criteria which determine the degree to which theoretical knowledge lends itself to generalization or extension. However, in speaking of the generalizability of practical knowledge, we are looking not for features which would enable us to apply it to the extension of knowledge but for those features which enable practical knowledge to generate <u>consistent</u> <u>practice</u>. Thus, for example, a feature such as the clarity of the terms used relates directly to standards of communication in the field. Physicists and psychologists have radically different criteria of clarity, but for both groups these criteria make possible that communication on which the extension of knowledge in the field is based. For practical knowledge, however, the criteria of clarity are not fixed but respond to the needs of problematic situations; in some areas a teacher may be able to operate very effectively with relatively unclear concepts (e.g. she may be unable to articulate clearly the nature of the classroom atmosphere which she intuitively, and consistently, establishes), whereas in other areas she may require concepts that are very clearly spelled out (e.g. a teacher of emotionally disturbed children may profit from a precise behaviourally-oriented scheme for maintaining control of the classroom).

In characterizing the structure of practical knowledge we have sought terms which would reflect the relationship to practice, to the teacher's experience and to the personal dimension. Three basic terms will be used: rule of practice, practical principle[2], and image.

The <u>rule of practice</u> is simply what the term suggests--a brief, clearly formulated statement of what to do or how to do it in a particular situation frequently encountered in practice. A rule of practice may be highly specific, relating to how to deal with a personality conflict encountered by a teacher in one of his classes, for example. Sarah has a rule for dealing with one student who is learning-disabled: she tries to show him "that he has my full attention <u>after</u> I finish all the instructions." Other rules may apply to somewhat broader situations, such as the organization of materials or the giving of assignments. But in either case the rule makes reference to the details of the situations to which it relates, to means; the ends or purposes of action are taken for granted.

The <u>practical principle</u> is a more inclusive and less explicit formulation in which the teacher's purposes, implied in the statement of a rule, are more clearly evident. Thus when Sarah speaks of trying "to make the kid happy to walk into that class," she states a principle directed especially to remedial work, to students with difficulties and the principle reflects her purpose of giving priority to the students' emotional readiness for learning.

In a study of practical reasoning, Gauthier suggested that the main use of practical principles is

> ... to bring past experience to bear on present problems. This experience is useful because the realm of the practical is necessarily a realm of uncertainty. To deliberate fully upon the consequences of future actions, or upon their possible grounds, would often be to ignore the practical context in which we must act.[3]

Practical principles originate in, and give us a means of profiting from, experience. The same, of course, is true of rules of practice. The practical principle, however, is more expressive of the personal dimension of practical knowledge, for while rules of practice may be quite idiosyncratic, the holder of a principle is an agent who can give a reason for his actions and who, we expect, will act in such a way that his behaviour over time is consistent with personal beliefs and goals. Thus we may say that a course of action chosen on the basis of practical knowledge, while it may not be precisely similar to courses of action chosen on previous occasions, is nevertheless 'principled'. Sometimes it will be possible to analyse principle, relating it to specific rules of practice. At other times, while principles may be quite clearly held, the complexity of the situation, the teacher's inexperience, the unavailability of necessary means, or other reasons may prevent the formulation by the teacher of explicit rules of practice. Practical principles may be derived quite formally from theoretical viewpoints, they may grow intuitively out of experience, or (most likely) may develop from some conjunction of theory and practice.

The third level, that of image, is at once the least explicit and most inclusive of the three. On this level, the teacher's feelings, values, needs and beliefs combine as she forms images of how teaching should be, and marshals experience, theoretical knowledge, school folklore, to give substance to these images. The image seems to refer to all of Sarah's teaching seen from a particular perspective. The "rhythm of the school year", and the notion of "nowhere to hide" in the Learning Course and hence of 'hiding behind' subject matter expertise, are very broad notions the uniqueness of which is drawn from the way they express Sarah's personal perception of her teaching rather than from the situations to which they are directed.

Each of the three terms reflects different ways of mediating between thought and action. A rule of practice is a guideline on or from which the teacher acts; it exists and she follows its dictates. She formulated it herself, in many cases, but for just this purpose of eliminating the need for thought. An image, conversely, is something one responds to rather than acting from. If the rule pushes us along with a demand for assent, the image pulls us toward it, inspiring rather than requiring conformity. Without thought, the image becomes meaningless since it is open, and takes on different senses in each situation. The practical principle, however, may mediate between thought and action in both ways. We may act on a principle, simply following its dictates, as we would a rule; or we may see the principle as embodying a purpose we aspire to realize.

Examination of the three levels of organization of practical knowledge may tell us a variety of things about the teacher and her knowledge. One way to assess the consistency and integration of practical knowledge is in terms of the interrelationships among the three levels. For example, do they hang together substantively, or does the teacher hold quite 'progressive' images side by side with rigid and restrictive rules of practice? We can learn something of the teacher's development and style from the three levels. Thus we might expect a beginning teacher to have fairly clear images, but few rules and inadequate principles to guide her work. We can also imagine different styles in the use of practical knowledge, and the three terms help to illustrate this. The following of rules of practice involves the teacher in a methodical and straightforward carrying out of her goals (which may be articulated or not). The use of practical principles, however, is largely a reflective activity, while images are used by the teacher in an intuitive way to aid in the realization of purposes. Undoubtedly, the use of knowledge is highly individual and there will be many different styles of knowledge use among teachers. But style will be determined, in part, by the choice of one or another level of knowledge as the preferred mode in which to work. In this chapter we will look at the three levels of organization of Sarah's practical knowledge to see by what means it is ordered and what uses of her knowledge the structuring elements make possible.

In looking for evidence of rules of practice, practical principles and images as organizers of Sarah's practical knowledge, we are not interested primarily in statements having the outward form of a rule, a principle or an image, but rather in the way such statements operate in structuring Sarah's knowledge. We shall see that a given statement may look like a mere description, yet function as a rule, a principle, an image, or sometimes in several ways simultaneously.

We should also recall that our access to the structure of Sarah's knowledge is largely through statements made in the interview setting. It is possible that Sarah's knowledge is structured differently in classroom use than in its after-the-fact articulation. Nevertheless, what she has to say about her knowledge provides an important perspective on this knowledge and on how she structures it, especially for its use in explaining and accounting for her practice.

This account of the structure of Sarah's knowledge will begin by illustrating briefly each of the three levels of structure. We will then consider the relationships among the three levels, how they develop and function.

Sarah enunciated rules of practice in all areas of concern to her. These rules took diverse forms: sometimes a brief statement, sometimes an extended description of practice from which a number of closely related rules could be inferred. In speaking of the organization of curriculum materials, for example, Sarah commented: "You don't want to do very heavy, demanding stuff the week before a holiday, or at the end of June. Nor do you want to start with very 'soft' stuff, like communications, group dynamics, at the beginning where the kids are doing no writing." Concerning the work of curriculum development in a group setting, she pointed out that the group's problems could have been dealt with by "the simple effort of trying to meet at open-ended time slots"--a rule never honoured, as we have noted elsewhere. In teaching reading, Sarah spoke of giving a variety of assignments to which she would "respond as expressively as the kids write," with her reply ranging from a personal comment to detailed correction of spelling and grammatical errors. These three examples constitute rules of practice, each translating a different area of Sarah's knowledge into a form immediately usable in practice.

Another statement of rules of practice is the following:

> I certainly try very hard to listen very actively to the kids, to paraphrase, to encourage them to paraphrase, and at most times to allow them to express their concerns and to discuss their concerns without judging them.

In this comment Sarah states a number of distinct rules: listen actively, paraphrase, encourage students to paraphrase, don't judge. These rules taken together constitute an approach to communication in the classroom which can be expressed in the statement of a principle (discussed in the next section). It is clear from the comment, however, that Sarah distinguishes a number of separate practices which she follows regularly and almost systematically in her teaching.

PRACTICAL PRINCIPLES

Like the rule of practice, the practical principle is a statement of what one should do, or how to do it, in a given range of practical situations. However, the practical principle is a more inclusive statement than the rule, and it also carries with it some indication of the reason for adhering to the practice in question. Some of the rules cited above are given their rationale in statements of practical principles. Thus, concerning group work, Sarah commented that "what we were preaching had to be practised." All of the rules of practice which Sarah formulated for facilitating the work in groups find their justification in the principle that communication is a skill, and a difficult one to acquire, necessitating both practice and the willingness to take risks. Insight alone is not enough to change the working of any particular group, nor of its individual members.

With respect to remedial teaching of reading or skills, Sarah held to the principle of beginning with the student's emotional state, by giving "unqualified positive regard" and by trying "to make the kid happy to walk into that class." This principle is related to a variety of different practices ranging from unstructured talk to working closely with a student to help him pass an upcoming chemistry exam.

Another important principle concerns the evaluation of learning and teaching. Sarah pointed out that "whatever I expected from the kids, I had to give them first;" "we have to <u>teach</u> the kids some things before we mark the kids on them." This principle, formed by Sarah in the Learning Course work, directed all of her subsequent teaching. Thus Sarah held principles relating to all the areas of her knowledge, and used them regularly in every facet of her work.

IMAGES

The image is a brief, descriptive, and sometimes metaphoric statement which seems to capture some essential aspect of Sarah's perception of herself, her teaching, her situation in the classroom or her subject matter, and which serves to organize her knowledge in the relevant area. The image is generally imbued with a judgment of value and often expresses in a particularly clear way some purpose Sarah works toward in her teaching.

For example, Sarah holds an image of herself

137

as "a good, energetic teacher." This short phrase
effectively captures Sarah's dual sense of self as
a resource and as a person at the service of
others. Her perception of the social milieu in
which she worked is expressed by Sarah's characterization of her relationship to students as that of
"an ally, working together to allow them to beat
whatever system is outside." In this statement
Sarah defines schooling as a 'system' and locates
herself and her students clearly in relation to
that system. The images Sarah holds of her teaching style reflect a sense of dichotomy: she
gives a "double message" in the classroom; sometimes she "gives too much, challenges too little."
Finally, Sarah's imagery of her subject matter
suggests the development her knowledge underwent in
the course of the interviews: the Learning Course
subject matter gave the teacher "no place to hide",
while conversely English literature could offer "a
window onto the kids and what they're thinking."
The significance of these images will be treated
more fully in Chapter 8, but it is clear from the
examples that Sarah holds a wide range of images
which serve to condense various aspects of her
knowledge. Let us now consider in more detail how
the images, practical principles and rules of practice operate. We will look first at the overall
structure of Sarah's knowledge: the relationships
among the three levels, and what knowledge is embodied by them. Then we will examine the development
of this structure and see how Sarah extends her
knowledge by means of rules of practice, practical
principles and images.

RELATIONSHIPS AMONG THE THREE LEVELS

Having illustrated each of the three levels of
structure in Sarah's practical knowledge, we can
now make several points. First, the three levels
are interrelated and serve one another. That is, a
principle or an image may give rise to a number of
rules which exemplify it; an image may grow out of
principles and rules which work towards it. This
interrelationship is not unidirectional, nor does
it always involve all three levels. Second, the
levels are not always discrete; but rules, principles and images can usually be identified in terms
of how they are used in context. Third, rules and
principles most often express instructional knowledge, while images serve to order all the aspects

of Sarah's practical knowledge.

A number of examples will best serve to illustrate the ways that the three levels interrelate. We pointed out that Sarah's instructional principle of giving "unqualified positive regard" was related to a range of rules of practice concerning instruction, including the rule of responding to assignments "as expressively as the kids write", and other rules for beginning remedial work with a new student: "We have a chat, and I try to pull out interest that the kid has, or strengths." The latter procedures are not always followed, however, for a corollary to the principle of "unqualified positive regard" is the notion of "catch-up"--"You have to give the student the support that will allow him to feel comfortable in the content area," even if that means spending several hours in some narrow and painstaking pursuit like helping a student study for a chemistry test. Thus, a given principle may enjoin several different and competing rules of practice appropriate for different situations.

Sarah's rules concerning the ordering of course materials and units are summarized not by a principle but by an image: the "rhythm of the school year" is held by Sarah to be the best rationale for ordering the materials in a course. This example illustrates the fact that the three levels do not always stand in a linear relationship from the concrete and particular to the abstract and general. There are in the interviews no principles articulated concerning the ordering of materials. Indeed, Sarah explicity rejects the notion of 'spiral curriculum', and the underlying principle that "everything has to come first...the kids are new in the school and they have to learn to cope right away." Having no clear principles in these areas, decisions about the order of units in the Learning Course must be made on an ad hoc basis. Consider the following set of statements:

The course should begin with the Communication unit, to establish a kind of atmosphere where kids can take more risks.

Nor do you want to start with very soft stuff, like communications, group dynamics, at the beginning where the kids are doing no writing.

139

We begin with the Communications unit....
Actually we didn't begin with it this time; we
began with the Reading unit, but maybe I'll
explain later on why we did that.

Here, the first two passages state conflicting
rules of practice, and the conflict is resolved not
by a higher-order principle but by a third principle from another area having to do with Reading.
The Communications unit must come first to establish the particular atmosphere necessary for the
course; but for other reasons (principles) the Reading unit may come first. Thus we have a movement
from rules to principles to images but it is non-
linear in two senses: one, in that it may skip from
rule to image; two, in that it moves from rules in
one content area to principles in another.

Another example of this movement is the following: Sarah's image of being an ally, helping
students to beat the system, seems to give rise to
the principle that students should be made aware of
"where they've been, and where they're going" in a
course. Her principle of fostering the ability to
communicate openly by establishing an atmosphere in
which students feel free to take risks relates both
to specific rules (listen actively, paraphrase, and
so forth) and to the image of being an ally of students.

The three levels of structure are not always
discrete, however. In discussing her view of communication Sarah's rules of practice are clearly
stated. She tried, for example, "to allow students
to express their concerns and to discuss their concerns without judging them." However, it is difficult to classify the following statements:

One of the messages there is that the kids
take risks and succeed in communicating more
openly.

If you want to stress the idea that listening
is a very active, difficult task, and that we
all avoid it by all kinds of tricks...I feel
much more commitment to getting the kids to
feel that, and to understand that.

I believe that these statements reflect a
practical principle in that they give part, at
least, of the rationale for the various rules of
practice relating to communication: they state the

relationship among listening, risk-taking and communication. Lacking is a statement of why open
communication is desirable in education; this is an
assumed good in Sarah's frame of reference. But
although there is no single, direct statement of a
principle, it is clear that the various rules of
communication reflect a 'principled' way of doing
things, a common purpose to be realized. Thus it
is reasonable to speak of a <u>practical principle</u> of
<u>open communication</u>. Taken together, the various
statements serve the function of such a principle.

We can say, then, that the structuring of
Sarah's knowledge works in several directions. The
particular, concrete rules of practice are grouped,
ordered, and sometimes dictated by practical principles and, less immediately, by images. Principles held contribute to the establishment of images
which, in turn, enjoin the articulation of particular types of principles and rules. And the various
principles and images relating to different content
areas are traded off against one another in the
course of decision making, determining which of
several conflicting rules is to be followed in the
given situation.

Almost all of Sarah's rules and principles are
directed to instruction. (The exceptions are the
few rules that relate to the work of the curriculum
planning group.) This is hardly surprising since
the task of rules of practice and of practical
principles is to order practice, and instruction is
that practice. However, most of Sarah's rules and
principles also embody knowledge of the other areas
of practical knowledge, as well as of instruction.
For example, the rules which tell Sarah to approve
of students' chatting during class, and to tune in
to chance events in her classroom, are drawn not
primarily from instructional concerns but from her
view of subject matter: language is everywhere,
talk is language, spontaneous events are as good as
(if not better than) planned lessons in fostering
awareness and active use of language.

Other principles reflect other aspects of
Sarah's knowledge. For example, the principle that
one should "link up what's happening in the literature to the kid's own development" reflects Sarah's
view of English as a medium for expression of values, and her personal wish for contact with students and her concern for their needs, as well as
being an expression of her instructional knowledge.
Thus it would be difficult, if not impossible, in

Sarah's case, to speak of the specific knowledge she uses to order instruction without making reference to the other aspects of her knowledge.

Likewise, the images which order Sarah's knowledge are drawn from and bring into play all the areas of her knowledge. The notion of the "rhythm of the school year" embodies curricular knowledge. The "good energetic teacher" reflects personal knowledge. Subject matter knowledge is captured in the images of "no place to hide" and "a window onto students" while knowledge of the milieu is expressed by Sarah's view of herself as an ally of students, helping them to beat the system outside. Finally, the instructional knowledge that finds expression in the range of rules and principles discussed above is also ordered by a number of images, in particular the notion of giving a "double message" in the classroom, and the related image of "giving too much, challenging too little." Thus it appears that much of Sarah's knowledge becomes available for practice through the medium of images, intuitively formulated. Let us then consider in more detail how the structural elements of her knowledge developed and how they function.

DEVELOPMENT AND USE OF STRUCTURE

It is not always possible to tell which level came first in the development of Sarah's knowledge. There are instances in which Sarah described the development of rules of practice as a result of the direct application of a principle. For example, she told of formulating an approach to a writing workshop in which she began by teaching students specific writing techniques (instead of beginning with free writing assignments) as an application of the principle that "whatever I expected from the kids, I had to give them first." In the course of the interviews, her statements of images generally emerged after she had been talking about practices concretely in terms of rules and principles. Some images, for example her sense of being "a good, energetic teacher" appeared to be strongly personal in nature and prior to the specific practices which Sarah followed. Often, images appear to influence the formulation of her instructional principles in indirect ways. For example, we noted that Sarah's view of English literature as a "window on kids' inner world" affected her instructional principles. Another instance is the principle that "whatever I

expected from the kids, I had to give them first";
this principle clearly accords with the image of a
good, energetic teacher who takes full responsibility for what students learn and refuses to see her
subject matter as a hiding place.

This account of the way that knowledge of
subject matter, milieu, self, curriculum and instruction is used to generate practical principles
and rules of practice is consistent with the view
presented in chapter 6. We saw that Sarah did not
tackle a new piece of knowledge analytically; instead she absorbed the information or approach, and
allowed it to 'work itself out' in practice. This
use of theoretical knowledge is largely intuitive,
and images are the tools which enable the working
out to proceed. There are a number of specific instances of this in the interviews.

For example, through discussion of the 'nonsense words' presentation Sarah became aware of a
difficulty in her teaching style. Although I had
presented the example to make a point about her
relationship with students, Sarah used it to focus
on the way that she sometimes used a spontaneous
event in the classroom but was unable to finish the
lesson well. The notion of the 'nonsense words'
presentation became an image (and the term was apt
in suggesting a lesson organized around a chance
event or device with no intrinsic meaning) which
Sarah grasped eagerly and which allowed her to
begin articulating a tension between spontaneity
and control that marked her teaching: "Well, that
whole epiphany I had about the nonsense words type
of presentation I give, is of extreme value to me,
because it--epiphany is the only word I can use, I
suddenly gained, light shone on it."

In another example, Sarah's use of the image
of "giving too much, challenging too little" served
her in working on the problem of her relationships
with students. This image was first mentioned in
the fourth interview; by the fifth interview nine
months later Sarah was able to comment:

> About giving too much: I play tricks some-
> times...I don't give as much, and it could be
> that that grew out of my awareness of it, from
> speaking about it.

We can say, then, that Sarah uses her images to
help extend her practical knowledge.

There are, thus, a number of respects in which

images constitute the main ordering feature of Sarah's practical knowledge. First, as just noted, she appears to use images in bringing the whole range of her practical knowledge to bear on her teaching, and in furthering the development of her knowledge. Much of the knowledge which is of importance to her would be unused if she did not rely heavily on images. Sarah had many rules of practice and practical principles concerning instruction, and her teaching was done in a 'principled' way, with the intent of realizing consistent purposes. But often principles could not direct practice because they generated conflicting rules, and were not stated clearly enough to be compared systematically as basis for a decision. Instead, such decisions were made intuitively at the level of image. An example is the decision concerning the way to begin the Learning Course; though Sarah had principles concerning how to proceed with communication and with Reading, the decision was not made by articulating these principles and deciding among them. Rather, the decision was an intuitive one resting on images--notions like the rhythm of the school year, or the classroom atmosphere helped Sarah to mediate among competing principles and to dissipate potential conflicts. The following passage illustrates this:

> I spoke last time of being much more organized, and now I've got this other thing: trying to make the kid happy to walk into that class, and I don't feel they're in conflict. I feel that combination is working toward a slightly different style.

Finally, images have a stylistic importance for Sarah's knowledge. Typically she uses descriptive statements to articulate both rules and principles: she gives an account of what she does and how she does it, and this account conveys both rule and principle. Sometimes a very apt word or phrase emerges around which the account coalesces, and the phrase then becomes an ordering image tying together a number of principles and rules. Both the visual quality and the intuitive appeal of the image are characteristic of all Sarah's knowledge.

We have seen that Sarah's practical knowledge is structured by and around a small number of images which reflect the entire body of her knowledge and serve to hold together the principles and rules

she uses in bringing her knowledge to bear on practice. Because of the centrality and scope of these
images, we can use them to draw a picture of
Sarah's knowledge that will pull together the analyses of Chapters 3 through 7. This will be the
task of the next chapter.

NOTES

     1. Joseph J. Schwab, "The Practical: A Lan-
guage for Curriculum," School Review (November
1969), pp. 20.
     2. The conception of· 'practical principle'
was proposed in an earlier paper: F. Elbaz,
"Schwab's 'Deliberation': Critical Analysis and
Implications for Teacher Curriculum Development,"
(University of Toronto, Qualifying Research Paper,
1975).
     3. David P. Gauthier, Practical Reasoning
(Oxford: Clarendon Press, 1963).

Chapter 8

COGNITIVE STYLE:
PRACTICAL KNOWLEDGE IN USE

Chapters 3 through 5 have set forth and analysed
the content of Sarah's practical knowledge, while
chapter 6 and 7 have indicated how she holds this
knowledge and have shown how it is structured.
Whatever portrait of Sarah's teaching may have
emerged for the reader from the necessary but sometimes obtrusive welter of detail, certainly a
strong sense of Sarah as a teacher has become real
to me through the process of setting down and ana-
lysing this data. It is now my task to make present to the reader this sense of Sarah's practical
knowledge in use, her 'cognitive style'.

I draw upon the term 'cognitive style' as an
equivalent for the notion of 'practical knowledge
in use' with something of Sarah's sense of relief,
in the second interview, at finding an appropriate
term to describe her own work. 'Cognitive style'
is particularly apt here for several reasons.
First, it connotes 'doing as informed by knowledge', thus balancing the emphasis in the analytic
chapters on 'knowledge as held and used'. Second,
it has antecedents in cognitive personality theory
which sought to balance cognitive and affective
variables, and in the phenomenological sociology of
Schutz who tried to account for the experiential
context of practical knowledge. Third, because
'style' is also a concept in aesthetics it helps to
bridge the gap between my world and that of Sarah
whose knowledge and work are profoundly shaped by
her education in and love of literature. Finally,
the term 'cognitive style' not only labels what
will be presented in this chapter but also hints at
its methodology. It will be descriptive, since
style must be described rather than analysed; it

147

will be appreciative, since to attain a consistent style in any human endeavour is a mark of achievement; and it will be general, for style is ultimately a generalization from many actions to a single manner of acting.

I will portray Sarah's cognitive style by speaking about her images, some of which were identified in Chapter 7. There are two reasons for doing so. There is an obvious connection, first, between style and imagery. As style is a generalization from behaviour to manner, imagery is a generalization from practical rules and principles to a metaphoric form of guidance for action. Second, we have seen that images were of particular importance to the way Sarah structured her knowledge; it thus seems likely that the specific images she used will be most telling in depicting her cognitive style. I will look, then, at Sarah's images for each of the content areas of her practical knowledge discussed in Part Two: curriculum, subject matter, instruction, milieu, and personal knowledge.

CURRICULUM IMAGERY

Although Sarah became involved in curriculum development work with great enthusiasm and a strong sense of commitment, we saw that her final achievement in this area was a mode of work in which development was largely ad hoc: rather than planning, researching, writing and preparing materials Sarah had more confidence, she concluded, in a process where she met with students, heard their concerns and then drew upon her existing resources to meet those concerns. This type of work emphasized responsiveness to students and improvisation, two qualities which suggest an artistic mode of operating (though artistic endeavour is not the only area in which responsiveness and improvisation figure). Another image bolsters this sense of curriculum work as artistic: Sarah spoke of the "rhythm of the school year" as a basic criterion for determining the sequence of instructional activities in a curriculum. The school year is thus perceived as a unified whole with a rhythmic articulation of its parts, much as a literary work or art object might be viewed. This type of image is not particularly dominant in Sarah's comments but it is suggestive. The pervasiveness of imagery in all the areas of her knowledge is, of course, also supportive of a view of Sarah's cognitive style as an artistic one, and this theme will be taken up again later in this chapter.

SUBJECT MATTER IMAGERY

As we have seen, there is a striking contrast between the two images which order Sarah's subject matter knowledge. Early in the interviews she spoke of subject matter in English as a 'place to hide', in contrast with the Learning Course which offered 'no place to hide'. By the fourth interview, subject matter was conceived no longer as a barrier, but rather as a window, a medium which allowed for contact and communication between teacher and students.

Opposed as they are, these images have in common an important feature: both view subject matter knowledge as intellectual and practical space. It is the arena in which students and teacher make contact, or fail to make contact because the teacher takes refuge behind the accumulated wisdom of the discipline. Subject matter is intellectual space insofar as it allows for the expression and clarification of intellectual content; it is practical space because it is the medium in which students and teacher share in the instructional process.

The use of so basic a category as space to convey her subject matter knowledge suggests that Sarah's view of her subject matter is a major determinant of her cognitive style. From the analysis in Chapter 4 it appeared that Sarah values subject matter less for itself (as worthwhile knowledge) than for what it enables her to bring about in the classroom encounter between herself and students. Nevertheless, the nature and the forcefulness of her imagery strongly suggest that subject matter is the intellectual space Sarah inhabits. In Sarah's terms, and those of current slang it is "where she's coming from" no less than is the part of her personality that expresses empathy and concern for students.

Further, Sarah's imagery reflects a very crucial insight that is begining to emerge in her practical knowledge. It is not merely a realization that it is difficult to teach learning skills apart from specific content. Rather, Sarah is beginning to appreciate the necessity of a tension between form and substance, process and content in the subject matter of instruction. (This lends support, too, to the conclusion, in Chapter 4, that Sarah was beginning to work on the idea that skills are shaped by the disciplines in which they are used.) This development is not surprising. Sarah's academic background and training were clearly a most significant influence on her practical knowledge, and it is thus to be expected that she seek ways of integrating English literature 'content' with 'skills' form.

INSTRUCTIONAL IMAGERY

If a sense of tension is beginning to emerge in Sarah's subject matter imagery, it is already well developed in her images of instruction. Sarah typically described her teaching by means of oppositions: she characterized her teaching style in terms of the opposition between spontaneity and distance, and her interaction with students in terms of giving versus challenging them. Although she was working on and resolving some of the issues raised by these dichotomies, the tension which marked Sarah's teaching did not seem to dissipate. Early in the interview sequence she spoke of wanting to be away from the pressures of the classroom, from the "breathlessness" of teaching; later she described her work in the Reading Centre as "done under pressure". It appears that the tension is not (or not merely) a characteristic of the situation but is something Sarah carries with her--a characteristic of her cognitive style. How can it be accounted for?

We can look at the tension Sarah experiences in a number of ways. The simplest, but perhaps least stimulating, interpretation is that such is the nature of teaching. Many writers have pointed to the fact that the teacher must attend to a multiplicity of variables, must balance conflicting needs and viewpoints.[1] Sarah spoke of "the peculiar condition of being an English teacher, and having to constantly be tuned in to so many things." But this does not account for our impression that Sarah actively seeks situations involving pressure, and that she purposefully construes issues in terms of dichotomies. Sarah values being 'shaken up', and believes that a degree of frustration is a necessary ingredient of learning. I would suggest that her cognitive style, as it pertains to instruction, is one of deliberately constructing a view of the teaching situation which challenges her, which has the potential for shaking up her existing mode of operating and for bringing about growth and change. The tension which is a characteristic of Sarah's cognitive style is, at least in part, a creative tension.

However, we can also view this tension as symptomatic of a dissonance within Sarah's practical knowledge. In Chapter 5 it was suggested that Sarah's practical knowledge of instruction was consistent with a subject matter comprised largely of skills. We saw that Sarah did not have a view of teaching that related to subject matter content: she rejected the 'transmission' view, and saw no alternative. But her subject matter imagery tells us that content was indeed an important matter for Sarah. In fact, even her instructional imagery shows this. Both 'spontaneity versus distance' and 'giving versus challenging' deal with responsiveness to students, on the one hand, and the direction of learning toward something outside the student, i.e. subject matter content, on the other. We saw that the skills content Sarah had developed was often ambiguous, did not always allow for the clear articulation of lessons, and seemed to suffer from the lack of grounding in the content of a specific discipline. This difficulty, I believe, also helps to account in part for the tension which marked Sarah's cognitive style with respect to instruction.

SOCIAL IMAGERY

Sarah describes her social milieu and expresses the social cast of her knowledge by means of an imagery of conflict, competition, and aggression. The imagery is varied and subtle; it slips by the reader of transcript almost unnoticed, but once attention is drawn to it the nature of this imagery becomes unmistakeable.

In her relationship with students, for example, Sarah had two kinds of perceptions. In teaching English she had been in a situation where "the class controls the teacher", manipulating her by their degree of interest in the materials she presents. Later, in the Learning Course Sarah saw herself as an "ally", on the side of students against the "system", helping students to "survive" in the school. Though she assumed radically different postures, in both cases Sarah viewed her stance in terms of two opposing camps.

Sarah's relationships with other teachers is marked by a similar perspective. The work of the Learning Course group was supposed to provide a sense of community, and to some extent did so. But the group's relations were fraught with interpersonal problems that "erupted" all at once; the prospect of becoming involved with a new group of teachers the second time was, for Sarah, "a whole new potentially dangerous situation." Afterwards, Sarah saw the work of the group as overly regimented, "like horses, all running on the same track at the same speed." In the Reading Centre Sarah's relationship with her colleague Ellen was basically a harmonious one, yet she still observed that each teacher had her own "territory" which included the particular students she worked with. Thus, despite a base of good relationships, teaching as a social activity was, for Sarah, conditioned by the perpetual need of the individual to protect herself from assaults on her right to work independently.

The school as a social setting was the arena for these conflicts and others stemming from the nature of the setting and the teacher's place in it. Sarah saw the school as an organized, sometimes hostile system with its particular politics; it was a structure that made demands on students with which they had to comply. As a teacher in the system Sarah felt subject to "occupational hazards" like a lack of time to reflect; she perceived herself as "being challenged by people who are suspicious of what I'm doing." Even in the more congenial context of the Reading Centre she felt herself "on trial for the future" and anticipated the need to "fight for staffing" for the Centre. As a group teachers were vulnerable, Sarah felt; following an unpopular teachers' strike they had been subjected to a "series of blows in the press" and, as result, "as a profession we felt completely emasculated."

Thus despite Sarah's extensive knowledge of her social milieu and the generally successful social adaptation which this knowledge allows her, her view of the social world of school is an unfriendly one. It is a fortress besieged from within and without, a place in which the teacher must strive to protect herself and her students. The danger is twofold: on the one hand, there is a fear of being drawn into meaningless work (the class controls the teacher; horses running on a track) and, on the other hand, there is the danger

that if the situation is not properly handled the
enterprise will dissolve totally (problems erupted;
group work was a dangerous situation; the profession felt emasculated).

IMAGERY OF SELF

Sarah speaks about herself in a matter-of-fact
way, usually without drawing on elaborate imagery.
In the first interview she spoke of herself as "a
good, energetic teacher", a description which suggests both a sense of responsibility and a feeling
of competence, two qualities which underlie Sarah's
view of herself. The phrase is a very general one,
and this reflects a reluctance on Sarah's part to
describe herself in detail (though she was not
unwilling to talk about personal concerns that
related to her work). For example, in explaining
her disinclination to seek promotion, she said, "In
terms of my own--the way I am, I don't want to seek
promotion."

Sarah does make repeated use of one characteristic to describe herself--her age. In the first
interview, to explain why she had become more aloof
and demanding, and her teaching more structured,
she pointed to the desire to inculcate skills, and
then added "I'm also getting older, and I think
that's a real factor. I'm thirty, and I'm not
twenty-five, as I was when I went into that school.
And the kids perceive me as thirty, and not twenty-
five." In the second meeting she gave a similar
explanation: "I think that less of the spontaneous
kind of thing is really a matter of being five
years older." And once again in the third interview, considering her relations with students,
Sarah said

> I think age comes into it a bit too. I don't
> have an image of myself as being a woman who
> looks 31 years old. I know that I am, and I
> know that I do, but I still, I think, have
> assessed myself as being a younger member of
> the staff. I think that the kids nowadays
> perceive me that way, although realistically
> it's just not true.

This preoccupation with age can be understood
in a number of different lights. Undoubtedly the
concern with age and ageing is a widespread phenomenon in contemporary society and especially among

153

women. But being perceived as a younger member of the staff is important to Sarah, one suspects, not mainly because of a personal need to feel or to be perceived as young but because it relates to her position as an "ally" of students. To be on the side of students means, in part, to be on the right side of an invisible line dividing between the young and the old. Sarah's instructional stance and her way of coping with social conflict both depend on this position; her view of subject matter supports it.

A striking feature of these statements, however, is their self-contradictory nature. Sarah knows she is five years older, and assumes she is perceived as such. But her own image of self, an image she knows is inaccurate, is that of a "younger" person. In short Sarah sees herself as unchanging (in some respects) despite the passage of time. This image of self as stable over time suggests that knowledge of self, and the personal dimension of practical knowledge in general, are of considerable importance for Sarah. Let us, then, next consider the implications of each of the images and their contributions to Sarah's cognitive style.

SARAH'S COGNITIVE STYLE

From the foregoing discussion of Sarah's images, we can construct a view of her cognitive style. We must begin with subject matter, for we saw that this provides Sarah's intellectual space. Sarah's practical reasoning starts with subject matter; the Learning Course work began with a view of the subject matter to be taught: thinking, according to a particular view of it. In the course of developing a new subject matter for teaching, two things happened. First, Sarah moved away from the area of subject matter (English literature); eventually she returned to this area with a series of insights gathered along the way. Second, what was initially not subject matter but instructional knowledge (communication and skills) was transformed into subject matter for teaching; the subject matter area seems to have a tendency to overtake other areas.

We can best understand the implications of subject matter in Sarah's practical knowledge by imagining the possibility of starting with, for example, the instructional area. A teacher might

154

well envisage her work as unfolding within a particular instructional space in which there are move-
ments between teacher and students. Subject matter
then becomes the material passed back and forth
within instructional space. Alternatively, the
setting for instruction might be elaborated primarily in terms of social relationships; instructional process could then be the form in which
subject matter content is embodied. (Note that the
starting point need not be conceived in terms of
space; however, space, and time, as basic categories, are likely clues to the ordering of knowledge
and the cognitive style to which this ordering
gives rise).

For Sarah, instructional knowledge provides
the material to work on in her teaching: she is
concerned to work in a detailed way not with the
intricacies of literature but with, on the one
hand, the students and how they are learning, and
on the other hand, her own teaching as it is evolving in terms of the conflicts between spontaneity
and distance, giving and challenging. It is in
this area that Sarah has developed the majority of
her practical principles, but frequently she works
at the level of the image. For example, she moved
toward a desired style of interacting with students
by reflecting on the notion of 'giving too much,
challenging to little' and trying out various
approaches without formalizing these via principles
or rules.

Sarah's social knowledge sets boundaries on
the exercise of all her practical knowledge. Sarah
perceives the social framework within which she
operates as constricting and even hostile to her.
We can see the choices she makes in other areas as
responses to this social constraint. Thus, for
example, she attempts to develop subject matter in
skills that is, ostensibly, value-free and does not
stir up questions of "what knowledge is of most
worth?", thus avoiding overt conflict with the
'system' and its representatives whose values are
opposed to hers. Further, as we have seen, the
exercise of this skills knowledge gives Sarah a
social modus vivendi she can accept.

However, although she is most careful to
respect social boundaries and expectations, Sarah
perceives her own values through the personal facet
of her knowledge. Awareness of her own values and
of the strengths and weaknesses of her teaching
allows Sarah to express her unchanging values

through sustained human relationships of a particular kind, through a steady commitment to the welfare of students, and through a striving for the attainment of rigorous standards in her work.

Sarah is a teacher who is mindful, respectful--of knowledge, of persons, of her own worth. She cares deeply about her students but knows that this concern must be both limited and channelled if it is to be helpful. She has a good measure of the discipline necessary to direct her concerns in useful ways and of the techniques for doing so. Up to now, though, it appears that her concern for students has stood in the way of her acquiring a clear and consistent sense of the subject matter within which she and her students move.

Sarah's cognitive style is, in many respects, the style of an artist. Sarah has a sense of the spontaneous. She is aware of the relationship between the form and the content of instruction. She uses tension creatively to further her own understanding and growth. There is, in her social imagery, an awareness of the constant need to wrest meaning from chaos, to give order to her work. And she works in the medium of a concrete embodiment, in the classroom, within space and over time, of her personal values and purposes.

Finally, underlying Sarah's concern for persons is, it seems, an unarticulated but profoundly radical social critique which Sarah prefers not to bring to the surface, because to do so would be to disrupt totally the delicate balance of the factors which comprise Sarah's cognitive style.

The notion of balance, finally, reflects both the aesthetic and the practical nature of Sarah's cognitive style. Her style is, we have seen, an expression of a number of crucial personal concerns that are not easily held in balance. Sarah's main purposes are in the instructional domain. She wants to teach students skills of lasting usefulness, as well as a way of being with others and of communicating: two tasks, difficult in themselves, far more so in combination. But she insists on doing so within the medium of subject matter that is both relevant to students and instrinsically worthwhile; again, a combination that is not easy to achieve. And both areas of concern are articulated within the context of a hostile social framework that, she feels, negates many of Sarah's purposes: the school structure makes it virtually impossible to follow individual students' progress for long periods; it subjugates interpersonal relationships to the concern for passing grades and moving successfully ahead in the system; it rejects students' needs for learning that is relevant to their lives in favour of learnings that the administrators of the system can display to warrant the public trust and public money they enjoy; and the school structure trivializes debate on the value of the knowledge being taught in schools.

Sarah, however, does not gather together these points (all of which she makes in one form or another) into a critique of the social system of schooling. Her critique is expressed through images rather than through an argument, and the metaphoric nature of her protest is what allows for the balance that is the accomplishment of Sarah's cognitive style. A theoretician with Sarah's knowledge would have all the ingredients necessary to construct a coherent argument; and having done so, she would become incapable of working within the system. Sarah's work is not theoretic but practical, personal, and artistic. She makes her statement through action. Her purposes, which conflict when viewed as simultaneous goals within the existing system, are realized in the process of an individual teacher's ongoing work. She often falls short of her goals, fails to accomplish what she intended. But within the rhythm of the school year, her purposes are worked out in a way that is at once an impressive creative accomplishment and a down-to-earth example of the adjustments and accomodations that mark practical knowledge in use.

NOTES

1. See, for example, Robert Dreeben, "The School as a Workplace," in R.M.W. Travers, ed., Second Handbook of Research on Teaching (Chicago: Rand McNally, 1973); Philip Jackson, Life in Classrooms (New York: Holt, Rinehart and Winston, 1968).

Chapter 9

REFLECTIONS ON METHOD:
THE PARTICIPANTS' PRACTICAL KNOWLEDGE

The interview process in which Sarah and I engaged
is itself an instance of the exercise of practical
knowledge on both our parts. In this final chapter
I want to look at this research activity and to ask
a series of questions about it. The first question
is, what kind of knowledge or understanding has
been produced by the activity itself? The second
question is, what have I learned about methodology
insofar as the joint involvement of teachers and
researchers in the study of curriculum and teaching
is concerned? The third question is whether the
process of articulating one's practical knowledge
can be initiated and pursued outside of a specific
research context. In the course of attempting to
answer these questions I will be looking back at
the study from my own perspective as a researcher
and teacher, but I will be concerned particulaly to
anticipate the questions that might be raised by
practitioners--teachers and other school people who
are wondering what implications this kind of study
has for their everyday work.

WHAT IS KNOWLEDGE OF TEACHERS'
PRACTICAL KNOWLEDGE?

In writing up this study I have experienced the
most difficulty not with the body of the work but
with a final statement in which convention expects
me to state the conclusions of the research, to
show that the questions raised at the outset have
indeed been answered. This difficulty, I now

think, was due to a confusion about the basic methodological commitments underlying such research. It is worth taking the trouble to sort out this confusion here, I believe, because a degree of clarity about one's epistemological assumptions, essential for the researcher , is equally important for the practitioner who wants to be actively involved in a research or curriculum development activity that comes his or her way.

It will be useful to draw upon the current distinction among three forms of epistemology and the different intellectual traditions to which they give rise: the empiric-analytic, the interpretive and the critical tradition. It seems to me that the present study responds, at various points, to concerns stemming from each of these perspectives, and thus gives rise potentially to three different forms of knowledge or understanding (though not all are equally developed here).

If we adopt an empiric-analytic perspective we commit ourselves to looking for law-like regularities in the behaviour of teachers. Given that the search for a "theory of teaching" has not led to dramatic results, many have argued that a preliminary phase of empirical work has been neglected: that is, we need a more complete and detailed understanding of the work teachers actually do, of the way they plan for instruction, of their decision-making processes in and outside of the classroom, in order to better ground the hypotheses we formulate about teaching, so that genuinely predictive theories can be elaborated.

While I do not believe that the search for a theory of teaching with explanatory or predictive power is a defensible undertaking, I can nevertheless detect, in looking at this study as an indicator of my own practical knowledge, the influence of the empiric-analytic perspective. For example, there is a sense at times that the study seeks to give a "true" or "correct" portrait of Sarah's practical knowldge. I entertained the notion of "triangulation"--looking at the same phenomenon from different perspectives--as a way of validating this portrait, noting that Sarah's use of knowledge in the interviews paralleled her use of knowledge in teaching. Thus her concern to answer my questions in the interviews confirmed my view of her "theoretical orientation" to knowledge as objective, such that questions asked have answers independent of the person asking them: "I could have

perhaps paused and thought more carefully of where
your question was leading rather than where I wanted to lead it. If I'm not answering the question
you're asking, let me know, because I probably can
answer it, and want to." (Interestingly, this
statement also illustrates Sarah's embeddedness
within the empiric-analytic perspective: she assumed that the search for knowledge was unidirectional, leading to truth; further, she had
expected to play the role of passive research subject who is kept in ignorance of the researcher's
intentions.)

Another instance of my use of triangulation to
verify the analytic findings is found in the parallel I drew between the interview situation and
Sarah's teaching with respect to the dichotomy
between spontaneity and distance. In the second
interview Sarah's participation had been easy and
spontaneous; she freely referred to problems in her
teaching and was openly self-critical. In that
interview Sarah suggested we try in the future to
look at how she plans a lesson. We arranged to do
so; but when the time came, Sarah kept me at a
distance. The lesson had been planned in advance
(for reasons we will consider later), and together
we could only review in retrospect some of the
rationale behind it; as a researcher I had been
effectively excluded from the process, just as
Sarah sometimes kept her students at a distance.
This procedure of verification was not adopted
wholesale in the study, however, because I felt
that it involved looking at Sarah's knowledge in a
fragmented way, as comprised of discrete bits of
understanding reflected in discrete episodes of
behaviour. But there are other ways in which the
study might offer starting points for empiric-
analytic work. I suggest the notion of "cognitive
style" as a possible conceptual tool to guide the
study of teaching; it is a tool which could lead to
the identification of a relatively small number of
distinct styles in the use of knowledge (intuitive,
methodical and reflective are the ones that I
imagined). Likewise in beginning to work with the
terms "rule of practice", "practical principle" and
"image", I had expected to focus primarily on practical principles as organizers of the teacher's
knowledge and had hoped to be able to articulate
some general statements about Sarah's use of principles which would have been testable in other

contexts. This did not come about, largely because Sarah's knowledge seems to be organized so personally around her images of schooling. But efforts to generalize in this way still seem to me to be valid and potentially interesting lines of research. I do not look forward to a theory of teaching arising out of such work but neither do I dismiss efforts to make empirical generalizations about teaching.

It is of course the interpretive perspective which is most apparent in the study, in my concern to find out how Sarah makes sense of her own work and to articulate the knowledge she holds from her own point of view; I saw her purposes as important considerations in explaining what she does, and wished to honour her own formulations of these as far as possible. Further, I was also concerned with the communication between Sarah and myself as an important source of understanding. I found that Sarah and I both had unexpressed needs and motives which operated to structure our discussion, and in one sense there was a striking complementarity between Sarah's position in the interview situation and my own. Though we did not discuss it, both of us were engaged in similar pursuits. Sarah was trying to establish herself in a new domain, a new area of interest. In that area the effort to develop a subject matter for teaching was also a search for recognition and enhanced professional status. At its best, this activity gave Sarah a feeling of "power and excitement about being able to schedule my own day and make my own projects," though in the course of events in the typical context of school, this feeling tended to fade away.

My position was not unlike Sarah's. I was engaging in the interviews in order to gather data with a view to completing a study. Like Sarah, my concern was a personal one, to demonstrate to myself as well as others mastery of an area of knowledge and of a style of research to which I felt a personal commitment. Sarah saw her own sense of professionalism (that is, her feeling of pride in being able to order and assume responsibility for her work) as being at odds with the school system and the demands it made upon her. I too experienced the "double bind" of research: to demonstrate a capacity for original and independent research, while respecting the accepted canons of the field.

In addition to the similarities of our positions, Sarah and I were dependent on one another in important ways. Clearly I needed Sarah to provide data for my study. More specifically I needed her to say things that I could interpret as evidence of her practical knowledge, and to act in ways that would warrant my use of an informal, personal and cooperative style of interviewing. Her behaviour was thus critical to both the form taken by my study and its content.

Likewise Sarah was dependent on me, though less critically so, since her work as teacher was in no way subject to my control (though it was undoubtedly influenced by our discussion). Sarah's dependence on me was indirect: I represented the academic world which, in her view, had some claim to set standards for her work. Our meetings occasioned for Sarah the need to call herself to account, not to me as an individual but to what I represented.

Though we made occasional reference to our mutual need of one another, neither of us confronted the strength of this need, nor did we speak about how it was influencing our discussion. Perhaps as a result, the influences are pervasive and subtle. We were sometimes apologetic (as when I spoke of "picking" Sarah's brains) or self-deprecating (as when Sarah wondered what "someone" with my knowledge and experience would have done with the Learning Course topics). We played a variety of roles with one another. I have already made reference to Sarah as the good student, eager to answer all my questions. In return, on occasion I lectured, expounded, justified the way I was conducting the interviews and the research. Sometimes, on the other hand, I played the student to Sarah as teacher. In the first interview when we realized there had been a systematic misunderstanding on my part of the Learning Course, Sarah very patiently explained the Course to me once more ("Maybe we'll have to go in reverse for a while, and go back to things that I've said before.") Throughout the interviews, I reminisced about my own high school days; generally these recollections, while relevant, did little to further the discussion. I was at a loss to account for them until I recalled that I was in fact a student, both in 'real life' and in the dynamics of the interaction with Sarah who was teaching me about her practical knowledge. It is not surprising that the role I was playing brought forth echoes of earlier experiences in that role.

The complementarity of the relationship between Sarah and myself is, however, most striking when it gives rise to behaviour that is clearly at odds with some of our deepest personal interests. The best example of this is our treatment of the topic of Sarah's teaching style. In the second interview I raised this issue in terms of the 'nonsense words' presentation Sarah had made in a class I observed. Sarah became aware of a problem she had in 'finishing up' lessons that began spontaneously. This insight was most significant for her. She referred to it as an epiphany, and was interested in pursuing it further. So was I. I had enjoyed observing and commenting on Sarah's classes, and felt that I had done so skilfully. Three interviews followed (one of which included an observation session). Several times we referred back to this episode, agreeing and promising that we would return to deal with it. Contrary to both Sarah's avowed interest and the purposes I had formulated for the research, we never did so. I can explain this only in terms of our respective needs to maintain our positions within the inter-view situation.

Dealing seriously with the problems of Sarah's teaching would have required of me a commitment to repeated observation of her classes. This would have taken up more time than I could then devote to it but, more important, it would have demanded either a detour in the study I had set out to do or, more likely, a complete restructuring of the research. I was not prepared to change my plans to such an extent. Apparently I was equally unable to admit to Sarah that a topic of such concern to us had to be ignored simply because it would delay or disrupt the completion of my project. I believe, however, that Sarah was also reluctant to deal with the topic (it was she who had suggested a planning session for just this purpose, yet planned the lesson in advance making the purpose unattainable), and for a similar reason. It had to do with Sarah's ability to realize successfully her purposes in the classroom. It is true that she had expressed a willingness to have her view of herself and her teaching 'shaken up'. But the particular period in which Sarah was working on a new subject matter, and moving into a new setting, was an inauspicious time to challenge her sense of compe-tence by calling into question the only aspect of

164

her work on which she could then rely, her ability to structure classroom learning. In this instance, then, Sarah's need to sustain her professional self-image joined with my needs, to eliminate from consideration a topic which, for sheer interest, was of prime importance to both of us.

Thus the interpretive perspective allowed me to become aware of the particular communicative situation Sarah and I were in as structuring my view of her knowledge. I was able to take my analysis of her knowledge of instruction so far, and no farther; perhaps on another occasion, with a different set of constraints we would have been able to pursue these issues, while other ones would have been closed to us.

The critical pespective, finally, informed the study indirectly but in an important way. As I have mentioned, the decision not to adopt a critical stance in the analysis was made quite explicitly. I had often felt that critical studies of teaching ultimately accomplished much the same thing as empirical studies: they judged the teacher against an external standard, and found her wanting. It was largely to avoid this judgmental posture that I chose a interpretive style of research which would credit the teacher with autonomy by taking up her own pespective. The idea that teachers are independent agents holding knowledge does not arise from a phenomenological study of things-as-they-are: we know that teachers often reject this view of themselves and see their teaching as determined by external constraints, though their view of these constraints is usually a narrow one limited to the demands of administration or parents. It was with a hope of finding ways to change this situation that I undertook the present study: my intention was not simply to present for its own sake a picture of the teacher as a holder of knowledge. Rather I assumed that to change our view of the teacher is to open up new possibilities for action. Further, since knowledge is power, to see oneself as holding knowledge is also to see oneself differently in relation to existing sources of power.

Thus I believe that the picture of Sarah's practical knowledge has the potential for opening up a critical dialogue. This did not happen in the interviews because both of us were embedded in our particular situations, and our need to preserve existing definitions of these situations was too strong to allow for the raising of critical questions. But I can venture some suggestions about the kind of issues around which such dialogue would be most likely to take shape, and the conditions which would support it.

In Chapter 6 I pointed to a form of academic bias in Sarah's work, evidenced by the way that the Learning Course was eventually re-directed to an academically-oriented clientele. Sarah's response to the charge of bias, I predict, would be to accept the assessment readily and to add that within the school system as it presently is, such bias is inevitable. Students have already been categorized by the time they come to the Learning Course, and if the skills learned in the Course are not going to be reinforced by other teachers, there is little point in wasting time teaching them.

Thus the academic bias, if it is that, surfaces is response to a situation where Sarah feels she can do little for her students. It would certainly be useful to bring this to awareness and to explore the reasons, but I would not be too hopeful that a fruitful dialogue could develop, for several reasons. First, the issue does not address a strength in the teachers' knowledge on which to build; second, the issue is not a pressing problem for Sarah; and third, I as a researcher have little to offer by way of remedy.

A more positive example should make this clearer. A major problem for Sarah was the evaluation of the Learning Course. She pointed out that it was difficult to assess what students had learned because the individual timetabling system in her school made it impossible to follow up all the students. This issue might have been a promising one to explore because of the ways it meets the three conditions just stated. Obviously it was important to Sarah to be able to assess her work, and she would likely have been willing to invest time and effort in doing so. It is also the case that she had strengths in the area: she was good at making the initial diagnosis of student needs and interests; she had simple and effective ways of evaluating ongoing student work; and she had a capacity for the kind of self-criticism needed to evaluate the impact of a lesson, though she was not always able to bring this to bear. Her difficulty with evaluation was threefold: first, the scope of the job was larger than what she had done before because it involved a whole course rather than

individual lessons; second, there was a problematic
longitudinal aspect to the evaluation; third, she
had the expectation that the task required a specific form of professional expertise which she
lacked. On the first of these aspects the help
Sarah required was technical, and I could likely
have provided it: it would have involved analyzing
the course content and coordinating the evaluation
of its various parts. On the second aspect it
would have been particularity valuable to discuss
the constraints which make it impossible to follow
the progress of individual students. In effect,
the innovation of individual timetables, which
ostensibly allows for maximum individualization,
actually renders each student something less than
an individual because no single other person in the
system has the time to treat him as a person.
Sarah was keenly aware of this paradox but had not
connected this phenomenon with broader issues
relative to the functioning of the school in
society. Finally Sarah's view of evaluation as an
"expert" function could have been examined critically. Following this, it would have been interesting to suggest that the problem of evaluating the
course was actually a research problem, and that
one way of dealing with it would be for Sarah to
conduct a case study, following closely the work of
two or three students to trace their development of
learning skills from the Learning Course onward.
In this way Sarah would have been offered not only
critical insights but means of dealing with the
problematic situation, and she would likely have
generated solutions of her own.

As a second, apparently narrow example that
has broad ramifications, consider the following:
the imagery Sarah uses in speaking of her social
milieu is imagery of violence and aggression.
Prior to analysis this imagery had passed unnoticed
to both Sarah and myself. The very taken-for-
grantedness of such strong and unequivocal imagery
forces a reexamination of the way Sarah, and all of
us, look at social relations within the school.
Are competition and aggression really so normal and
taken-for-granted? If so, what might we do about
it, and do we want to? The power of Sarah's imagery suggests that there is a real concern here; as a
researcher I can offer both the initial observation
and the view that Sarah's ability to articulate her
feelings through such imagery constitutes a real
strength, a source of knowledge. I can also share

my own sense of the competitiveness and hostility which are found in the academic world. Discussion is one concrete form of pratical action that can be undertaken here; it is at least conceivable that because teacher and researcher have different perspectives and experience they may be able to offer one another new insights and suggestions for action.

The foregoing discussion has , I hope, demonstrated how the articulation of a teacher's practical knowledge can be a starting point for a critical understanding that grows out of the teacher's concerns and is validated in practical action. The knowledge of teachers' practical knowledge which has been obtained by this study is primarily an interpretive understanding of one teacher's work as seen by one researcher; but it is also potentially a critical understanding of how that knowledge funtions in a social context, and it is this latter form of understanding that I hoped to promote by the study.

THE PARTICIPATION OF TEACHERS IN RESEARCH

When I set out to study Sarah's practical knowledge I formulated a series of high-sounding statements about research as a shared endeavour in which the interests and purposes of both teacher and researcher were to find a place. I proposed to invite the teacher's participation in every phase from the formulation of precise question to the final analyses of the data. I found that it is extremely difficult for two persons to simply come together, to talk, to explore ideas, much less to analyse data and interpret findings jointly. Inevitably the social frameworks out of which they operate will condition their discussion. Does it follow that the effort to conduct research based on the assumption that researcher and 'subject' are both persons, is a wasted effort? I do not believe so.

This worry seems to stem from an implicit assumption that there is some truth to be attained by the research which is obscured by the exercise of practical knowledge. Rather, the difficulties that two persons have in communicating are potentially the most illuminating features of discussion for the purposes of this research. Such difficulties highlight aspects of the teaching-learning situation which would otherwise go unnoticed.

Nevertheless, I will be more cautious in the

future in speaking about shared research efforts. To begin with, the research activity is embedded within a particular milieu; it is the business of the researcher to formulate researchable problems to obtain funding for their investigation and to publish findings. In doing so he or she must be responsive to the ethos of the academic community, not the needs of teachers. Teachers can play little or no role in these very crucial aspects of the work. Second, the researcher inevitably brings his own perspective to bear on his work, as does the teacher; the development of a common perspective takes much time and shared experience, while the option of taking up the teacher's perspective exclusively is largely impossible. Third, the interests and responsibilities of teachers will not always warrant their extensive involvement in research.

What can, however, and should be shared by teachers and researchers is an understanding of what the research is trying to accomplish and what each party will contribute and take away from the endeavour. Teachers will be participating actively in research being carried out within their classes if they have a clear view of what kind of knowledge is being sought (the threefold distinction among types of research involved above would be a useful tool for this purpose), if they understand what is expected of them and agree to provide it, and if they can share these understandings with the researcher. Teachers often have unexpressed motives for participating in research projects: it may confer prestige within the school, or it may be difficult to refuse a request from one's principal. Obviously they are not likely to admit to such motives so long as the researcher remains an outsider who comes into the school to serve her own ends. But if the researcher is able to bring to awareness her own implicit motivations and is willing to share these with the teacher the process will become a joint activity regardless of how research responsibilities are actually divided. In short, specific details of method seem much less important than the researcher's willingness to be open about her own assumptions and presuppositions.

I believe the most important lesson to be learned from this study is that it is possible for teachers to become aware of and articulate their own practical knowledge, and that this process can lead to greater self-understanding and professional growth. Certainly Sarah indicated that her knowledge was developing and that the fact of talking about it contributed to this change. The study was not intended to influence her development and I did nothing is particular to foster it--in fact,as I pointed out, our avoidance of some of the more pressing issues may have impeded the development of her knowledge. So it is likely that the same activity carried out under different auspices could have led to more dramatic results.

The process of articulating one's practical knowledge does not require a research context nor does the second party have to be a researcher--it might be another teacher, a non-teaching but curious friend, or a notebook. The process must, however, be distinguished from mere talk, telling stories about the hard day one had or trying to understand the behaviour of one's principal. A measure of formality is required because the process is one of giving form to one's knowledge. The categories used here can serve as a convenient starting point, a checklist to help the teacher make sure that no essential aspects are being overlooked. Undoubtedly as one goes along more appropriate terms of analysis will suggest themselves. The teacher could begin as I did, by making an inventory of the content of her knowledge, adding to the list over a period of several weeks until it is relatively complete and then looking at each aspect of content to identify the orientations taken and the rules, principles and images which are involved in each area.

An alternative procedure might be to write down critical episodes in one's teaching and, when a number of these have been collected, to reflect on the series to see what recurring problems and strengths are revealed. This task, in fact, is one I undertook at the very outset of this study. I found it very exciting to be able to generate explanations of the small number of resounding successes and (memory being mercifully selective) the equally small number of dismal failures I had experienced as a teacher at the elementary and secondary level. The polarization of success and failure seems to be useful in giving rise to explanations that may initially be simplistic, but which are refined as one applies them to less extreme cases. For myself this effort allowed me to formulate a number of aspects of the teaching-learning situation that I held important--such matters as treating students positively, viewing them as active learners, connecting in a realistic way with the knowledge they already had--and I soon realized that these themes applied equally to teachers and learners; evetually this line of thinking gave rise to the notion of 'practical knowledge' which became central to my own practical knowledge as a researcher.

I have sketched two contrasting processes-one might term them deductive and inductive--which are certainly oversimplifications of a complex form of reflection. The process will likely be further complicated if two teachers join in reflecting on their work. One principle of all research should be borne in mind: that the phase of muddling through a large mass of disorderly data is apparently essential; it does not pay to impose a premature ordering on the information. The teacher who is patient, and prepared to tolerate the exposure (even to a notebook) of what appear to be failings and incoherences, will find the task personally rewarding in itself; more important, I am hopeful that it can lead eventually to the opening up of new possibilities for teaching as social action.

NOTES

1.   Yonemura has involved teachers in a similar process; her work is reported in "Teacher Conversations: A Potential Source of their own Professional Growth," Curriculum Inquiry 12:3 (1982). Chris Clark and his colleagues at the Institute for Research on Teaching at Michigan State University have also worked with teachers on the keeping of journals of their planning.

APPENDIX

THE DATA SUMMARIZED

In this appendix the data collected through the series of interviews and the two observation periods is presented. The presentation will follow the sequence of the study, summarizing each interview and observation session in turn. The plan formulated prior to each discussion will be outlined, and the extent to which it was followed will be assessed. The various topics of discussion will be indicated, and the content summarized, after which illustrative selections from the transcript will be provided. Comment will also be made on the style and emotional tone of discussion, on its movement from one topic to the next, and on the understandings and misunderstandings which it produced.

A general comment is in order concerning the quality of the data. The interviews were informal; most took place in the home of either the teacher or the writer, and were taped on a simple cassette recorder. The teacher could have been invited to the university, to record the interviews with professional facilities. The informal setting was preferred because a comfortable, relaxed atmosphere seemed more important than optimal recording conditions in securing the quality of data. In fact, all the interviews took place in relative quiet; interruptions (for coffee, snacks or a phone call) were few and brief. Initially even the familiar cassette recorder was somewhat intrusive, because it required watching to determine when the cassette had ended. (Once only, a short portion of discussion was lost.) At other times, the relaxed atmosphere prevailed to such an extent that the quality of recording suffered, as both Sarah and I forgot

to speak up for the tape. However, while the recording quality was sometimes poor (especially in
one interview which took place in Sarah's school
after observation), and there are unclear words or
phrases (indicated on the transcripts), it rarely
happened that the sense of a passage was lost. The
transcripts are thus accurate renderings of the
discussion.

The transcripts were edited for readability;
certain phrases and sentence structures which pass
unnoticed in speech but which are awkward in written material were eliminated (e.g. "sort of",
repetitions, run-on sentences). However, passages
which indicated confusion or difficulty in articulating an idea were preserved intact or edited only
slightly. The reader aware of the editing policy
can take this into account as he makes his own
interpretations.

Much of value is lost in tape recording--for
example, the gestures and facial expressions which
we use to interpret one another's meaning--but
conversely, many qualities unnoticed by participants are revealed on tape. Moments of awkwardness
or embarrassment often pass quickly and are forgotten; on tape such moments are preserved, as are the
manoeuvres by which they were overcome. Laughter,
sighs, uh-huhs, and the like which were apparent on
tape are indicated on the transcript, but it must
be remembered that their meanings vary widely:
laughter may be good-natured, self-mocking, embarrassed; uh-huh may indicate assent, "I hear you,"
or even "I don't agree but I am following your
argument." Occasionally, a return ·to the tape
recordings was helpful in the course of interpretation. But generally, the transcripts are sufficient for understanding, evaluating and suggesting
alternatives to the interpretations made.

One datum of the research process which must
be recorded here is that the procedure of transcribing the tapes was unusually taxing. This may
be merely a personal phenomenon. It seems to be
due to a combination of factors: transcribing tapes
is a challenging job, technically; it is difficult
to transcribe smoothly when the role of interpreter
is being played at the same time, and equally difficult to 'turn off' this role when one is highly
involved in it; transcribing one's own voice is em-
barrassing at best, but more so when one is also
acutely aware and critical of the way one is handling the job of interviewing. This difficulty had

two consequences for the research process. It interfered somewhat with my intention to give Sarah a copy of the preceeding interview transcript before each successive meeting (the third transcript was not ready at the time of the fourth meeting), and also meant that the plans for some interviews had to be drawn up on the basis of general impressions, rather than detailed analysis of the preceeding interview.

The interviews are presented in the first person, to convey the informal way in which they were conducted. I have tried to express Sarah's point of view as far as I was able to perceive it on reading the transcripts· and notes made during observation. These summaries rely on straightforward description of content, and on immediate perceptions and feelings; they are prior to and independent of the more complex interpretative and analytic work presented in the text.

INTERVIEW I   May 1976

Planning

The background to the first interview was several informal conversations I had had over the previous year or so with Sarah concerning her teaching. She had told me about an experimental course that was being set up in her school, and in which she was involved. I was interested mainly in her involvement in the curriculum development process, and had largely forgotten the specifics of the course itself. When I first contacted her about the interview, I spoke of a single meeting, and said that I would like to record it; I did not tell her how I planned to use the material, as I had not yet made such a decision myself. I did, however, assume that she would be interested in talking further about her work and that such a discussion could be mutually beneficial as earlier discussions had been.

Discussion

We met on a weekday evening in my home, drank tea and chatted; I adjusted the recording equipment and we began. I had prepared only two very broad questions. I asked Sarah first what purposes and needs motivated her involvement in this experimental course, and how these purposes were being met by her ongoing work; and second, what knowledge was she drawing on in this work.

Sarah commented that she would have preferred smaller, less exhaustive questions, and she wondered if I was suggesting that there existed professional materials more adequate than the ones her group had developed. She then described the evolution of the course.

An English teacher in her school had formulated the notion of a "Thinking Course" based on the conception that "reading is a function of thinking." This teacher, Liz, and a vice-principal, Dave, were people with whom Sarah had frequent contact; they formed the nucleus of a group working on the "Thinking Course". After a while the group limited its focus to a more modest concern with 'learning', and finally to "coping with the kind of work you get in our high school...strategies for succeeding in the particular politics in our school."

Sarah mentioned several problems that had motivated her to work on the course: there was a concern with the 3 R's (a much-debated issue at the time) that joined her own feeling, while teaching Grade 13, that students were ill-prepared for the work demanded and that her own efforts were therefore wasted; she also felt that her previous participation in professional development activities had been diffuse and lacking in reinforcement, and she saw the course as an opportunity to develop professionally by working in a supportive, communal framework.

Sarah then described in detail the planning process, the components of the Learning Course and their sources. She mentioned some ways in which her work on the course had influenced her English teaching, and vice versa, and spoke of her emotional commitment to the course.

Two interesting gaps in the communication became evident towards the end of this interview. First, it became apparent that while Sarah had been emphasizing the highly-structured nature of the Learning Course, I had consistently been noting its loose aspects (for example, the diffuseness of the interdisciplinary subject matter), and Sarah took pains to correct this impression.

The second gap in communication was one in which I felt that an important point I made was ignored by Sarah. She had been expressing her concern that she was relying too heavily in her tea-

ching on the study habits which had been effective
for her in high school but for which she could give
no external justification. This point was exciting
to me because, in beginning to work on the notion
of practical knowledge, I had been concerned to understand the varied outcomes of my own teaching
experiences, and had concluded that a reliance on
my personal learning skills had sometimes enabled
me to teach effectively. I described this (enthusiastically but probably too briefly) to Sarah,
and was astonished when she made no reply and went
on to a different topic.

We concluded with a discussion of the problem
that had been latent in much of the interview--
evaluation. Sarah was concerned with this on two
levels: evaluation of student progress and evaluation of the Learning Course and the way it had been
developed. Despite her doubts, Sarah closed on a
positive note, pointing out that her own reading
skills had been improved by the use of techniques
taught in the course, and this gave her some hope.

The portion of transcript which follows presents the beginning of the first interview.

F. I guess we talked about it, but let me try to
    formulate very briefly the kinds of things I'm
    after, and then just go at it any way you
    want.
S. O.K.
F. You were involved in a really major planning
    effort, something you didn't have to do. You
    could, I'm sure, have got materials, or had
    materials...
S. Mm-hmm...
F. You could have done without this. So I'm in-
    terested in why you did it, what purposes of
    your own you were trying to serve by doing it,
    what needs there were in the classroom, what
    needs there were in you and in your teaching
    that made you want to get involved in it, and
    how you see those needs or those purposes as
    working themselves out in the course of it.
    So that's one thing. And the other aspect of
    it is: what kind of knowledge you used and how
    you used it in order to work through the
    thing, whether it's theoretical knowledge,
    discussions with other people or just in-
    tuition or your own experience; just the kinds
    of things that you're aware of drawing on in
    order to formulate and to plan the things you

177

were going to do.

S.   O.K.   I'd probably feel more comfortable if you asked little bits of questions one at a time at the beginning, but I wanted to clarify something first.   Are you suggesting that by calling up someone or getting in touch with a certain library--there's one specific person who's doing research-we could have gotten a package which was a whole course-- "Learning Course"?

F.   No.

S.   I thought you were suggesting that that was a possibility, and we chose another possibility, of putting things together ourselves.

F.   Well, I wasn't, but now that you've brought them up there are those possibilities, so maybe we can get into it that way--why <u>didn't</u> you choose that other possibility?

S.   I think, mainly, because none of the people who fooled around with these ideas for months before anything arose out of it knew an advocate or had a connection that we though could help us.   There was a connection for getting material in Communications, there was a connection for work on reading, but nobody that we knew--and we were from pretty varied backgrounds--knew anyone who had set up a course like this, or who had spoken about formulating a course like this.   By the way, it started out being called a "Thinking Course", and the evolution from "Thinking" to "Learning" I think is a very interesting one, because in a sense it's a huge evolution of copping out.

What mainly happened is that the original person who gave birth to the whole idea left us in June for a promotion.   She--I don't know whether I told you this before-- she was someone who had been given a semester (half a year)--free, and an office in the school, from the English department--she was an English teacher--to set up a kind of core language program, or at least set up a Grade Ten core language program.   She took a course in Reading offered to one representative of each school by the Board, and got very interested in the aspect of reading that the professor presented as "Reading is a function of thinking, and if the kid is taught to think, then reading, if it isn't a perceptual problem, won't be a problem". And, by her proximity to a vice-principal in the school, I think she enlisted his enthusiasm, and I was communicating quite frequently with both of them, because I was interested in what Liz was doing in English, and Dave, the vice-principal, was the person I went to with teaching problems.

So we thought that maybe we could get a group working on 'thinking', and for months the course was called in our own minds "this course is about thinking", and only at the end of August and the beginning of September did we realize that we weren't doing anything about thinking because we didn't know anything about thinking (laughter). But we probably could do something quite minimal in the sense of getting the kids to cope with the demands that are made of them by other teachers in various courses in the school. So the course got named, "This course is about learning." And I think the better name for it now would be "This course is about coping with the kind of work you get in our High School during the four years you're here." And it's much more modest, but I feel more in control of that, because none of us really had any theoretical knowledge of 'thinking', or even of what 'learning' is. Or rather, we knew that there had to be strategies for succeeding in the particular politics of our school. And what you have in front of you (indicates course outline) is really a collection of different ways of coping with school, of being successful.

F. Was that the original problem that worried you, the students who were 'not successful'?

S. Well, there were a couple of problems. We, although we said we weren't, I think bought into the statements about the three R's having disappeared, and we have to go back to the three R's. Well, I don't think any of us was naive enough to think you go back to the three R's, but certainly we had to go somewhere. And I think we also felt, each one of us who was strongly involved, felt alienated from our own particular staffs, our Department staffs, and felt that the philosophy, or the lack of interest in professional development on our own staffs, made us seek a community of our own, which basically became the little community which worked on the course and is working on the course.

I have a file that I can get for you--Dave will get it for you when you're at the school--of the different memos that trace the development of the course. One of the things that happened was that we sent out an invitation to any teacher in the school, asking them what kids couldn't do, that they would like the kids to be able to do. A physics teacher replied that the kids couldn't read the actual English on the questions. History teachers said the kids can't read, but it's up to the English Department to teach the kids to read. It was Liz's premise throughout the whole thing that Reading belongs to the whole school, it doesn't belong to the English Department, specifically because the type of reading that kids do in English is so different, and requires such different perception than the reading of hard factual theoretical prose, that the kids have to do so much...

F.   And there are probably ways that they learn to not learn in English, and to maybe fool you into thinking that they're learning, that don't work for fooling a physics teacher.

S.   I was going to mention something else...something that again came from Liz; it'll come back to me, I'm sure.

F.   Can you recall some of the...I'm guessing but I don't know if I'm guessing right about the kind of feelings that you had about your own teaching, that told you that you needed something like this.

S.   Well, I don't know. I expressed this to someone recently, and I expressed it in a very tentative way, and I liked the way it sounded, and now I'll express it more definitely, but I really don't know if I'm catching what actually happened. By a kind of accident of allotting teachers to courses, I was locked into teaching Grade 13 for 18 months, three semesters, and I realized that the kind of work that we were demanding in terms of reading comprehension and writing from Grade 13 had no basis in the way that we were reading, or grading the courses up to Grade 13. And I felt in the department that I was in--that mainly comes with the leadership or the lack

of leadership or the type of leadership in the
department--I could never contribute to any
kind of policy in the department I was in.
And--maybe I shouldn't go into it in detail, I
think the teachers in the department are quite
competent but I don't think they...because
they're swamped...So I was feeling dissatis-
fied with the Grade 13 situation, and...

F. In other words, you were having to demand more
of the kids than they had been prepared to...

S. Well...I was reducing my demands in many ways,
and I was also seeing that Grade 13 is certainly not the place for a good, energetic
teacher to be. And I had put a lot of faith
in Liz that she would set up some sort of core
program and I would become pretty active in
that. That didn't happen: her core program
eventually ended up being the Learning Course.
I think there was a kind of...

F. What was she teaching before that?

S. She had been teaching English.

F. At lower grade levels?

S. She had been a Head, they're not called head,
a Chairman of a department in a Junior High
School, and she had left that position to come
into high school, and...The thing that I was
going to say before was that she felt that a
great key to learning was learning how to work
in groups. So that a lot of the course as it
was originally envisioned was the dynamics of
groups and practising different behaviours.
And that's changed a bit, largely because I'm
not sure we can teach kids how to function in
groups. I think a lot of it's disappearing
next year.

I also have always felt that there have
been few opportunities right in front of my
nose to develop professionally. I'm not a
reader of educational magazines or anything
like that, and every course that. I've taken
always inspired me in some way, but there was
no kind of community of people to mutually
inspire each other around the school. So...

F. It kind of stopped there.

S. Yes, it stopped at the end of the weekend or
the end of the session or whatever. And
trying to implement those gems that you learn
is very haphazard, and those things self-
destruct, because you're alone in them, and
you're over- enthusiastic and overdo it

without thinking about it carefully. I guess
to summarize, I'm feeling a kind of loneliness
in the actual work I was doing, and also feeling that there had to be a way to give kids
writing skills and reading skills that wasn't
being done in the English department as it
existed in our school.

The people from other departments who were
interested in the Learning Course seemed to me
to be interested because their kids weren't
reading or writing well. There's this funny
evangelical feeling among geography and history teachers that if they can get hold of the
kid for a while they can teach them how to
read and write, but they're too busy with
their content. The other thing, which is part
of a whole general trend I sense in this
Board, is getting away from curriculum development in specific areas and opening up to
more general skills and ...development, also
the personal development of the teacher. So
there weren't as many opportunities being offered to 'professionally develop' in English.

F. Was the Learning or the Thinking course origi-
    nally supposed to be part of the English de-
    partment, or was it spread out?
S. No...
F. Were other people involved in it?
S. No, the other people were quite involved. One
    person from the Geography department was in-
    volved all the time, probably more actively
    than others at the beginning, and there were
    some science teachers who were involved, and
    then stopped being involved, I don't know why.
    That's in answer to the question of whether it
    just came from the English...
F. How did you feel about...getting involved in
    something that was so diffuse in terms of the
    subject matter?
S. Well, can I backtrack for a minute, because
    there's something I wanted to say. The origi-
    nal idea was that no teacher would teach the
    course more than once, and this is part of
    Dave's theory of professional development by
    means of 'seeding', where you get teachers who
    in some sense are influential, and you incul-
    cate something in them, and they, just by
    their changed behaviour 'seed' their separate
    departments, and they don't at all have to be
    in positions of leadership. So that, in a

way, teaching the Learning Course was for teachers' own professional development. It turns out that there has been a need to keep someone continually in the course, and it's turned out that it's been me, so far... I'll remain in it, next year. I've forgotten what your question was.

F. Oh, it doesn't matter. How do you feel about that, about 'carrying the flag' for this thing?

S. Well, it put me in a funny position, a position that I worried about all during the semester, because--and I express this worry a lot--by the end of the first semester, there was a course there. It was a course that was very clumsily put together, and it had a lot of flaws, and we were aware of the flaws, but I still felt some commitment to it. I felt that with the two new people who were coming in, I would sort of say, "This is the way it is", rather than "Here's a file of materials and dittos and references for us to use and reshape." So I felt strange about that. Also, the experience of working with two other teachers, not as a team in the teaching but as a team in planning and reflecting, was a very, very heavy experience, with a lot of problems that erupted all at once very late in the course. And I didn't relish the thought of going into a whole new potentially dangerous situation there.

What has turned out is that I don't feel that I own the course, and there is definite input from the two people who have never taught it before. But I am kind of--I don't know whether I'm using the right word--I'm usually one step ahead of them, because I know what's coming next. So, for instance today, I met with the librarian in the resources centre for what we'll be doing two weeks from now. And the other two people really have no idea what we'll be doing two weeks from now. So that's my function, more or less, at the moment, as the person who is continuing with the course.

F. Do you want to go into what you described just now as 'things that erupted at the end of the course'?

S. Yes, it's very ironic. Because of Dave and his interests at the moment and over the past few years, the course had a very heavy emphasis on group dynamics and communication, communication blocks. He's a trainer in professional growth seminars and things like that. The course had a very heavy 'socializing' content, and one of the things that we kept harping on was the idea of a group having two functions, a task function and maintenance function, and we would want the kids to...

F.   Do you want to explain the terms?

S.   The task function is getting the job done, the maintenance function is keeping good feeling going in the group. Well, we tried to show the kids that even if they were in a group project where they couldn't intellectually contribute very much, there are so many things you could do in terms of paraphrasing, in terms of supporting other people, in terms of sensing what someone feels like out in a group, that would keep the group going and facilitate getting the task done, and making the people feel good about the task and wanting to work in groups again.

Well, after preaching so much, you'd think that some of that would have rubbed off on our little group of five. It turned out that we were all harboring these separate, different burdens of grudges, and feelings of inadequacy and jealousy, that we never had time to expose to each other because we were always so busy with the task of "What are we going to teach tomorrow?" or "Where are we going to get these materials?" or "Can we order that kit before next week?" Also the tension of the impending strike worked on all of us, one of the people on the team was the Ontario Secondary School Teachers' Federation rep in the school, and the...well, anyway, we met for dinner and an open-ended meeting. And the atmosphere of the meeting, and the tension of the impending strike, and the fact that Liz was there, and she was feeling a bit, more than a bit hurt, I think, that the course had changed so much since she had conceived of it. We just vomited out all the grudges, you know: You didn't use my plan for that unit, and I feel inadequate because you're so organized, and you know, it all became very obvious once the people started verbalizing that I think that would have helped us very much, except that we had this hiatus of $2\frac{1}{2}$ months afterwards, when we were on strike. So I think that I've really learned a lot--I learned that you must practise that.

After the first interview, I felt that some direct
experience of the Learning Course would enable me
to understand it better. Sarah agreed to a visit,
and shortly after the first interview, I joined her
at school. The class I observed was a group of
about fifteen Grade 10 students; Sarah described
them as quite docile, "like tadpoles," and they
appeared cooperative and cheerful. Except for one
girl who remained near the door, students sat in a
circle and participated freely in the lesson.
Sarah was relaxed, friendly and casual. There was
some goodhumoured joking about Darryl who did not
do the assignment; he was sent outside to complete
the work but shortly returned, unsuccessful, and
another boy went out to help him. This seemed to
be a common procedure.

The topic of the first lesson was "Collecting
and Classifying". The students worked orally
through a series of exercises they had done as
homework. They were asked how they would classify
the contents of their desk drawers, cupboards, etc.
Values and personal perspectives arose quite naturally. One boy classified everything as "expensive
or cheap," and said he separated them because
otherwise the expensive things would look cheap.
Sarah added, "Or the cheap might look expensive".
The atmosphere was one in which the two opposing
attitudes toward material wealth could both find
acceptance. (Later Sarah told me the boy, at se-
venteen, ran two stores in the local market. She
also noted that his attitudes toward money did not
arise in an earlier unit on values clarification,
and this made her wonder, in retrospect, about that
unit.) One girl organized her clothes cupboard for
colour coordination, and another boy separated his
clothes into those he wore and those his mother
wanted him to wear. The exercises made the point
that classifying is a familiar activity we all do
in different, individual ways; although the role of
'purpose' in determining classification was implicit, it was not articulated.

The second half of this double lesson was on
different kinds of reading for different purposes.
Sarah asked students to suggest three nonsense
words, and she wrote these on the board. She then
used each one to refer to a different type of reading which she defined and illustrated. Students
were then asked which type of reading they would

use for various tasks. At the end of this segment, Sarah gave students the correct labels (scan, read intensely, read for pleasure) but, interestingly enough, some students had difficulty letting go of the nonsense words; clearly, they were 'taken in' by this device.

The atmosphere in this class was open and friendly. One task in the first segment of the lesson was to classify the activities of the Learning Course; students most often chose the dimensions 'boring' and 'interesting', and readily told Sarah which activities (including, for some, the present lesson) were boring.

This visit also enabled me to observe Sarah in the school. She took me to the English staffroom; she had a desk there but spent little time at it because of her negative feelings toward the English department. However, we had tea there and I noticed a chatty note in her handwriting telling people how to make use of the tea facilities, which she had set up. This incident caught my attention immediately; it seemed likely to be an indicator of the way Sarah made herself at home in her school.

Planning

Following the first interview and observation session, several months were spent developing the plan
for the study, using the first interview as a pilot
study.   Thus the first interview had been subjected
to close examination, and I brought to the second
interview a list of questions and topics for discussion.
    I was concerned to disclose to Sarah my own
purposes in carrying out the study and my conception of the research as a cooperative effort between teacher and researcher. With respect to specific issues, I wanted to probe her conception of
skills, and especially the view that there are
content-free learning skills. If there was time, I
wished to discuss her view of her role and relationship to students, as well as any topic she
might raise.

Discussion

I opened by telling Sarah of my surprise that despite my best intentions I had told her little, in
the first interview, about my work or my purposes
in conducting the interviews. I asked her what she
guessed my intentions to be. Her answer was reaso-
nably accurate: "I think you're trying to get
closer to the factors that influence a decision in
whatever he decides to do in the classroom, or
whatever he decides to do in his preparation for
being in the classroom." She added two insights
that would, she felt, necessarily limit her ability
to provide what I was interested in: first, the
fact that thinking "in operation" at school is different from thinking done while reading or studying
(and she wondered if I was trying "to bring those
two things closer together"); and second, the fact
that whatever she was telling me during the interviews might be remote from her actual school experience.   But she could do no more than try to
answer honestly.
    I then spoke at length about my own purposes
and ideas. I expressed my respect for what teachers do, and my dissatisfaction with the conceptualization which assumes teachers have experience
while academics have knowledge about teaching. I
was trying to conceptualize teaching in terms of

knowledge, understood broadly as experiential and as involving the teacher's values and purposes. I added that this work was important to me in making sense of my own experience. I expressed my discomfort at confronting her as academic versus teacher to take apart her experience, and wondered whether she too was sensitive to this.

Sarah replied that the "particular type of modesty" which came across in discussion was not part of her everyday experience; in fact, she was often challenged and had to put on a bit of a front "and assume that I know more than I really do."

I asked what interests Sarah had in holding these conversations. She said she had been prepared simply to help in my research, and even expected to remain ignorant of what it was about. But she found it a strong experience to reread the transcript, and to find that "words do capture experience, and even one's words transcribed on a page still have a life in them." One consequence for her of the first interview was that she could now admit that the course in which she had taught Othello was simply a bad course. She hoped there would be further insights of this sort, but expected nothing and was simply open to the process.

I then described the research conception I was working with, and my wish to deal with her openly and to share the insights and understanding arising out of the interview. Sarah for her part asked me to make sure I pushed her to answer my questions, as she felt she had rambled at times in the first meeting. She also confirmed that the opportunity to reflect on her own experience appealed to her (although she had more opportunity now to do so than formerly).

I suggested we discuss the concept of learning skills, but it soon became apparent that much had changed recently in Sarah's work, and she outlined these developments. She was no longer teaching English, but taught the Learning Course to one class and spent the rest of her time in the Reading Centre, where she met with students who came for help in reading and study skills. She also told me of various events which had, in effect, terminated group work on the Learning Course (though other teachers, as well as Sarah, continued to teach it).

We returned to the notion of learning skills, and Sarah spoke of this in terms of her concern to help students make sense of the many tasks they were asked to carry out. I tried to express my appreciation of the need for this, but also to formulate a possible criticism. Using as an example the lesson I had observed on Classification, I distinguished Sarah's view of classification as a useful, everyday proceedure, from a 'realist' position which claims that a classification scheme marks off existing distinctions. But, it seemed to me that on Sarah's view, classification was an arbitrary proceedure. Student responses in class had made it clear that their classification systems were related to the perspectives and values they held; Sarah readily agreed to this. I said that, for me, the point should have been made explicit, and pressed further. My point was that, while general skills like classification do exist, they are not neutral structures which function identically in any field, but vary across disciplines depending on the perspective of the person using them.

Sarah was interested, but somewhat puzzled, and said (in a portion of discussion accidentally lost) that she would need time to deal with this. Personally, I felt that the single example had been inadequate to fully convey my point.

We went on to discuss 'mystification'-- students' sense that school demands were beyond their understanding. We shared some personal experiences of mystification, and agreed that a degree of frustration was essential for learning. Sarah saw students latching on to mistaken clues (e.g. typing makes an essay better), and felt that what she offered, such as research skills, though not guaranteeing learning, were at least relevant clues, coping skills. I suggested that her goals seemed confined to things students might not need after finishing school, and asked if she felt satisfied with this. Her reply was that she put great emphasis on hidden curriculum, on the "human experience of being in the classroom." And she was pleased that in her work now she was giving empathy to students not around the subject of their personal problems but concerning how they were coping with the demands of school.

I then presented another example from the lesson observed. I had been struck by Sarah's use of nonsense words to capture students' attention in the discussion of reading styles, but noticed afterwards that students had some difficulty letting go of the nonsense words. I suggested that this device, admirable in its way, was also a kind of mystification.

This led us into a discussion of Sarah's teaching style. The use of nonsense words was a type of device she associated with a 'hyper mood'; it was a spontaneous technique which seemed to carry the interest of the class though it invariably lost some students, and which often didn't finish well because the mood faded before the activity was over. Sarah felt she used this type of technique less than she used to, partly because she was older, less rushed, less anxious to do several things at once; but "I can feel that mood coming back even as I talk about it." She was now aware of giving a "double message" in the classroom, of spontaneity combined with a sense "that I know where it's leading." I tried to clarify these notions in terms of 'mystification' and distance between the teacher and students.

Sarah mentioned an important new influence on her style, a humanistic approach to reading which she was exposed to in a Reading course. She was taking a broad view of language now, so that conversation and digressions became more acceptable, and she had an overriding concern for making kids feel happy in class and for projecting "unqualified positive regard". I asked for examples and she described the techniques she would use to begin work with a new student (e.g. an informal chat about his interests, rather than a questionnaire probing his various difficulties). Later, she gave various kinds of writing assignments, some carefully structured and others more open-ended and expressive. In choosing the kinds of assignment and the way she treated them, she took account of student needs and learning styles.

Although this approach seemed opposed to her concern for skills carefully structured and ordered in units, she did not feel any conflict in her teaching. I agreed that the conflict seemed to be a theoretical one. Sarah added that she had felt the conflict more acutely in the first interview, but that it was related to "the conflict between my confidence and my lack of confidence"--she felt highly competent to deal with specific cases but fumbled in the effort to give a broader, theoretical view of her work.

At this point the conversation seemed to open up onto a great many avenues, which both of us were reluctant to enter at that late hour. We agreed to stop, but feelings about the interview continued to spill out. Sarah described the discussion of the 'nonsense words' presentation as an epiphany for her, and expressed the sense of a great gap between the strategies she used in teaching and "what learning is." For my part, I expressed the feeling that I had not adequately backed up my point in the discussion of classification and learning skills.

Sarah then suggested we "look into how I plan to do something...all the things that are left up to chance, and mood, and time of day." She felt that she had a tendency to stop short, leaving things unfinished; "and I think that I need some practice in becoming aware of when I stop short, and why I stop short, and I think it would be beneficial to me to articulate that." We ended with a comment from me about how the discussion seemed to flow (towards the end) when I let go of my agenda and concentrated on listening to Sarah and the topic at hand.

In the excerpt which follows Sarah talks about her view of learning and her teaching style.

F. We were talking about mystification, and you had said that in your work you were responding to the idea that, this sense that kids were mystified by the demands that you were making on them. And we both tried to recall experiences that we've had of being mystified. And yours was in learning yoga, and not being able to get one's body to do what one wanted it to do. And mine was in doing pottery, and that sense of not having a clue what was being asked.

S. I think that what happens in school is that kids get a clue, and it's a mistaken clue of what's being asked, and they get these, well, they're very obvious, funny things-- if you underline things prettily, you're doing a better job, or it's so widespread that if you type it, it becomes a better piece of work. (laughter) Or, if you give back to the teacher verbatim what he said about a poem, it's good.

F. And, well, quite naturally, it's not their fault, to confuse the fact that in some circumstances you get a better mark--I guess statistically, it's been proven that you do if you type, and underline. I want to try and connect a few things. Maybe they're too many things to try and put together. The idea of mystification, the idea of the kid feeling that he's out of his depth or that he doesn't really know what's expected of him: the reason that I asked you whether you'd had that experience is because of one of my own convictions about teaching. It's not—I experienced it, and then I came across it in print as well, and I really buy it—it's the idea that it's important for the teacher to have a sense of what it is to be a learner, and what kids feel like. And...

S. I would add that it wouldn't do me much good to decide that I wanted to be a learner, and then to go out and learn something that I have a knack for. But in a sense whatever experience I'm having in yoga, I desire it because it has the frustration that I certainly didn't have, in high school or in academic work.

F. I think that's what makes an experience worth anything, that you're pushing against something. I once had the experience of being told by a teacher, I read this and it's a good paper but I don't feel that you learned anything. And it was true that I had taken a lot of stuff and put it together and ordered it, but I hadn't learned anything. I had been marking time in writing that paper. And I suppose a lot of what kids do in school is marking time in that way.

S. Could I latch onto that, for a second? I heard you making a distinction between collecting facts, or whatever it was that you had to do for that piece of work—you had put them together, but you don't know what you had learned. It would be my feeling that, under any circumstances you would have had to collect things and put them together, and either the learning would happen or it wouldn't happen, but perhaps if you hadn't collected those things, and if you hadn't known where to find them, for sure the learning wouldn't have happened.

F. Yes.

S. And I think that maybe that, in my own mind, links back to the idea of it not being called a Learning Course, but sort of a coping with school, coping with what you're asked to do in school assignments.

F. Do you confine it to that, though? Do you see it as, are you content with teaching students things that they're not going to need, say, when they leave school? That aren't going to make any difference later on? Is it just, I can't believe that. I guess I shouldn't have asked the question in a negative way--that you're teaching something that is just enabling them to get through these four years.

S.   Well, I guess in answer to that I would depend on the--I guess by now it's a pretty cliched notion--the second curriculum or whatever it's called, what the kids learn from the human experience of being in the classroom and the way an adult reacts to them and the way an adult, I guess, helps to create an environment where they react to each other. And all those, that's where I've put my money about learning. I'n not really sure how much learning goes on in the so-called assignments kids do, but I think that a lot of important, sometimes spectacular and sometimes really destructive things happen in the classroom, and I suspect that that's what the kid leaves high school with. And I guess the coinage, or the medium that I'm using lately is saying to the kid, I care about you, not the way the guidance counselor gives the message "I care about you and all your personal problems", but I care about you and how you're surviving around here. And I think that in my reference to 'coming from' a different place of my personality or my relationship with the kids, lately I've felt that I'm giving a lot of concern and a lot of empathy, and it's feeling sincere to me, but the subject at hand is not the kid's stepmother or abortion or whatever it used to be in past years, but rather how the kid is coping with the demands being made on him in the classroom. It's a completely different experience for me.

F.   I guess it has to do with who you are with the kids. Let me just throw something else at you, because it was something nice that I watched, again in that lesson, and I guess it's as appropriate here as anywhere else. You remember you were talking about different kinds of reading- scanning, and reading...

S.   Oh, was that...the time you were there?

F.   Yes, I think it was the first half of that lesson.

S.   Oh yes, it was sort of dovetailing...it wasn't

dovetailing, it was ending one thing and beginning something else (laughter).

F.   Yes. And you started off by asking them to
give you three nonsense words, which you wrote
on the board. And then you used each one for
a different kind of reading.

S.   Mm-hmm.

F.   And you asked them, and they gave you examples, and so on. And then at the end, you
said, okay, these things are called 'scanning', and 'reading for pleasure', and--I
forget--whatever...

S.   Intensive reading, inventory, or some such
thing.

F.   And one little thing that happened was that
some of the kids had trouble letting go of the
nonsense words.

S.   Mm-hmm.

F.   And it worked--as evidenced by the fact that
they didn't want to let go of the words afterwards, and they maintained interest in what
wasn't a particularly exciting lesson.

S.   (laughs) That's for damn sure.

F.   So it worked. But then I thought, well,
there's something else there, though, and
it's, in a way it's mystification too, of a
somewhat different kind, in that they didn't
know what you were doing with the nonsense
words, at the beginning.

S.   Mm-hmm.

F.   And maybe at the end they figured it out, I
don't know. I don't know to what extent they
reflect on teachers and teacher techniques, to
think about why you had done that. Do you
think they would have thought about it, or
been aware of it, or not?

S.   My main thought about that is that that type
of thing I do usually isn't planned; I know I
didn't plan that. I don't remember exactly
why I did it, but it's usually the kind of
thing that comes at a very 'hyper' moment,
that happens to me maybe five minutes before
the class, or...I'm usually feeling--now it
might have been your presence. It might have
been, I remember it was a rushed day, or something extraordinary happened that morning, I
don't know, or it felt as if it had. And I'm
also aware, in that particular kind of activity, that the 'hyperness' on my part often
leaves before the activity is over, and that

those things don't get finished well. O.K., I don't think I would have had the presence of mind to say, "Look, I used those nonsense words and we had some fun with them, but let me explain why I used them." I think perhaps that one of my reasons for using them was that I didn't...let's say the word 'inventory' was one of the words that I wanted to replace. Maybe I felt that they knew the word 'inventory' in another context, and I didn't want to start dealing with that at the beginning.

F. Mm-hmm.

S. I don't know, I don't want to give myself that credit, because I think it did come in a hyper mood, and I do that far less often than I used to, I think I have fewer hyper moments in the classroom. But I can feel that mood coming back even as I talk about it.

F. Yes, I'm sort of...I'm not criticizing it, I have mixed emotions about it, and they're emotions much more than judgments. Because my on-the-spot reaction to it was to psych into what it is that makes you a good teacher, and, well, I guess, to have a sense of the hyper feeling, and to kind of admire it. But later on, I thought, well, what's happening here is that there's something you know, and the kids don't know.

S. Mm-hmm.

F. To go back to what you said before, about kids assuming that the teacher knows the answers. You put it very well before, that kids expect the teacher will punish them for not knowing what's inside the teacher's head. And so you're injecting a little bit of that, and it's putting a certain distance between you and the students. Whether or not he thinks about it, perhaps more so if he doesn't think about it. And that's one small element, and not a negative one either, not a negative one because...well, I suppose one part of your job is to be distant from your students, to bring certain things to their attention and engage them in those things, and not to be a teaching machine that just is there, obviously (laughs). So it's a distance, but it's...that particular item of it might not have been calculated, but the general stance that you have is calculated.

S. Mm-hmm. Something that I've become aware of,

not very recently but in the last couple of years, is that I do give a double message, and both aspects of that message are obvious to me. A message of spontaneity in the classroom, but also a message that I know where it's leading, and I think that that particular business of the three nonsense words would be a good example of that. I'm not sure which, if I had to lean more in one of those directions, I'm not sure which,--well, I shouldn't say I'm not sure because I guess that my behaviour lately has been more in the direction of "This is what we're up to next, and this is what we've been doing," and then, I guess within that...

F.   Is that--which one is that, of the two directions? I know where it's leading?

S.   I think that's the one that you spoke of in terms of distance.

F.   Well, but there's a big difference between... you know, there can be distance with mystification, and there can be distance without it, and setting out for them where things are leading, and why, is deliberately trying to avoid mystification. (pause) I can't think of an instance of it now, but I think that I've had it, and you've had it, and we've all had it, of the teacher who was very spontaneous, gave the impression of being with students, and yet was mystifying all the time, in the sense that it was the teacher's personality that was kind of holding the whole thing together. So that there was a lot of control being exerted just by the charisma of the personality, with nothing much rational about it.

S.   Mm-hmm. I can think of some teachers in the school where I work. I guess they annoy me because they seem to carry things off so easily on the basis of a certain type of energy. They seem to be much more consistent. I'm much more...harrassed, a lot of the time (laughs). There's a kind of clarity in what they're doing. But on the other hand, I'm not sure I like what they're doing. There is a certain type of kid that likes that.

F.   I don't think it does very much for independence, for the kid. (pause) I recall that the last time you talked about that as well, and it was related to the notion of learning skills, that as a result of focusing on learning skills, you were doing more of this kind of thing--planning out the course of where you were going, and providing that for kids.

S.   Mm-hmm.

F.   Do you see that your teaching is changing as a result of that exposure, or as a result of the new things that you're teaching? The different kinds of concerns, for skills, and for setting things out? (pause) Is it related to doing less of the spontaneous kind of thing?

S.   I think that less of the spontaneous kind of thing is really a matter of, as I said in the last conversation, of being five years older. That hyperness has disappeared because I'm not rushing from one thing to another, I'm not in a hurly-burly of a lesson and a discussion with a kid after a lesson, and catching a kid I want to speak to before the next lesson begins. I'm walking into the lesson much more slowly, and I'm probably breathing a lot more slowly as I walk up to the front of the room, so I think that what isn't happening before every class is a factor in what is happening. Another influence on me lately, and I hope this isn't throwing a curve into what you're trying to do, is that, in the interim between the last conversation and this conversation, I've taken two courses and am in the process of taking a third, which nominally deal with reading, but the subplot of the whole thing, I guess, is a humanistic approach to the classroom and to working individually with the kids, and a new set of vocabulary, like "unqualified positive regard", and...

F.   What?

S.   Unqualified positive regard, and I don't like the sound of it, but it...I think it's obvious that when dealing remedially with kids with a whole history of failure, maybe you can institute a change through having the kid see himself and perceive the problem in a different light, and that often is achieved by looking at the kid much more positively than he's been looked at before. Those ideas, plus some new ideas about language that I've been exposed to through lectures, but haven't had a chance to do much reading about yet, are making me realize how...well, it's a very simple idea that language is everywhere, it isn't only in the essay that the kid writes, and it isn't only in the written work that the kid does. But those are influences that have changed my teaching. I'm delighted to see two kids chatting during a class, which would have never happened before. I'm much more willing to stop and tune into something else that is happening in the class, and almost throw the lesson out the window.

So those are influences on me that are changing the teaching, and it's a funny combination, because I spoke last time of being much more organized, and much more compartmentalized into units, and now I've got this other thing that's on my mind a lot, which is trying to make the kid happy to walk into that class, and I don't feel they're in conflict. I feel that combination is working toward a slightly different style. You know, if you were to walk into the classroom, you might not notice it, but I feel it inside. The nice thing about this third course that I'm presently taking is that I've never seriously taken a course while I'm teaching; it's always been in the summer, or on leave from school for a couple of days. And it's very nice to have the idealism and the new ideas on Tuesday night, but still to come from the reality of Tuesday, and back to the reality of Wednesday. I think it's a much better learning experience for me.

Planning

The second interview had been highly satisfying to
me because of the sense of mutual exchange that I
took away from it. However, I was unprepared for
the magnitude of the change Sarah had made in moving from the teaching of English to work in the
Reading Centre. Thus, although the discussion of
Sarah's teaching style and the content of the Learning Course had raised many questions, it seemed
advisable to postpone these questions until the
background to the change in Sarah's work had been
filled in. The questions I formulated for the
third interview dealt, therefore, with this change.
I wanted to know when and on what basis Sarah had
made her decision, the influence on this decision
of her feelings about teaching literature, the contribution she hoped to make, and the training she
had obtained. Also, I was interested in her feelings after three months of work in the Reading
Centre, what subject matter she was drawing on in
the work, and what role she was taking vis-à-vis
students since she had stressed being 'on their
side' in the Learning Course. In fact, the topics
discussed in this interview followed this list of
questions closely, but also in what seems to be a
natural sequence. The use of a list of questions
did not appear to be the hindrance it sometimes was
earlier.
     When I arrived for the interview, it became
apparent that Sarah was preoccupied with an important personal matter. As the interview had been
scheduled in advance and had necessitated travel on
my part, the question of postponing it did not
arise, as it certainly would have under other circumstances. The interview proved to be the longest
one in the series. I suspect that Sarah was concerned to fulfil her commitment despite her personal situation. For my part, I made an effort to
direct my questions toward matters of information
and did not try to probe sensitive issues. Thus
the discussion that resulted was extremely matter
of fact, detailed and in some respects superficial.

Discussion

We began by exchanging responses to the transcript
of the previous interview. I expressed embar-

rassment at the lecture I had given Sarah on my
views and purposes, but she told me she had found
this reassuring. We both confirmed a sense that
the discussion had moved in mutually beneficial
directions, and Sarah also said that reviewing her
comments about the Reading Centre helped her to see
and appreciate progress that had been made since
she began working there. However, while the second
interview had given her a sense of new ideas and
directions to work on, she had been unable to make
use of these. The discussion of classification, in
particular, inhibited her; she felt a challenge to
restructure the lesson, but did not know how to go
about it. The next time around, there had been
sufficient practical constraints to justify simply
eliminating the lesson.

I asked about the background to Sarah's decision to move into Reading, and she explained this
at length, describing the English department she
left, and her feelings about teaching English literature. We then talked about the professional
development activities in which Sarah had taken
part over the years, and about her concerns with
communication, group work and writing.

We went on to discuss Sarah's work in the Reading Centre: her tasks, the various resources on
which she was drawing, some typical incidents, problems she was working on, basic ideas she made use
of and so forth.

Finally, we talked about Sarah's role in the
classroom and about her relationship to students.
I suggested that Sarah was putting herself on the
side of students, helping them to function in the
system and to cope with its demands. She responded
that she was comfortable with this formulation and
with the role itself, for she had found the situation in which she was perceived as the one who judges students, passes or fails them, to be a "very
phony structure." I commented that there seemed
to be two opposed modes of teaching behind our
discussion: one that of dispensing knowledge, the
other that of dealing with students and their immediate experience. I pointed out that there were
alternatives to these two, for example the possibility of dealing with students' experience in such a
way as to articulate it as knowledge. Sarah and I
both agreed that perhaps in teaching Reading this
option was not available to her, and it seemed that
such an alternative had not been available to her
as an English teacher.

The following portion of transcript deals with Sarah's decision to become a Reading teacher, and with her view of English teaching.

F.   I'd really like to know how you came to the decision to move to the Reading Centre.

S.   Well, lately I've begun to see most of the decisions I make as coming through the back door rather than the front door. This was definitely a back-door type of decision. Quite casually in a conversation with Dave, the vice-principal I worked with on the Learning Course last year, I--he was in charge of Professional Development in the school, which meant that he had a box of brochures on his desk (laughs), that I would snoop through every once in a while and go to a lecture or a weekend or something like that, and he had posted a notice that Professional Development courses for the summer were available-- applications were available in his office. I wandered in one day, and it was probably a day when I had a spare at the end of the day and nothing that I really wanted to do in it, and I asked him if he had an application for the Reading course, which, I guess, was understood by both of us to be the course that the Ministry offers. He asked me if I was interested in Reading, and I said, not particularly in Reading, but, considering that I've been at the school for five years, and have been teaching English for five years, it seems to me that I'm in the process of running dry, and that within the next five years, I'd like to develop some kind of lateral--some way of doing a different job without necessarily having to seek promotion, because in terms of my own...the way I am, I don't want to seek a promotion, in the...(unclear). So he said, "Oh, so you're interested in reading? "And I said, "Well for the time being anyway." But (laughs) he said, "Well, would you like to do Reading at the school next year?" And I said, "I don't know, I'll think about it."

     I might actually be telescoping two conversations now. But my idea certainly was to start getting qualified in another field, or in another couple of fields, so that by the time I'm 35, 36, 37, I could perhaps be away from the pressures of the classroom all

day long, and be into something else, without
having to become a department head or who
knows what. So I did take the Reading course
--I felt forced to take it after I had, within
a week, committed myself to doing Reading in
the school. Now there is a precedent, there's
a woman who was hired last year to do English,
and then in a staff shift she became a Reading
teacher. So what the school had decided to do
was to staff the Reading Centre all day, and
they did some manoeuvering and finagling, and
I became a Reading teacher also.

The immediate payoff for me was that I
began to realize how uncomfortable I was in
the English department, in the human aspect of
the English department. I think I mentioned
before that everyone was moving right, very
rapidly, and becoming very rigid and narrow,
with all these newspaper articles about getting 'back to basics', and things like that.
So that I looked upon the prospect of doing
Reading--well, I welcomed the prospect of
working with Ellen, because I liked the kind
of things she had been doing that year, and I
was happy to get out of the English department, for a while. And the challenge of doing
something new interested me. And I especially
liked the idea of being away from that hotbed,
in the English department. I personally was
in a funny position in the English department,
because I felt my credibility slipping, almost
hour by hour, and the kind of discussions that
were going on constantly there were annoying
me to a point where I think I wasn't functioning in the classroom the way I usually do.
That's a summary of the back-door ways I got
into Reading.

F. Certainly it's very...condensed. How, first
    of all, does it connect up with the Learning
    Course?

S. In terms of the structure of the day?

F. No, when you started to get interested in Rea-
    ding you had already planned the Learning
    Course?

S. Oh, the interest in Reading came out of my
    responsibility to do the unit on Reading in
    the Learning course. What I did was, I spent
    not long at all, maybe it was just a couple of
    hours at the professional library. I went
    with some ideas, and then they were reinforced

by what I read, and then when I set up a unit and went to Ellen, just to look at it and give me some suggestions for exercises, she seemed excited that I had reached these conclusions that she had reached on her own also. She could provide me with materials that I didn't know about. So that the interest in Reading really came from that responsibility I had in the Learning Course.

F.   So it was after that, that you thought to move into Reading?

S.   Yes, Mm-hmm.

F.   Had you, at that point, already taught the Learning Course?

S.   I was into teaching it a second time already. All of this transpired around May of last year.

F.   I see. It was probably just around the time we met.

S.   I might not even have known about it.

F.   Perhaps you didn't.

S.   I'm sure I would have mentioned it.

F.   I think so. I know that I knew about this, but I don't think I knew specifically... (unclear)...Okay...(long pause) ...Can you fill in a bit about the English Department, because I know about 'back to basics', but I can't really understand how that could have been affecting you teaching in ...(unclear)... I just don't know enough about the context.

S.   Well, what happened in the English department was that the Head and the Assistant Head seized upon the 'back to basics' business in the press as a justification for returning to the grammar and highly structured, "composition" approach that had been, basically, the approach that I learned under, fifteen years ago. And the Head of the department set up all kinds of structures where people who were working on certain courses or certain grade levels would meet together to set up criteria for the following year. What happened was that he chose people to be the chair-people of these committees, who more or less were dancing to his own tune, and I attended several of those meetings and heard things that seemed to me to be ridiculous.

Now I must have been pretty unbalanced, at that time, in my own opinions, because I remember the venom I felt toward the other people. But it was the kind of thing where they would set down a list of requirements for Grade 10, and one of them would be, "A formal essay". And then they'd go on to discuss the next requirement, which would be "Survey of poetry, from the 16th-20th centuries", let's say. And--I felt that I was screaming--I kept on saying, it doesn't do any good just to write those things down. We have to think of ways, if we want a formal essay, first of all, let's decide if Grade 10 is the best place for it, and second of all, wherever it is, we have to realize that we have to teach the kids some things before we mark the kids on them. And it seems to me that this whole approach of giving a list of the finished products of what we want kids to do isn't getting us anywhere.

The other thing is that they had developed all these structures, that if a kid makes five spelling mistakes he loses five marks, and if he makes six, he loses five and a half marks, etcetera. And I kept on saying that this isn't improving the standards (laughter); being punitive does nothing to improve the standards, and what are we doing to encourage kids to write, and to encourage kids to feel that writing is a valid form of expression, in the same way as their clothing or the way they play basketball. Actually I've forgotten the question...(unclear)...(laughter)...but maybe in summary I can say that the climate in that English department was very, very alienating, for me. And I think it's obvious that no matter how firm I felt in my own beliefs, it made me shaky in the classroom. You know, when you've just come from a meeting talking about all the grammatical structures that are going to be taught, and then you go into a classroom and have an informal conversation about something for a few minutes, I think you feel a fair amount of guilt, no matter how strong your own views are. So that's the kind of thing that was happening in the English department then.

The other thing that I argued for very strongly--maybe more strongly than I really felt--was that it wasn't absolutely necessary to teach Shakespeare every year. I tried to show people that, for a student, learning

Shakespeare was like learning a foreign language, and that I didn't think a quarter of the course should be taken up teaching the student what he felt was a foreign language. To circumvent learning the foreign language, he would go to things like Cole's notes, and then regurgitate them on an essay, and I felt that was quite futile. But there were certain people in the department who sounded as if I was cursing motherhood or something, so there was no communication about that. (pause) It was quite an uncomfortable situation for me.

F.   Mm-hmm. (pause) Last time you said something about, "I'm not defending literature anymore." And I wondered about that: first of all, what you meant, and second of all, whether that kind of feeling had something to do with your making this change.

S.   (pause)...Well, I think that in what I was talking about, I was really referring to a concept that I've been very aware of lately, of how the class controls the teacher. If you come into a class, and are excited about a poem or a story or something, and the kids catch that excitement, that reinforces you, and it reinforces you the next time you plan that lesson, let's say the next semester you're teaching it. If consistently a class registers very lukewarm responses to things, or understands something on a level that's so far below your own expectations, I think that eventually that kind of feedback becomes very, very debilitating (laughs). And...I guess the best way I can describe the change in my feelings about teaching literature is that last year, when I was teaching literature, I could hear my own voice an awful lot of the time (laughs), which makes me think that I was being quite self-conscious about what I was saying. And I certainly don't have that now when I teach the Learning Course, and I don't remember it from past years.

The other thing to remember is that, in the courses that I've been allotted to teach, I haven't been teaching a lot of literature lately, because I've had a Writer's Workshop, which was a writing course, obviously, and a Grade 13 Themes Course, which was more a course based on ideas. We would take something like Walden, or Walden Two, and read

excerpts of it, rather than "literature"--
James Joyce, T.S. Eliot, something like that.
So I had been away from a straight literature
course, the way that Grade 11 course was, for
a long time, and maybe I felt the difference.
I was never the kind of teacher who would get
up and read a soliloquy and break into tears,
or something like that (laughter). I think I
was known as a teacher who wasn't too up in
the clouds at all, and very often I'd get a
response in student evaluations at the end of
a semester, where the kid would say, "You're
the first English teacher I've ever understood," or a kid would say, "I'll always remember the conversation we had about such-and-
such." So I wasn't 'defending literature' in
the sense of trying to convince them how great
Shakespeare was, but I did feel an obligation
to open them up a bit to an appreciation of
literature, and as time went by that seemed to
be more and more of a futile process. There
was also the problem of teaching, let's say
Portrait of the Artist as a Young Man, to kids
who didn't read, who didn't read for pleasure.
So that the gap there was tremendous.

F. Did you have much choice about the material
you would teach?

S. No. In the system I work in, the texts are
pretty well prescribed, but because no one
comes and visits your classroom, you have a
fair amount of autonomy in how you're going to
treat the courses. I'll give you an example:
there are some teachers who treat Othello as a
jumping-off point for talking about Freud, or
modern psychological interpretations of jealousy, or talking about women's liberation in
terms of Desdemona and Emilia and Bianca. And
that's quite exciting for the kids, actually,
but it's not studying Othello.

F. Would they go through a course, taking the
prescribed texts and relating them to contemporary issues?

S. Yes, that's an approach that some teachers
take. I get the impression from what I see--
I'm much more mobile in the school now, because I'm always running down to the office,
or going to talk to a teacher about something
while classes are going on, and I see a lot of
English teachers, more than I used to, I
think, standing at the front of the class tal-

king. You very rarely see a teacher in a pose of listening to the students. Kids don't seem as sleepy as they used to; they all seem quite alert, but it's the teacher talking up there and there's no doubt about that, at least in the English wing of the school.

F. Do you think that's got something to do with the 'back to basics'?

S. Definitely. I think that the English department has really been bitten by something, and in feeling so threatened, their vision has considerably narrowed.

F. Can you explain a bit more?

S. Well, I think that the strike made teachers very paranoid, and it made them a bit 'holier-than-thou'. And then, when they got this second series of blows in the press--I think it was sometime in late winter--about literacy, and the lack of it, they...I think as a profession we felt completely emasculated. I think that business of the narrow vision is very strong, in the sense that, well--if kids aren't writing the way they used to, and if they used to learn grammar, then therefore if we restore grammar they'll learn better. And just because that sounds logical (laughs), doesn't mean that it's the truth. (pause)

F. I'm curious about this: In the time that you were teaching English, what sort of things did you seek out in terms of professional development? What directions did you go?

S. Well, I was aware a long time ago that talk was important in the classroom, and even in a class that seems very active, it's only, let's say, 10 out of the thirty people who are talking--I think the teacher usually perceives it as extremely active if there's an exchange among ten--but it's not an interchange, it's a ping—pong ball always going back to the teacher. I realized that group work was probably the answer, or one answer, but--you have to do more than just put kids in groups, and you have to do more than put them in groups with a highly-structured task. So, I remember attending a workshop at OISE (The Ontario Institute for Studies in Education) called, "The teacher as group leader", and I had either misinterpreted the pamphlet, or else the pamphlet was very ambiguous, but what they were really trying to do was train teachers to be in positions of committee leaders and project leaders, and it was professional development for teachers among teachers. But I did get some of those insights that are quite in vogue now about shared leadership, and establishing goals, and maintenance tasks and keeping the group feeling good about what it's doing rather than just pushing it to get the job done, and each person recognizing his own strengths in a group, and working from those rather than trying to conform to an image of a certain kind of person who is terrific in groups. Well, all of that made me realize how complex the idea of working in groups was, and fortunately I had the Learning Course where we actually had a unit called "Group Work", and we could do a lot of these structured exercises. So the Learning Course eventually became the outlet for that series of sessions on group work.

I was always very alert to listening for ideas in writing. I didn't take a year of teacher training at college, so I never got taught how to do things (laughter)...

F.   Those two facts may not be related at all (laughs).

S.   But I never learned, let's say...Apparently D. was the important teacher of poetry, and he had a method, but I never learned the method, so I never had to go beyond the D. Method, because I didn't know what it was. But I always assumed that there was something wrong, even in my early years of teaching, in having the only thing the kids wrote being literary criticism. It seemed to me that kids have to write from a more personal side of their personality. So a lot of what I looked for in books or in bookstores, was practical ideas on how to get kids to write using voices other than that very austere voice of literary criticism. So that was professional development that I sought in books and workshops.

<u>Planning</u>

At the close of the second interview, Sarah had
suggested we meet for a session in which she planned a lesson so that we could follow this process
through to the actual lesson, to see what was provided for, and what left up to chance.   The third
interview had provided a comprehensive picture of
Sarah's work up to and including her job in the
Reading Centre.   I was eager, therefore, to return
to the questions of planning and teaching style
that had been raised earlier.
    The topic of the lesson to be planned and
taught was not agreed on in advance--partly for
technical reasons but largely because Sarah's major
concern seemed to be with her teaching style and
this, I felt, would be equally accessible to us
regardless of the subject matter of the lesson.
However, when we met for the planning session,
Sarah informed me that she had already planned the
lesson I would observe the next day.   I was somewhat disappointed, but also puzzled because the
suggestion to conduct this particular exercise had
been Sarah's, and I had put no pressure on her
beyond asking her to choose a lesson which raised
issues of importance to her.

<u>Discussion</u>

Against this background we began the discussion
with rather lengthy mutual apologies.   I commented
that the goal of simulating a planning session had
been an artificial one; it would suffice for my
purposes if Sarah merely indicated typical kinds of
concerns in planning.   For her part, Sarah explained that she had planned the lesson in advance
because of the need to be sure xeroxed materials
would be ready.   She then described at length the
steps she had already taken students through in
working on essay writing.   This description led to
the fact that students had requested a week's break
to read and take notes for their essays, and because she had been unwilling to go on to one of the
long units remaining in the course, she had opted
to fill in with some 'left-overs'--lessons on reading and study skills which she considered important, but which had no fixed place in the course.
The lesson I was to observe was on 'Inventory', a

technique for close learning of dense factual material, which involves reading the passage (by paragraphs if it is long), deciding on the main idea, and then covering it sentence-by- sentence asking, and answering, questions about each sentence and making predictions. Sarah explained the preliminary work already done and the lesson itself; she had chosen a passage from a Grade 10 science text on the nitrogen cycle on which to try out the inventory technique.

Sarah listed a number of concerns: she would be unable to deal with questions on the scientific content of the passage, if any arose; she was afraid some students would be baffled by the text; she didn't know how long the task would take--and had prepared additional work if needed; and she mentioned a student with a learning disability, whom she found it difficult to deal with, and with whom she wanted help.

I remarked that Sarah's comments were mainly intended to assist me in observing the lesson; I wondered what her 'notes to herself' were. She expressed, first, her concern to present the techniques as useful for all studying, not simply as tasks performed in the Learning Course; and she reminded herself that students would have difficulty following instructions. Sarah pointed out that she generally went into class without a detailed lesson plan, but with extra materials to keep students busy if they finished early. She then indicated several broader concerns. The first was related to the general intent of the course: she felt it was preparing students for tasks which teachers were not demanding (i.e. teachers were not using textbooks, were not expecting well-researched and carefully structured essays) and which students would never practise. In part this was due to the fact that the academically-oriented course was being taught to non-academic students, a problem which would be solved by offering the course on a higher grade level next year. However, it seemed to me that the issue was more fundamental, since the original intent of the course had been to provide basic learning skills. A second major concern was with Sarah's teaching style: she felt she "gave too much, challenged too little." After some examples, we concluded. Here is an excerpt from the discussion.

S.   What I can do is go over with you some of the

decisions that were made in the making of tomorrow's lesson, and they're quite typical, I
think, and not very artificial at all. The
reason the lesson is planned is that I had to
prepare some material after school today, and
what with Xerox machines and everything, I'm
never competent about (...unclear).

I have been working with the kids in a
very slow,and for me painstaking, series of
steps that take place up to the writing of a
formal essay. Now the whole question about
whether these particular kids should or should
not be equipped to write a formal essay is
something that maybe we could discuss, but my
justification for it is that it was originally on the course, and that in themselves the
steps perhaps have some value.

F. Mm-hmm
S. Would you like me to go into that series of
steps, because it explains why I'm not doing
any more on the essay work tomorrow. The
kids chose topics which...most of them chose
them from a list which had been prepared by
the librarian and myself, based on what the
kids seemed most interested in, the kind of
paperbacks that kids were requesting and the
library was buying. Subjects like rape, gam-
bling, adoption--as I mentioned before, the
stock market, Jimmy Carter, things they had
picked up interest in through the newspaper--
ESP, things like that--dreams, sleep.

They spent a week--five lessons--in the
library with the teaching librarian there, and
she took them through a series of steps that
supposedly work in doing any kind of research:
setting up alternatives, subject headings,
using magazine index, vertical files, reference materials, things like that. They were
tested on that, and then they set up a trial
bibliography, which had them investigating
various sources of material. And then they
started note-taking, and I was quite stringent
about how I wanted them to take notes, and
supervised it quite closely for a while, making sure that they weren't doing straight
copying all the time, and making sure that
they were getting a fair quantity and that
they were previewing the material before they
started writing from the first paragraph,
etcetera.

My original plan was to give them not very long for the note-taking, and to collect the notes and make sure that they were adequate, then begin to have private conversations with the kids about the form that they saw this essay taking, and I had already done some work on taking a series of notes and classifying them in different ways. I thought that all of that could be done as one unit, without bringing in any other work or any other units, but the kids were objecting quite strongly to a lack of time, and they said that they wanted more time to take notes.

So what I did, basically, was left them on their own to take notes for about a week, and started something else, which is what I'm more or less rounding off tomorrow. It doesn't organically grow out of the essay writing work, but the other alternative would have been to start the Values Education part of the course or the Communications part of the course, the group work part of the course, and I didn't want to do that because those are two units that I want to work with someone in the Counselling Department on. I'm not satisfied with the units the way they are, and I can't go farther on my own. And the other woman who's teaching the course wants that equally. We had originally planned to do that at the end of May and first few weeks of June, and we left it like that. So what I'm doing now is something that I think should be on the course, but it's stuck in at not a very appropriate time. What it is, is mainly material taken from a reading series called Tactics in Reading, which as far as I've seen is the best approach to reading non-fiction.

The particular unit that we're dealing with now is called "Inventory". Inventory is, as I see it, a study skill, and it's used when you have material very dense with facts that you have to commit more or less to memory. Basically, what you do when you take inventory is that you read the passage, or if the passage is very long you read a paragraph at a time. You decide what the main idea is, what's going on, in one or two words. Then you go back and, as it says, take inventory. You read a sentence and then ask a question about the sentence and then answer the question. Once you're sure that's okay, you go on to the next sentence. And as you get more adept at it, you learn which sentences you don't have to take, that are put there to keep the reader's interest or as an additional example or whatever. And in some cases, at the end of a certain part of the material, you predict what's going to come next, and prediction is a very important part of the reading process as I see it.

So, on Friday, the kids got the preliminary exercises which I had xeroxed, on inventory. There were a lot of absences--it was a Friday afternoon class--and because the class is so small, I think it was three absences all together, it made it seem like a very empty class. Today, Monday, we spent most of the class doing the next two exercises together, and gave the kids who had been absent a chance to catch up. Now, all this seems kind of useless to me unless the kids can find a way, or it can be demonstrated to the kids that this approach works on real life materials that they encounter. Well, there's no one subject that all of them take, and the reading level in the class is very divergent: there are good readers, kids who are reading at Grade 10, 11 and 12 levels, and then there are some readers who I would say, if they were tested, were reading at a Grade 5 or 6 level. And what I tend to do, I think, is to take more into consideration the kids who are the lower readers, and try to give them a feeling of success. What I did for tomorrow is I xeroxed a very short section of the Grade 10 textbook, a Grade 10 Science textbook. It's about three or four paragraphs long, and the title of it is "The Nitrogen Cycle", and as a series of paragraphs, the're self-contained.

What I'd like to do is...hopefully, the kids will be baffled by it on a first reading ...and give the kids a chance to try out the inventory method and see if it works. So what I have with me in this file is the passage, and the work that they did on Friday and Monday so that you can see what they've been exposed to already. I'm unsure about a couple of things. First of all, I have no background in science, and if they start asking me what are bacteria, or what is nitrogen, I'll have no way of answering. And I really didn't feel like equipping them with science dictionaries or anything like that, because I don't feel that's the object of the exercise. So I'm concerned about that. (pause) I'm also concerned that a couple of kids will be lost, still be overly baffled by the material, and I also have no idea how long it's going to take. We have a forty-minute period in the morning, and another forty-minute period in the afternoon, and the way I presented this is a study method used when you have to commit a lot of facts to memory. We've done other work on skimming and scanning, and getting the general idea, previously. And if it doesn't take very much time, there's something that I've been meaning to do for a long time, and it seems to me that I need about half an hour for it, and I've prepared for that, although we might not get to it.

What it is, you're familiar with it, I'm sure, is when you have to commit to memory a list that makes no sense to you--one example that I have is the names of the Group of Seven--I'm sure that a lot of teachers demand knowing the seven names. You put the names in a list, and take the first letter of each name and you make up a sentence that does make sense to you, and then you remember the sentence forever, and you can always rhyme off the names of the Group of Seven (smiling). Now that's fun, and I have two lists for them. One list is taken from a Grade 12 Biology textbook, about the characteristics of living organisms, which someone did have to commit to memory, someone who comes to the Reading Centre. So I know it's a kind of task that the kids do have to do at the beginning of a course they might be taking next year, and it's a fun way of doing it, and I think it might have some carry-over in other subjects.

That's basically the kind of thing we're going to be doing tomorrow. I can't say whether it's very characteristic of the type of work we do, The material is here if you want to look at it.

F. Okay.

S. So, that's what's happening tomorrow. The kids have to hand in their notes for the essay on Thursday, so some of them will probably be concerned about that, and ask me about that. There's one thing that I'd like you to be aware of in the class, because I'd like some help with it. There's one particular student who has a learning disability and I suffer a lot of tension with him (laughs). I've noticed that things that he does rile me and upset me, that can be done a second later by another student and elicit a smile from me or a shrug of my shoulders. I don't particularly want to go into why this kid upsets me, but the fact is that he does, and the fact is that I show it. An additional fact is that he was absent one day last week, and it was idyllic for me. So I want you to be aware of that; his name is Mark, and unless he's intimidated by you, and I don't think he will be, his behaviour is very noticeable. So that's a feature of the class that's always there.

Observation II

I spent the day with Sarah at her school (following the first part of Interview IV the previous evening). During the morning I observed her work in the Reading Centre, and one session of the Learning Course class. After lunch, I attended the second session of the Learning Course class, and we then returned to the Centre to discuss it.

The Reading Centre consisted of two small, adjoining offices, used by Sarah and her co-worker, Ellen. Sarah's room was windowless but pleasantly decorated. I sat at a corner desk, perused the selection of books on the shelves, and listened in on the sessions Sarah had with two of her regular students. Joe, a genial grade 12 student, brought in his Biology text and wanted help in studying for a quiz. Sarah went over some of the material with him, following the text and helping him to define terms.

Mary, whom Sarah mentioned yesterday (Interview IV, Part I), came in to work on the novel she was assigned in her English class. It was evident that Mary had been thrown into near panic by this assignment. She worked along with Sarah, reading and discussing brief passages, with Sarah doing a good deal of advance explaining to convey to her the basic dilemma of the story. Mary seemed to be comprehending the explanations, but when Sarah left

216

the room briefly and a fellow-student in Mary's English class stopped by, Mary's panic reappeared and she wailed that she did not understand the book at all. The boy gave her a brief explanation, which she seemed not to hear, repeating again that she simply did not understand. Mary seemed to be paralyzed by the book, and I wondered whether there was any comprehension in her passive acceptance of Sarah's explanations. I was struck by the unfairness of this blow delivered to a weak student who had just begun to make progress in reading. Sarah's comment about giving too much, challenging too little, also came to mind: this student had been dealt a challenge she could not meet, surely; but it may be that she was being further debilitated by Sarah's well-intentioned and correct help.

We went on to the Learning Course, which met in one of several prefabricated structures on the school grounds. Nine or ten students, lively and friendly, were present. As Sarah had anticipated, there was much chatter and questionning about prior assignments, scheduling of the next few classes and completion of the essay work. She handled this in a friendly but businesslike way, terminating the discussion after a few minutes with "I wasn't opening up discussion for complaints." I wondered how Sarah would introduce me, and whether she would involve me in the class; she said simply that I was a friend who wanted to come to school with her. A student sitting in front of me struck up a conversation, and another made sure I received material Sarah handed out, but for the most part I was ignored. When the text was distributed, Sarah learned that about half the students had just studied the nitrogen cycle in science. She expressed regret, but asked them to do the exercise anyhow. She reviewed with the class the steps involved in inventory, and students began to work independently on the passage. Sarah moved around the room, assisting and discussing the work with individual students. After a while, she threw out a few questions: How did the process work? What would students change in it?

I tried the exercise and soon learned the point of it. After writing down a few preliminary questions, I wrote one central one, "What are the steps in the nitrogen cycle?" When I attempted to answer this, it became obvious that the question was too broad to be answered easily, and therefore it was useless in helping me to learn the material.

From comments made around the class, it appeared that several students were having the same experience. One comment Sarah made was that, "You can't shove all this information into your head in one lump." Most students seemed to get the point of the exercise by the end of the lesson, but there was no class discussion of it.

We went to lunch. There had been some rumor during the morning of students smoking marijuana on the school grounds. The students were reported by a teacher whose class they disturbed, and whose dilemma vis-à-vis her own students was discussed in the lunchroom. One of the students reported was a member of the Learning Course about whom Sarah had been concerned earlier. When we returned for the second session of the Learning Course after lunch, there was some buzzing among students about this episode, as well as much complaining about the heat. Sarah gave a mini-lecture, brief and sensible but with a faint edge of frustration in her voice: "We can't control the weather, or the fact that this classroom is uncomfortable, but we can control our own behaviour and attitudes--we can wear light clothes, avoid spending lunchhour in the sun (which, of course, students had done) and we can try to accept the weather and its limitations on us, rather than complain about it." Gradually the class settled down and did two exercises in memorization; working individually and then checking work with the whole class, they developed mnemonic devices to remember the names of the Group of Seven, and eight characteristics of living organisms.

I was struck by the low-keyed emotional tone of these classes, especially in contrast with the lesson observed a year earlier. Students seemed quite free in their behaviour and comfortable in the class, and they were allowed an opportunity to express whatever concerned them, but these concerns were not allowed to enter the life of the classroom. Worry over assignments, the weather, drug use, all were carefully put in their places outside the limits of the lesson. In retrospect I realized I had not identified the student Sarah had described as learning-disabled; I asked her after class and then recalled the boy pacing about, asking many questions. But his behaviour did not seem unusual to me during the lesson, nor did Sarah's behaviour toward him. I wondered if some of the emotional flatness I perceived had to do with her efforts to master the tension his presence apparently generated in her. After the lesson, we returned to the Reading Centre to record the second half of our interview.

The intent of the second half of the interview was,
of course, to discuss and analyze the lesson.
However, the interview came at the end of a long,
hot and tiring day, and this, combined with the
particular qualities of the lesson itself (i.e.
there was nothing immediately striking about it)
gave rise to a brief discussion that summarized a
few important points but did not probe them.

Sarah's assessment was that she seemed to have
accomplished her purposes; yet she was disappointed
with the lessons, because they had lacked any feeling of insight or excitement such as she had felt
initially when she discovered that the techniques
allowed her to make sense quickly of unfamiliar
material.   Early in the lesson, she had realized
she could not simulate her experience for students,
despite the fact that students had been allowed to
discover the point of the inventory exercise for
themselves. With respect to the memory work, Sarah
felt she hadn't given students sufficient opportunity to draw their own conclusions, but she felt
that all the techniques accumulated to give students a sense "that sitting over the book for an
hour isn't studying." We digressed for a moment to
talk about studying, a topic Sarah had raised with
the class on several occasions, and returned to
comment on several of the students' experiences
with the lesson.   Sarah felt she had made the
point--though to individuals rather than to the
whole class--that the techniques could be useful
when modified to one's own needs.

I commented that this task was necessarily a
plodding one, not likely to be greatly exciting to
students. Sarah agreed, and cited this as a reason
for her discontent in the course at this time. She
now saw the course as largely her own creation, and
"it doesn't respond the way an English classroom
can respond." She would be teaching the course
again next year, along with a non-academic English
course using interesting new materials (involving
group work and democratizing the classroom) that
she thought would also be useful in the Reading
Centre. But, it seemed to me, she was experiencing
a pull back to English literature; in her words,
she wanted a window onto students and their thinking, and also wanted "my window to be more open."
And this seemed to require "English as a medium for
getting to talk about different values and expe-

riences." She did feel that her training in the Learning Course and in Reading would make her a more effective English teacher. On this note, we concluded.

The following excerpt records Sarah's response to the lesson.

F. You said two things: you were kind of disappointed in the way the lessons went, but on the other hand, it seems that you accomplished what you intended.

S. Mm-humm.

F. And you said that you were... just the fact that some of the kids had already encountered that material...

S. Mm-hmm, yes.

F. And that they copped out, some of them, in the middle.

S. Mm-hmm.

F. I thought, what was quite nice, because I did the exercise and I did the same thing--I copped out in the middle. And it seemed to me that a couple of the kids, anyway, I was sure of a couple of the kids, and they realized they had copped out and that it wasn't very good.

S. Mm-hmm.

F. In other words, when you went on and asked them to now use the questions to review, they realized that having written so few questions didn't give them enough tools to review with. And a few of them seemed to really catch on-- most of them, I think, caught on to that.

S. Mm-hmm.

F. And I think that it's better that it happened that way, pedagogically, than had they been obedient little children and done it right, and then they would never have realized the advantage of it, and they might, some time later when they wanted to use the technique, not have done it all the way and not realized what was wrong.

S. Or on the other hand, had I said, "Now there's a trick here, because you might fall into the trap of writing a vague question for which you are really not prepared to write down the answer."

F. Yes. So I thought it was very good that you gave them that freedom and that they were able themselves to realize what could go wrong with the method.

S.   I guess what disappointed me is that when I did this myself yesterday, I had a lovely... I got a kick out of the passage making sense, after it had made no sense at all initially at the end of a long day. And I realized, once I got to the class, that I could not translate that to the class, that I was simulating a simulation which was a simulation, and when I realized that--I realized that quite quickly--I changed my tone, so that I didn't expect them to get a kick out of the passage, but rather expected them to practise a technique that hopefully will be practised again in the next few weeks with success. So that was something that I learned very quickly around ten o'clock today. (laughs)

F.   I had a feeling that they saw the technique as useful.

S.   Well, there's an interesting new dynamic in that class. Can you identify Jack? Do you remember who Jack is?

F.   (nods)

S.   Jack--I mentioned him last night--he was a terrible problem. He would come and sit like a blob, he would make negative remarks, he caused other kids problems. He didn't write a word for a couple of months. I spoke to his parents, I spoke to him. And now he's on this new track, and part of the new track seems to be flattery, flattery, flattery. And I don't need it, I like it sometimes, but everything we've done lately, he'll say, Oh yeah, I can use it here, I can use it there; oh, those techniques, well, I can't use them this year but I think I'll be able to use them next year. And he's just yes-manning me so much, I think the kids are wondering what's going on. And he talks so much, and so positively, that I'm not getting a chance to get a sense from the other kids of what they think of a technique or whether they think they can use it. It's as if the class has changed personality, because he's quite strong, whether he's being negative or positive.

F.   Well, I heard some mutterings from Eddy who was sitting behind me...

S.   M-hmm.

F.   Which I couldn't interpret because I don't know him, and I don't know whether he really thinks it's useful, but doesn't like to admit that anything that goes on in a classroom might be useful, but when pressed, he did admit it. I didn't know whether he was admitting it because he had to be fair, and was playing it down because he didn't want to seem too enthusiastic, or whether he was being a good kid and saying it was great, but would forget about it as soon as he walked out.

S. Eddy is a very fair, honest, fun-loving, swinging kid; he's almost archetypal. I'm very fond of him. And he comes from a very cultured home, so I'm hoping that--you know, he's getting more and more pressure at home, and he comes to the Reading Centre about once every two weeks and just works on a paragraph or something very limited. I hope that he'll stick around the school, and maybe get into an academic stream where there's more challenge for him; I think he's quite bright. (pause)

I had another thought, and it just escaped me. (pause) What would be nice from now on, and I'll encourage it, is if kids come up to me, and this has happened in the context of the Reading Centre, they come up with another thing to learn--15 lines of memory work, of French verbs, and I suggest a method, which usually works because I think, anytime you believe that a method works, for the first few times it will work.

Oh, I know what I was going to say. In presenting the idea of a list making sense or not making sense, I'm sorry that I wasn't more careful, because--this is one of the big revelations for me this year in reading the book by Frank Smith called Reading and Comprehension. He has a section on memory, which is just about the only thing on memory that I've been able to find, although I've asked the professional library a couple of times if they have material on memory. If something makes sense to you, it goes into your memory much more easily, and you can make sense out of absurdities by applying your own game to them. And probably with some more thought I could have either presented a concrete situation, where something that made sense would have been memorized more easily, like words rather than nonsense syllables, and have them draw the conclusion rather than having me spit it out at them, and they really didn't understand that whole business.

F.   Yes.

S.   I preferred, at that time, though, to leave it, because I realized that there were some kids for whom that list about qualities of living organisms would make sense, and there were a lot for whom it made no sense.

F.   It's plodding work, you know, when you sit down to the exercise and it suddenly makes sense to you it can be like a light turning on, for you, because you can see the implications of it immediately because you already know how to study, and it's just one more technique maybe, that you plug into your set of 'knowing how'. Whereas for them it's like a little tiny piece of light being uncovered. Nothing stupendous is going to happen when you're teaching those things.

S.   Mm-hmm. Well, I think you've hit on one of the reasons why I'm not delighted with teaching the course for the fifth time next year. It's as if I've created this monster, because it's largely mine (laughs). There has been some very valuable input, but I think most of it is mine, and it doesn't respond the way an English classroom can respond. And I think the course is looked upon by the kids as not really a course. Although that's okay; I'm not competing with the very stringent standards of science courses, or some of the other courses in the school. But, as Jack once said, You're not a teacher, you're a Learning teacher, or it was You're not like the other teachers, you're a Learning teacher. And I think there was something positive in that, but it still made me long for other situations. And my other teaching commitment for next year is 22 English, which is these kids taking English (laughs).

Planning

The fifth interview took place some nine months after the fourth; it was intended to consolidate some of the topics previously discussed and to validate interpretations I had begun to make of the data. Before we began, I asked Sarah to read through the transcript of the previous discussion. My purpose, as I explained to her at the beginning of the session, was not to review the issues raised in the fourth interview in a systematic way, but rather to summarize what had arisen from our discussions about the Reading Centre. I also wanted to begin to present some of my preliminary interpretations to Sarah for her comment.

Discussion

I began by telling Sarah the general topics I wanted us to discuss; I was interested in how the Reading Centre was now organized, what kinds of work Sarah was doing to keep it functioning, how it fitted into the school, and what her priorities were with respect to the different kinds of work she took on. She explained that the beginning of the semester was a slack time in the Reading Centre, and also as she had no classroom duties this semester she was "feeling a lot of power and excitement about being able to schedule my own day and make my own projects."

Sarah then told me about various technical changes in her work, and about the repertoire of planned lessons that had been developed. She also described a new style of work that had evolved for giving workshops--beginning with the problems and materials that students brought in, and making use of preplanned lessons as required instead of according to a fixed schedule.

The Reading Centre was now more firmly established in the school; Sarah described various ways she communicated with other staff members about her work. She was also investigating new directions for her work: she disliked the one-time lessons and had begun to develop, as an alternative, an ongoing working relationship with a geography teacher in which she was trying to learn his approach and provide him with assistance concerning the literacy of his students. She had also become aware of new research on study skills which she expected to examine further.

I then mentioned two issues which had arisen in the previous interview: first, Sarah's feeling of "giving too much and challenging too little", and second, the problem of working with students under pressure in situations which seemed to hold little chance for real learning. Sarah described some new ways in which she had begun to handle such situations.

In closing, Sarah commented that while she was very happy with her work in the Reading Centre, she felt that, if the position came to be eliminated for budgetary reasons, she would nevertheless "carry most of it with me back into the classroom," that it constituted good professional development for English teaching. I expressed surprise, since I had noted great disparities between English teaching, as she had described it in her school, and the Reading Centre work. I pressed her to explain the relationship between the two kinds of work but she was not able to do so. We concluded our discussion with Sarah's comment that our earlier discussion of her teaching style had sharpened her awareness of problems, and had influenced some of the changes she had made.

In the segment which follows Sarah describes her role in the Reading Centre.

S.   Maybe I'd better fill you in on a strange experience I'm having right now. We're beginning a new semester now, I think it's about the sixth day of the new semester, and a very funny thing happens where you forget everything that went before. And as you probably sensed, the beginning of the semester can be a very slack time in the Reading Centre. So when you ask me what I do, I almost feel guilty (laughs) because, literally, in the past few days I haven't appeared to do very much. The other thing I should say is that last semester I was teaching two classes, which is two thirds of a work-load in the classroom, and was assigned to the Reading Centre only one period a day. As it turned out, I would spend that period of the day working on Reading Centre things, and also lunchhour, and whenever a kid wanted to spend time in the Reading Centre after school I would stay after school. So I think that from the way my day was divided up and my attentions were divided, I was overloaded last semester. And I wasn't able to do the kinds of things that I'm excited about doing now, as prospects. Because I do have the time--I have no teaching duties right now, no classroom courses to teach. I'm in the Reading Centre all day--I have a legal spare, but I can float that, and I'm really feeling my oats. I'm feeling a lot of power and excitement about being able to schedule my own day and make my own projects. I'm feeling, for the moment, terrifically professional (laughs)--I know it'll disappear, but I'm really enjoying it. By disappear, I mean I know that feeling of being in control of my day and my time will disappear. So those two points, I feel, are necessary, if you want to be filled in on my situation right now.

F.   So maybe we can start off by talking about how the Centre is organized now, as oppsed to last year.

S.   Well, we're in a different room. Ellen and I worked in two separate rooms last year. And what I realized is that, although we met quite frequently, both informally over a cup of tea, and formally when we scheduled a meeting a couple of days in advance, we weren't really aware of how the other person operated. I'm sure we respect each other very much, but we weren't terrifically curious. Working in the same room is interesting because, whether you want to or not, you absorb a lot of the other person's attitudes and techniques, and you realize that certain kids are "territory" of the other person. And even the whole issue of territory becomes important; for me, for a while, the issue of voice volume became important. So that's a startling difference, working in the same room.

Another thing that happened is that Ellen was pregnant and then had her baby in November or December actually. And she was feeling quite tired and naturally dragged down, and the tone of her relationships with kids and with other teachers was very low-keyed. And I might have picked that up, and what made me realize this is that when her substitute came for three months, I immediately realized what a different personality the substitute has.

And Lynn, the substitute, had a marvellous
effect on me, first of all because she looked
upon me as a certain kind of expert. She
would come with all these questions, which I
had to think of answers for (laughs), and in
many cases I realized I had answers, and in
others I found it was fun to work out an answer with her. And also, her years of experience teaching English came across in how she
helped kids, and I learned a lot from her.
She's subsequently gone on to start a Reading
Centre in another school. So that was a
change because I was holding the fort for a
while in the fall. And... maybe you'd better
ask another question.

F.   How much time do you have to spend preparing
in the Reading Centre now? Did that... The
last time we talked, I was almost overwhelmed
by how much you were having to do... preparing
lessons to take into different classes, preparing for workshops, that kind of thing. You
talked, the time before the last, about wanting to set up lessons to have on hand for
kids who came in. You were very concerned
about doing that, and then realized that maybe
that wasn't a good thing to do at all, that
there were better ways of structuring things
than having to set up a lot of work programs
and have them ready.

S.   Well, a couple of things have become second
nature. For example, we worked up a forty-
minute lesson on memory, which we were invited
to give by several teachers; I was getting
sick of going into classes and talking about
it. We called it Memory SCAR as an acronym.
I really felt it was a routine, it was quite
entertaining. It was a bit of background on
short and long-term memory, and some advice
about selecting materials and time-management,
a few mnemonic techniques and then a general
answering of questions. And we tried to adapt
each little seminar that we gave to the course
that we were teaching--it was mainly language
teachers who invited us in. Well, that's in a
file, and I suppose that if I didn't teach it
for the next seven years, I could go and pick
out the file and within five minutes, be ready
to give that lesson.

So, by this time both Ellen and I have a
repertoire-we have a common repertoire, and

she has things that she does that I've never
seen her do, and wouldn't know how to do, and
vice versa. So I'm pleased about that.

I realized another thing through Lynn,
Ellen's substitute. I was too busy to initiate on my own one of those Effective Reading
workshops, because I had steady customers
every lunchhour during the week, plus an ex-
tracurricular program that I'm involved in.
So I would have been quite happy not to have
an Effective Reading seminar. But Lynn said
that she wanted to see one, so that she could
take the format to the other school, or see
how she could adapt it. So--this story takes
a little while to tell, I hope you don't
mind--

F.   No.
S.   Anyway, we scheduled a week for it, and I put
up dittoed signs around the school, "Effective
Reading Workshop: Try to improve your comprehension; Learn about studying," and just sort
of make a lot of promises. Lynn was in the
English office one day, running off some
dittoes, and the Head of the English department came up to her and asked what the workshop was about. And Lynn, of course, didn't
know; the purpose of the workshop was for her
to find out. But she was so terribly diligent
that she improvised an answer. And then she
came back, very apologetically, and said that
she had told him, that she had bluffed, and I
asked her what she told him. And she said,
"Well, I told him that it was a workshop, and
not a course, and workshop meant that the kids
came with their own concerns, and we saw what
concerns were common to them, and what concerns were individual, and over the next four
days we dealt with the strongest concerns. Is
that what you do?" And I realized that that
was a wonderful idea. Rather than taking out
the file from last year which has five preplanned lessons with all kinds of xeroxes of
material that the kids couldn't care less
about, why not start with where the kids were
and with the things that they were concerned
with. And basically, I guess I had enough
faith that they would be concerned with the
things that were preplanned. So we did that,
and it was delightful. Only five kids showed
up; I knew some of them before, and I think

Lynn knew one. We put a long list on the board of things that were difficult at this time of the year, and looked at the ones that were common concerns, and shaped up a program for the next four days. Then we stated very openly that if a kid wasn't interested in what we were going to do on Thursday, just not to show up. And we had a great time. We would talk about whatever problem the kid was having; for example, one girl was very concerned about reading a story, thinking it was just a story, and then the English teacher would ask her to write about the theme. And she could tell everything about the story, but she didn't know what 'theme' meant. She felt it was some mystery that she could never get to the source of. I talked about what I thought would be a reasonable approach, for a while, and then Lynn would just fill in things that I had missed. I was improvising, and there were obviously holes in what I was saying, and Lynn just came back and made something more concrete, or gave another example or whatever. I think we worked really well together on that.

I mention all this because I'm prepared, at this point, to have much more confidence in that kind of process than in a process of planning and looking for materials and things like that. I think the kids bring with them the materials that they really need to work on. And it's a matter, on the one hand, of my listening, and on the other hand, of having confidence that I can deal with things at the moment. And that idea served me very well because I didn't have time to prepare last semester.

F. Okay. What about the place of the Reading Centre in the school now? Is it still a public relations issue for you, to look busy and to have people know what you're doing?

S. I think that things have moved in that direction. First of all, Ellen invented a new word: it's now called the Study Skills and Reading Centre, and my tongue would trip over it for months, but I'm quite pleased with it now. And I think some things have moved well in some directions that we were looking for. I've tried to develop some continuing conversations with a couple of people on the staff. One, for example, is the head of the Math department, who sent me a couple of students, with whom I did math, but more from the point of view of... in geometry, let's say, making sure that they did have a diagram before they started working on a problem. Or being there so that they could talk about a problem out loud, without my offering very much advice. Anyway, through the referral of these kids I started a kind of ongoing communication with the head of the math department, and we realized that there's a lot that we can do together in terms of kids not reading problems, and kids having trouble with vocabulary in problems and kids panicing and just racing through a problem. I attended one of his classes, and realized that he gives an awful lot of what I thought was vocabulary overload. I think I copied down eleven new words that he used--words like axiom and theorem and postulate, that I think are very difficult to grasp in any more than just a passive way in one class. So that kind of communication is growing. If you're interested in some new directions that I'm thinking of...

F. Yes.

S. I'm not really pleased with these one-shot deals, walking into a classroom once and giving them a speech on memory, or a speech on previewing a textbook. The one thing that we did add was that a month later, we'd come back for ten minutes for some feedback on whether the kids had used it, or if it had made them aware that they could try other methods. The feedback was usually positive, very few people said it was a waste of time, and the questionnaires were anonymous. I don't think that's very effective, and...

F. What's not very effective, the one-shot deal?

S. Yes, the one-shot deal. What we do is, we pick up one or two kids from every class who come in for a couple of lunch-hours to work on something specific. I had an idea, in Ellen's absence, that something I'd like to do during this semester when I'm only in the Reading Centre, is to attach myself to one teacher in the school, who isn't an English teacher, a discipline that's quite foreign to me, and attend some of that teacher's classes, watch how the kids perform on tests, become aware of some of the literacy problems the kids have in relation to that particular subject. And I thought of being a slight burden to the teacher involved, but also providing some services, like maybe helping to mark tests or providing bibliography or suggesting things, and create a kind of team of two people. I looked upon it much as a learning project for both of us. I think what happened is that because I had no time to act on it, I just sat on the idea for too long, and I got some doubts about it, and I got cold feet. I tried to think of a teacher whom I respected very much, whose style was very different from mine, and with whom I already had some kind of relationship. And I thought of Dan G., who worked with us on the Learning Course and taught the Learning Course. He teaches excellent courses with very high standards. I originally thought of him because a girl came into the Reading Center with a thirty-page essay on STOL aircraft, and he had gone through it very, very carefully, making all kinds of criticisms, and offered her a chance to rewrite. He had given her a full month to rewrite, and we worked on it a few times. But when I saw the thoroughness with which he marked that essay, I was... I felt very guilty about my own marking, and I was very impressed.

Anyhow, I dropped in to his office one day, about two weeks ago, and explained to him that I had more time than I've ever had before in the Reading Centre, and I wanted to get some more professional development for myself, and I had a suggestion to make to him. And the suggestion was, basically, "Dan, can we work on a team concerning the literacy of the kids in your classes?"........
Another thing that I picked up at random... well, at random (laughs) I picked up a guidance journal in which there was an article about the latest investigations about study skills. And what they seemed to point to-- actually, it was devastating for me, and it makes me realize how naive I was--is that these traditional study skills, like SQ3R and previewing, work very well, it seems, for a certain kind of thinker: someone who, I guess, likes to organize things and break them down into little bits and be a bit compulsive,

and things like that. But there are millions of people who attack problems in different ways, and apparently endless lectures on study skills and practice just don't do any good. They might in some way appreciate that that's a valid method, but they would never use it. The latest research seems to suggest that the best method is a blending of some study skills advice presented in a very structured way, along with anxiety-reducing techniques and, some people call it self-monitoring, and the idea is that study skills alone, even for kids whose thinking patterns can be adapted, won't do very much good unless there's some affective change going on. So what I did a few months ago was to contact some people at a university who are combining these two things in workshops for kids--anxietyreduction and study skills--and I got hold of the articles that they were working from, 40-50 page articles, and when I get some time I'm going to try to look at it and try to get some teamwork going with the guidance department. So, if they wish, they can undertake one part of that, and Ellen or I can pick up the other things.

F.   What do you do for the kind of students who don't take to the study skills in the way that

S.   Well, I have a feeling that that's a very crucial question, and your mild way of asking it masks a lot more (laughs).

F.   No, I don't know! You just finished saying that those techniques work for certain people, and so I'm wondering if they've come to any conclusions about how you work with all the other people.

S.   No. Well, I'm in the process of tracking down the bibliography from that article. But my only conclusion, now... Well, first of all, I don't force things on a kid. If a kid comes in with a history essay to do, I don't say, "here's the technique." I do a lot of talking. I do much more non-directed talking with the kid about the assignment. By non-directed, I mean most of what I do is paraphrasing, to make sure that I've understood, and also so that the kid can hear it played back to him. And for some kids, I'll say, I guess intuitively, why don't you come back on Thursday and let's talk some more about how

you're getting along? And what has happened
with a couple of kids is that I've never seen
their essay. At most I've recommended a book.
And they come back and say, "Ya, I'm doing
fine. Kind of wondering, though. You know, I
read this, and that, and think I'm ready to
start reading this." And most of what I'll do
is try to be supportive, and get them to talk
more about what they're thinking, even though
they haven't commited anything to paper, no
plan or anything like that.

I might say something like, "Well, if I
were a reader, I'd want to know pretty early
on in the essay about suchand-such." But I
don't ask them to do that; I just say, If I
were a reader, this is what I'd like to know.

Summary

Having reviewed each of the interviews, a comment
is in order concerning the overall movement of the
interview sequence. We can look at the movement
from several perspectives. In terms of style, the
first interview was the most formal, tense, and
directed; afterwards discussions gradually became
more relaxed and the effort to take the discussion
in particular directions was less and less prominent. More significant, however, is the degree of
interest and involvement in the interview process.
In this respect, the second session was a high
point. Sarah and I both felt that we were contributing to one another's learning and development,
and that the interview process offered many possibilities for continuing to do so. After the second
meeting, however, this feeling declined. The
fourth session was somewhat disappointing to both
of us, to Sarah because the lesson did not achieve
as much as she had hoped and to me because we did
not carry out the intended simulation of a planning
session. The lesson apparently did not stimulate
my thinking or generate many insights into Sarah's
teaching. Thus, the fourth session was a low point
in terms of interest. The third and fifth interviews, however, were relatively 'neutral' in terms
of personal involvement: both these meetings were
'task-oriented', and the task was for me to ask,
and for Sarah to answer, questions that would contribute to a comprehensive picture of her work.

BIBLIOGRAPHY

Apple, Michael. "Behaviorism and Conservatism:
The Educational Views in Four of the 'Systems'
Models of Teacher Education." In Perspectives
for Reform in Teacher Education. Edited by
Bruce Joyce and Marsha Weil. Englewood
Cliffs, N.J.: Prentice-Hall, 1972.

_____. Ideology and Curriculum. London and
Boston: Routledge and Kegan Paul, 1979.

Barnes, Douglas. From Communication to Curriculum.
Harmondsworth: Penguin Books, 1976.

Bowers, C.A. Cultural Literacy for Freedom: An
Existential Perspective on Teaching, Curricu-
lum and School Policy. 2nd ed. Eugene, Ore.:
Elan, 1974.

Britton, James. "What's the Use? A Schematic
Account of Language Functions." Educational
Review 23, No.3 (June 1971): 205-219.

Bussis, Anne M.; Chittenden, Edward A.; and Amarel,
Marianne. Beyond Surface Curriculum. Boul-
der: Westview Press, 1976.

Clark, Christopher M., and Yinger, Robert J.
"Research on Teacher Thinking." Curriculum
Inquiry 7, No.4 (1977): 279-304.

Connelly, F. Michael. "The Functions of Curriculum
Development." Interchange 3, Nos.2-3 (1972):
161-177.

Daniels, L.B. "What is the Language of the Practical?" Curriculum Theory Network 4, No.4
(1975): 237-261.

Dewey, John. Experience and Education. Kappa Delta
Pi, 1938; reprint ed., New York: Collier
Books, 1963.

_____. Logic: The Theory of Inquiry. New York:
Henry Holt and Co., 1938.

Doubrovsky, Serge. Pourquoi la nouvelle critique?
Paris: Mercure de France, 1966.

Dreeben, Robert. "The School as a Workplace." In
Second Handbook of Research on Teaching.
Edited by R.M.W. Travers. Chicago: Rand
McNally, 1973.

Elbaz, Freema Luwisch. "Schwab's 'Deliberation':
Critical Analysis and Implications for Teacher
Curriculum Development." Qualifying research
paper, University of Toronto, 1975.

_____. "The Teacher's 'Practical Knowledge': A
Case Study." Doctoral dissertation, University of Toronto, 1980.

Elliot, John, and Adelman, Clem. "Innovation at
the Classroom Level." Open University Course
E203, Unit 28, pp.43-92. Milton Keynes: Open
University Press, 1976.

Esland, G.M. "Teaching and Learning as the Organization of Knowledge." In Knowledge and Control. Edited by Michael F.D. Young. London:
Collier-Macmillan, 1971.

Fullan, Michael. "Overview of the Innovative Process and the User." Interchange 3, Nos.2-3
(1972): 1-46.

Gauthier, David P. Practical Reasoning. Oxford:
Clarendon Press, 1963.

Giorgi, A. Psychology as a Human Science: A
Phenomenologically-Based Approach. New York:
Harper and Row, 1970.

Goodlad, John, and Klein, M. Behind the Classroom
Door. Worthington, Ohio: Charles A. Jones,

Greene, Maxine. "Curriculum and Consciousness."
Teachers' College Record 73, No.2 (1971):
253-269.

_____. Teacher as Stranger: Educational
Philosophy for the Modern Age. Belmont,
Calif.: Wadsworth Publishing Co., 1973.

Hudson, Liam. The Cult of the Fact. London: Jonathan Cape, 1972.

Huebner, Dwayne. "Curriculum as a Field of Study." In Precedents and Promise in the Curriculum Field. Edited by Helen F. Robinson. New York: Basic Books, 1965.

Hunt, David. "Teachers are Psychologists, too: On the Application of Psychology to Education." Canadian Psychological Review 17, No.3 (July 1976): 210-218.

Jackson, Philip. Life in Classrooms. New York: Holt, Rinehart and Winston, 1968.

Keddie, Nell. "Classrom Knowledge." In Knowledge and Control. Edited by Michael F.D. Young. London: Collier-Macmillan, 1971.

Kelley, Earl C. Education for What is Real. New York: Harper and Brothers, 1947.

Kelly, G.A. The Psychology of Personal Constructs. New York: Norton, 1955.

Kuhn, Thomas. The Structure of Scientific Revolutions. Chicago: University of Chicago Press, 1962, 1970.

Mann, John. "Curriculum Criticism." Curriculum Theory Network 2 (Winter 1968-69): 2-14.

Maslow, A.H. Toward a Psychology of Being. New York: Van Nostrand, 1962.

Merleau-Ponty, Maurice. Phénoménologie de la perception. Paris: Gallimard, 1945.

Parlett, Malcolm, and Hamilton, David. "Evaluation as Illumination: A New Approach to the Study of Innovatory Programs." Occasional Paper 9. Centre for Research in the Educational Sciences, University of Edinburgh, 1972.

Peterson, P.L., and Walberg, H.J., eds. Research on Teaching. Berkeley, Calif.: McCutchan, 1979.

Pollard, Andrew. "A Model of Classroom Coping Strategies." British Journal of Sociology of Education 3, No. 1 (1982): 19-37.

Reid, William A. and Walker, Decker F. Case Studies in Curriculum Change. London and Boston: Routledge and Kegan Paul, 1975.

Ryans, D.G. Characteristics of Teachers, Their Description, Comparison and Appraisal. Washington, D.C.: American Council on Education, 1960.

Sarason, Seymour B. The Culture of the School and the Problem of Change. Boston: Allyn and Bacon, 1971.

_____; Davidson, K.; and Blatt, B. The Preparation of Teachers: An Unstudied Problem in Education. New York: John Wiley, 1962.

Schutz, Alfred. Collected Papers, Vols. I-III. The Hague: Martinus Nijhoff, 1962-73.

_____, and Luckmann, Thomas. The Structures of the Life-World. London: Heinemann, 1974.

Schwab, Joseph J. "The Practical: A Language for Curriculum." School Review 78 (1969): p. 1-23.

_____. "The Practical: Arts of Eclectic." School Review 79 (1971): 493-542.

_____. "The Practical 3: Translation to Curriculum." School Review 81 (1973): 501-522.

_____. "What Do Scientists Do?" Behavioral Science V (1960): 1-27.

Shavelson, Richard, and Stern, Paula. "Research on Teachers' Pedagogical Thoughts, Judgments, Decisions and Behavior." Review of Educational Research 51, No.4 (1981): 455-498.

Skilbeck, Malcolm. "School-Based Curriculum Development." In Supporting Curriculum Development. Open University Course E203, Units 24-26, pp.90-92. Prepared by William Prescott and Ray Bolam. Milton Keynes: The Open University Press, 1976.

Smith, Louis M. "An Evolving Logic of Participant Observation, Educational Ethnography, and Other Case Studies." In Review of Research in Education 6, 316-377. Edited by Lee S. Shulman. Itasca, Illinois: F.E. Peacock, 1978.

_____, and Keith, P.M. Anatomy of Educational Innovation. New York: Wiley, 1971.

Stenhouse, Lawrence. "The Humanities Curriculum Project." Journal of Curriculum Studies 1, No.1 (1968).

Strike, Kenneth E. "On the Expressive Potential of Behaviorist Language." American Educational Research Journal 11, (1974): 103-120.

Tyler, Ralph. Basic Principles of Curriculum and Instruction. Chicago: University of Chicago Press, 1949.

Walker, Decker F., and Schaffarzick, Jon. "Comparing Curricula." Review of Educational Research 44 (1974): 83-111.

Wann, T.W., ed. Behaviorism and Phenomenology: Contrasting Bases for Modern Psychology. Chicago: University of Chicago Press, 1964.

Westbury, Ian. "The Curriculum and the Frames of the Classroom." Paper presented at the annual meeting of the American Educational Research Association, New York 1977.

Wilson, Stephen. "The Use of Ethnographic Techniques in Educational Research." Review of Educational Research 47, No.1 (Winter 1977): 245-265.

Yonemura, Margaret. "Teacher Conversations: A Potential Source of their own Professional Growth." Curriculum Inquiry 12, Vol.3 (1982).

Young, Michael F.D. Knowledge and Control. London: Collier-Macmillan, 1976.